LIBRARY IN A BOOK

RACIAL PROFILING

Fred C. Pampel

Facts On File, Inc.

RACIAL PROFILING

Facts On File, Inc.
132 West 31st Street
New York NY 10001

Library of Congress Cataloging-in-Publication Data
Pampel, Fred C.
Racial profiling / Fred C. Pampel.
p. cm.—(Library in a book)
Includes bibliographical references and index.
ISBN 0-8160-5592-0
1. Racial profiling in law enforcement—United States. 2. Racial profiling in law enforcement. I. Title. II. Series.
HV8141.P26 2004
363.2′3′089—dc22 2003025845

Text design by Ron Monteleone

Printed in the United States of America

MP Hermitage 10 9 8 7 6 5 4 3 2 1

This book is printed on acid-free paper.

CONTENTS

PART I
OVERVIEW OF THE TOPIC

PART II
GUIDE TO FURTHER RESEARCH

PART III
APPENDICES

PART I

OVERVIEW OF THE TOPIC

CHAPTER 1

OVERVIEW OF RACIAL PROFILING

"Driving while black or brown" and "flying while Arab": Are these behaviors worthy of police investigation? Some believe that, in certain circumstances, they might be, but others strenuously say no.

Racial profiling involves law enforcement actions based on race, ethnicity, or national origin rather than on the criminal behavior of an individual. In practice, it may lead police to stop and inspect selected people passing through public places—drivers on highways, pedestrians in urban areas, visitors crossing national borders, passengers on airplanes—for the reason that these people fit a statistical profile based at least to some extent on group membership. It goes beyond stopping individuals who fit a description of a specific suspect that may include race, ethnic, or national origin characteristics.

For example, racial profiling might involve stopping

- young black men driving rental cars on interstate highways between Florida and New York City because they are viewed as commonly involved in drug crimes;
- minority bystanders on urban streets because they are present in a high-crime area;
- Hispanics near the Mexican border because illegal immigrants often travel certain routes after entering the United States; and
- Arab flight passengers because extreme Muslim groups have committed acts of terrorism.

In each case, race, ethnicity, and national origin contribute to suspicion and investigation.

The practice of racial profiling by police, government agents, and business personnel has over the past decade generated enormous controversy that shows no sign of disappearing. The nature of profiling has changed but not the motivation for its use. In the early 1990s, it often stemmed from efforts to fight drug distribution and sales. It also stemmed from the use of community policing practices that aimed to anticipate and prevent crime by stopping small offenses before more serious ones occurred. However, lawsuits and political opposition generated by racial profiling have done much to end such practices.

More recently, concern about high levels of illegal immigration and the September 11, 2001, terrorist attacks have led to other forms of profiling that relate more to national origin and ethnicity than race. Police and border agents responding to high levels of undocumented passage across the Mexican border may target Hispanics in the United States to check on citizenship. In their efforts to prevent terrorism, government agents and airline personnel may give special attention to young men who appear to be Middle Eastern or Islamic. Recent proposals from the U.S. Department of Justice to locate and apprehend members of terrorist groups give special attention to the Arab-American community.

Why does this practice generate so much controversy? On one hand, members of minority groups feel victimized by their race, ethnicity, or national origin rather than their behavior. They claim that stereotypes wrongly depict them as involved in drugs, crime, illegal immigration, or terrorism. Indeed, only a small part of any group participates in illicit activities, but racial profiling treats all members of the group as suspects. Profiling may violate civil rights of minority groups, reduce public support for the police, and ultimately increase crime. Many states have thus enacted legislation to ban the practice.

On the other hand, efficient use of police and government resources is aided by relying on statistical probabilities. Based on known information about the characteristics of those involved in crime, young black men in a high-crime area, young Hispanic men near the U.S.-Mexican border, and young Muslim men in airports present a higher risk of offending than women, older persons, and white men. Using race, ethnic, and national-origin traits in investigation is more effective than stopping people at random on highways, in neighborhoods, or near borders. If these traits are only one of many used to define a profile, then their use does not, according to defenders of the practice, amount to racial discrimination. Indeed, some claim that the failure to investigate reports about the possibility of terrorist attacks before the September 11, 2001, attacks stemmed from concerns over using racial profiling to check on Arab men in flight schools.

Is membership in a group ever a sufficient reason for special investigation, or do such actions always violate civil liberties? How common is racial profiling according to the available evidence? What actions have opponents taken to end the practice? The answers given to these and other related questions reflect highly charged controversies.

BACKGROUND OF RACIAL PROFILING

A report done for the U.S. Department of Justice provides the most complete and precise definition of racial profiling: "Racial profiling is defined as any police-initiated action that relies on race, ethnicity, or national origin rather than the behavior of an individual or information that leads police to a particular individual who has been identified as being or having been engaged in criminal activity."[1] This definition contains several important components.

First, it refers to police-initiated actions. Typically such action involves law enforcement personnel stopping vehicles or pedestrians in their search for evidence of the commission of a crime. Along with local and state police, the actions of federal immigration, customs, and law enforcement officials would fall within the definition. So would the actions of private security guards who have authority in malls, businesses, and office buildings. The actions initiated by police may occur in a variety of circumstances. They usually involve traffic stops on highways or roads and pedestrian stops on city sidewalks but can also involve stopping travelers in airports, train stations, and bus stations. Police often use the stops to check for contraband (for instance, banned or controlled substances such as drugs, weapons, or illegal goods). The actions can involve asking simple questions, requesting documents, and explaining the reason for stopping. More seriously, they can involve searches of cars or of individuals.

Some believe the definition should cover more than police action. Minorities complain that salespeople ignore them in stores, clerks watch them closely for shoplifting, and cab drivers refuse to pick them up. Consciously or unconsciously, teachers and other school personnel may use race as a factor in school discipline and punishment. Persons may be victims of hate crimes such as assault or even murder based only on their race, ethnicity, or national origin. Such actions reflect private discrimination, use of stereotypes, and forms of racial profiling, but they differ in an important way from police-initiated actions. Since police have the legitimate authority to use force and make arrests, the consequences of racial profiling by police are particularly serious and have special importance. Hence, racial profiling most often refers to police actions.

Second, the definition is limited to the use of race, ethnicity, and national origin without information on a specific suspect. The Supreme Court has ruled that it is permissible to use race, ethnicity, and national origin to help determine if a person fits the description of someone suspected of a crime. Police searching for a suspect identified by the victim as a white male, approximately five feet 10 inches tall and 180 pounds, and wearing a blue jacket could legitimately use race in their search. In contrast, racial profiling relies on general racial, ethnic, and national-origin categories rather than information on the characteristics of a specific individual. It might involve stopping only black drivers on a certain stretch of highway used often by drug couriers or stopping Latino drivers on highways near the border. Since racial profiling judges an individual on the basis of membership in a racial, ethnic, or national-origin group rather than on the basis of individual action, it could represent a form of prejudice or discrimination.

In principle, racial profiling applies equally to whites as well as to black, Latino, Asian, and Native American minorities. Whites driving in a minority neighborhood known for drug activity may be stopped because of a racial profile, and white members of motorcycle gangs or skinheads may face special attention from police. In practice, however, racial profiling adversely affects members of minority groups—it involves the use of power by dominant groups against less dominant groups. Since whites of European heritage tend to have more power in the United States than other race, ethnic, and national-origin groups, they are rarely subject to profiling. Members of minority groups, in contrast, feel commonly victimized by the actions of police.

Third, racial profiling requires police discretion, or the freedom to make decisions and choices. In observing a serious crime in progress, police have little discretion about whether or not to stop the crime. In such cases, where clear evidence of serious wrongdoing exists, racial profiling seldom comes into play. However, the enforcement of more minor crimes leaves the police much room for choice. For example, more motorists violate traffic laws such as those against speeding than can be ticketed; police have to make decisions about which speeders to pursue. Similarly, determining whether pedestrians are involved in suspicious activity allows for a good deal of subjective choice: Does standing on the corner, walking quickly, or looking around reflect suspicious or normal activity? Racial profiling occurs most often in circumstances where police have high rather than low discretion. Police develop their own methods for making choices in high-discretion circumstances and sometimes may intentionally or unintentionally rely on racial stereotypes in making choices.

To the extent that it involves the legal exercise of discretion, however, racial profiling differs from police brutality. Both may reflect discrimination and produce anger and protest among minorities. Yet, racial profiling stems from the use of race, ethnicity, and national origin in determining suspects of crime, while brutality involves the unlawful use of excessive force. Racial profiling may be legal and occurs in determining who to stop and search, while brutality is illegal and occurs after a stop.

Fourth, racial profiling differs, at least in principle, from criminal profiling. Criminal profiling involves identification of a set of behavioral characteristics of persons likely to be involved in crime. To be effective, the profile characteristics need to have a proven or well-known statistical relationship with offending. For example, a hostile personality, association with known criminals, or evidence of recent spending of large amounts of cash might signify criminal activity. Similarly, evidence left at the scene of the crime by a serial killer may suggest that the perpetrator lives alone, has problems with authority, and harbors rage against a certain class of people.

Racial profiling incorporates race, ethnic, or national-origin characteristics in one of two ways. It may use race as the *sole* grounds for a police action, or it may be *part* of a larger criminal profile. As the sole grounds for suspicion, racial profiling assumes a link between crime and race, ethnicity, and national origin—factors over which individuals have no control. As part of a larger criminal profile, use of race, ethnicity, and national origin assumes a connection between race and crime only when other behaviors or characteristics are present. As users of the term do not always make clear their meaning, it helps to keep the distinction in mind when considering arguments for and against racial profiling.

LEGALITY

Is racial profiling illegal? It might appear so on constitutional grounds. The Fourth Amendment to the Constitution of the United States of America, ratified in 1791, states, "The right of the people to be secure in their persons, houses, papers, and effects, against unreasonable searches, and seizures, shall not be violated." Searches based on race, ethnicity, or national origin may qualify as unreasonable because they are based on skin color or appearance rather than behavior. The Fourteenth Amendment, added to the Constitution in 1868, guarantees equal protection of the law to all persons. Designed to protect the rights of recently freed slaves, the amendment has come to be used to protect against racial discrimination in law enforcement. Racial profiling, because it treats some race, ethnic, and national-origin groups differently than others, may violate this amendment.

In answering the question about the constitutionality of racial profiling, it helps to consider the distinction between types of profiling. Use of race, ethnicity, or national origin alone to initiate a police action, sometimes called "hard profiling,"[2] has few supporters and clearly violates constitutional protection for equal protection. Use of race, ethnicity, and national origin as one of several characteristics in a profile ("soft profiling") appears legal in most circumstances. Proponents of racial profiling support the latter use, while opponents argue that use of race, ethnicity, or national origin in any form violates the constitutional rights of citizens.

The U.S. Supreme Court has ruled in a 1975 decision, *United States v. Brignoni-Ponce*, that the use of ethnicity as the sole reason for making a stop violates constitutional protections. Ethnic appearance alone, for example, does meet the standard for reasonable search and seizure. However, the Court has not ruled that use of race, ethnicity, and national origin as part of a larger profile violates constitutional rights. It has not explicitly ruled in favor of this type of racial profiling either. Still, a variety of related decisions suggest that the Court would support this procedure if there is evidence of an association between race, ethnicity, or national origin and offending.[3]

Many states have passed laws with the intent to eliminate racial profiling, but federal legislation to do the same has not yet passed. In June 2003, President George W. Bush issued guidelines for federal law enforcement agencies that bar them from using race or ethnicity in routine investigations. Since the guidelines do not apply to state and local law enforcement officers, some city police departments, most notably New York City, have instituted prohibitions on their own. Otherwise, racial profiling has not been outlawed.

Debates over the legality of racial profiling relate to larger disagreements over how to balance two rights or goals.[4] On one hand, citizens want to maintain constitutional rights that guarantee protection from unreasonable search and selective enforcement of the law. Such rights protect innocent persons from government interference and guilty persons from government abuse. On the other hand, citizens want to protect themselves from crime. To some degree, these two goals conflict with one another. Police efforts to protect citizens from crime can violate constitutional rights, but efforts to protect constitutional rights make it harder for police to fight crime.

This conflict defines a crucial question society needs to answer: Where should it draw the line in balancing interests of protecting individual rights and fighting crime? Liberals tend to favor more emphasis on constitutional rights, while conservatives tend to favor more emphasis on protection from crime. Liberals tend to side with the interests of disadvantaged, less powerful groups who they feel most need protection from the power of the government. Most oppose racial profiling in all forms as immoral and unfair discrimination. Conservatives tend to side with the interests of advantaged, more powerful groups that they feel most need protection from crime. Most support law enforcement agencies in dealing with crime problems, including their use in some circumstances of racial profiling. Many exceptions exist to these generalizations—politicians from both the Democratic and

Republican Parties oppose racial profiling. Still, political beliefs play an important role in the debate over the use of racial profiling.

STOP-AND-SEARCH RULINGS

The Supreme Court has approved three police practices that, by making it easier to employ racial profiling, have become the object of considerable controversy. First, in *Terry v. Ohio* (1968), the Supreme Court ruled that police can briefly stop and quickly search persons if officers have a reasonable suspicion that a crime is occurring or about to occur. When possible, police should obtain a warrant from a judge for a search based on probable cause or the reasonable belief that they will obtain evidence of a crime. In some circumstances, however, police cannot obtain a warrant in time to prevent a crime but can still act on the basis of reasonable suspicion.

The court, lawyers, and law enforcement officials make a distinction between probable cause and reasonable suspicion that relates to racial profiling. *Probable cause* refers to a reasonable belief that a crime is being or has been committed by a specific person. By requiring an officer to have a clearly expressed, objective, and factual basis for the belief, it limits discretion and prevents use of racial profiling. In contrast, *reasonable suspicion* gives officers discretion in making stops and more easily allows for the use of race, ethnicity, or national origin in police decision making. Critics highlight the breadth and vagueness of the standard for reasonable suspicion. It allows, they believe, for prejudice, discrimination, and mistreatment of minorities to enter into police judgments.

Second, the Supreme Court in *Florida v. Bostick* (1991) ruled that police can ask for consent to search personal property or cars. In principle, once police stop a car, they cannot search it without a warrant or probable cause that evidence of a crime will be found. However, if the driver voluntarily consents, a search can occur even without probable cause or even reasonable suspicion of a crime. Because citizens have the right to say no to the request, consent searches do not violate, according to the decision, the rights for protection from unreasonable search and seizure. Moreover, police do not have to warn individuals that they have the right to refuse the request.

From the viewpoint of critics, however, persons with less power feel a greater sense of coercion to agree to the request. Even among those carrying illegal goods, many agree to the search because they fear what will happen if they refuse. With consent giving police the right to search without probable cause and reasonable suspicion, it heightens the potential for use of racial profiling and discrimination against minority groups.

Third, in *Whren v. United States* (1996), the Supreme Court ruled that police can stop vehicles for a traffic violation as a pretext to check for the evidence of more serious crimes. *Pretext* refers to a motive put forth to cover the real reason. In this context, it involves stopping vehicles for minor violations with the real purpose of looking for evidence of more serious crimes—even if the police do not have probable cause to suspect a more serious crime. The Court ruled that if a traffic violation occurs, the police have the right to make the stop regardless of whether or not they have other hidden motives. The Court reasoned that judges cannot concern themselves with the subjective motivations of officers but can focus only on objective behavior. A pretext stop for a verifiable traffic violation, however minor, thus remains constitutional.

Critics of the ruling note that nearly all drivers commit minor traffic violations, which gives police much discretion in determining whom they should stop. Police can use minor traffic violations as an excuse for stopping minority drivers and weaken constitutional guarantees for equal protection under the law. In the words of one critic, allowing a pretext stop "permits officers who lack probable cause or reasonable suspicion to manufacture a pretextual basis for suspicion . . . [and] allows officers who have no more basis for suspicion than the color of a driver's skin to make a constitutional stop."[5]

Historical Practices

Although the term *racial profiling* and debates over its legality have emerged only recently, the use of race, ethnicity, and national origin in police-initiated actions has a long history in the United States, a history that has created much resentment in particular among African Americans. The history dates back to the period of slavery, when slave codes defined special laws and punishments. For example, a slave could not leave a plantation without a pass, and whites had the authority, even the obligation, to stop blacks and apprehend any who were "unable to give a satisfactory account of himself."[6] Under the code, whites could use skin color to detain and question without probable cause or evidence of a crime.

With the end of slavery, white politicians devised other means in southern states to restrict the freedom of movement among blacks. Mississippi and South Carolina passed "black codes" near the end of 1865.[7] These codes outlawed use of "insulting" gestures and language by blacks and made it illegal for blacks to assemble. Some southern towns had curfews for blacks and required all blacks entering the city to have their papers checked, and others required blacks to register so authorities could check their papers on demand. In northern cities, the white authorities also sought to control the movement of blacks. They did not have the same discriminatory laws as southern cities and states, but police could use laws against vagrancy, loitering, disorderly conduct, and other minor infractions to limit the activities and free movement of blacks.

Responsible for enforcing racist laws, the police became the object of black resentment and anger. According to one historian, "Already, at the end of the nineteenth century, resentment against the police and the system of local justice was a constant fact of life in the emerging Southern ghettoes, ready to be ignited by seemingly minor affronts."[8] In Atlanta, violence between blacks and police became common during the 1880s, as crowds tried to rescue blacks arrested by police. Police departments in both the North and South seldom hired minorities, which further widened the gap between the races. One fact perhaps best highlights the strained racial relationships: From 1920 to 1932, white officers were responsible for more than half of the murders of black citizens.[9]

Similar tensions between African Americans and the police persisted throughout the rest of the century. The pictures of southern police suppressing peaceful civil rights demonstrations during the 1960s remain vivid in the minds of many. In 1964, riots in the Harlem area of New York City were sparked by the shooting of a 15-year-old African American by a white policeman; in 1965, riots in the Watts area of Los Angeles were sparked by a confrontation between police and African-American onlookers after a traffic stop; and in 1967, riots in Detroit, Michigan, were sparked by a police raid on an African-American drinking establishment. Although many causes help explain the emergence of race riots during the 1960s, the belief of blacks that police discriminated against them played a role.

Over time, racial profiling became a symbol of larger conflict between police and the African-American community. Problems of poverty, social isolation, economic stress, and cultural differences persisted, and police became the first line of defense in dealing with the resentment and violence that resulted from these problems. Continued inequality and segregation today make racial conflict a crucial component of concerns over racial profiling.

Other minority groups also experienced early forms of racial profiling. Latinos have throughout their history in the United States faced special police attention because of suspicions that they have entered the country illegally. Asian Americans faced extensive discrimination as they began immigrating to the United States in the late 19th century. In perhaps the broadest instance of racial profiling, the U.S. government during World War II interned 120,000 Japanese Americans in special camps and confiscated their property. The internment did not rely on evidence that Japanese Americans had aided the enemy during World War II but used national background alone to justify the roundup. Despite the Supreme Court's approval of internment at the time, it is now viewed as a serious injustice.

These historical instances of police and governmental discrimination against minority groups have made minorities sensitive to racial profiling. During the 1990s, racial profiling emerged important in four areas: the war against drugs, the growth of quality-of-life policing, the control of immigration, and the fight to prevent terrorism.

CURRENT AREAS OF RACIAL PROFILING

WAR ON DRUGS

The war on drugs took on special intensity in the 1980s, during the administration of President Ronald Reagan. Heroin and cocaine had become illegal early in the 20th century, marijuana in the 1930s, and other drugs such as LSD in the 1960s. Federal, state, and local agencies had worked to apprehend both sellers and users. In 1973, President Richard Nixon established the U.S. Drug Enforcement Administration to merge diverse agencies in the fight against drugs. However, during the early 1980s, it appeared that large amounts of illegal drugs, particularly cocaine, were being funneled into the United States from South and Central America. Drug cartels in Colombia had grown powerful, even bringing Latin American military leaders and politicians into their distribution efforts. The public became increasingly concerned about the drug problem.

In 1982, the Reagan administration established the Vice President's Task Force on South Florida under the direction of Vice President George H. W. Bush. The task force aimed to stem the flow of drugs into the United States by stopping smuggling into the country. It also aimed to disrupt the flow of drugs from south Florida to large markets in the northeastern United States by capturing drug couriers. Working with the task force, the Florida Highway Patrol in 1985 issued guidelines for the police to identify drug couriers who transported drugs across American highways.[10] The guidelines warned officers to look for drivers using rental cars, carefully following traffic laws, and wearing gold chains and expensive jewelry. They also noted that certain ethnic groups—Hispanics and blacks from Caribbean nations—and gang members had become involved in the drug trade.

The war on drugs took on renewed urgency beginning in about 1985 with the emergence of the crack cocaine epidemic. Crack is a powerful form of cocaine that users smoke rather than sniff through the nose or inject. Inhaled as smoke, the drug reaches the brain quickly—in just a few minutes—and a higher proportion of the narcotic chemicals enter the bloodstream. The potency of the drug makes it less expensive, usable in small doses, and powerfully addictive. Police first noticed its use in New York City in 1985 and saw it spread quickly. The growing popularity combined with the powerful addictive properties of crack devastated many neighborhoods. The *New York Times* ran a front page story on the new drug and its terrible effects on neighborhoods already facing poverty and crime.[11]

Publicity about the horrors of crack cocaine grew. Stories in the media on babies born with an addiction, women prostituting themselves for the drug, gangs using drive-by shootings in their battles over the illicit trade, and the spread of the distribution networks into new towns made the use of crack in ghettos into a major crisis. Around the same time, Len Bias, a basketball star from the University of Maryland who was signed to a rich contract with the Boston Celtics of the National Basketball Association, died from a cocaine overdose. Bias did not use crack cocaine, but the publicity about his death heightened concern about cocaine abuse. In 1985, only 1 percent of Americans identified drugs as the most important problem facing Americans, but in large part as a result of media attention to the issue, 64 percent saw drugs as the most important problem by 1989.[12]

Congress responded to the crisis with passage of the Anti–Drug Abuse Acts of 1986 and 1988. The 1986 act created mandatory minimum penalties for drug offenders and specified particularly severe penalties for selling crack cocaine. For example, possession of only five grams of crack—compared to 500 grams of powdered cocaine—triggered the mandatory minimum sentence of five years. The 1988 act established the Office of National Drug Control Policy to coordinate international and national efforts to reduce use, manufacturing, and trafficking of drugs, and drug-related crime and violence. The first director of the office (known informally as the drug czar), William Bennett, contributed to antidrug efforts by working to make drug use socially unacceptable. The battle against drugs has continued into the 1990s and the 21st century.

Enforcement Actions

At the local level, the war on drugs led police to concentrate on users in minority neighborhoods. Crack use appeared more commonly in these neighborhoods than in white suburbs and affluent parts of cities, where users preferred powdered cocaine and other drugs. Gang warfare related to crack cocaine also led police to focus on young men from minority groups who appeared likely to belong to a gang. Wearing a certain style of clothing or colors led, often wrongly, to the assumption of gang membership, and gang members were sometimes falsely assumed to be involved in the drug trade. Many viewed racial profiling as a central part of the war on drugs.

Police attention to minority groups certainly resulted in many arrests. About 75 percent of persons in prison for drug offenses are minorities, and more than 90 percent of offenders sentenced for crack offenses in federal court are African Americans. According to results from one 1995 study, 32 percent of black men ages 20–29 (compared to about 7 percent of white men in the same age group) fall under court supervision in prison, on probation, or on parole.[13] Yet, surveys show similar use of drugs among both young white and black men. Although the drug laws say nothing about race, they have had the outcome, according to critics, of leading to discrimination by race in arrests and convictions.

At the state level, efforts to interdict highway drug traffic emerged. In the early 1980s, troopers in New Mexico noted that increasing numbers of traffic violations along the interstate highways resulted in drug seizures. Much the same happened in Maryland and New Jersey, where Interstate 95 connected Florida to large cities in the Northeast. Concluding that the U.S. highways had become arteries for drug transport, these states established drug interdiction programs.

Success at the state level led in 1984 to the establishment of Operation Pipeline, a nationwide highway interdiction program that focuses on private motor vehicles. The program trains officers across the country in the law, drug trafficking trends, and key characteristics shared by drug couriers. It also teaches the use of pretext stops for traffic violations to check for drug evidence by questioning the drivers, looking inside the car, and asking for consent to search the trunk. It does not, according to official statements, allow or encourage racial profiling.[14]

However, instances of racial profiling in the mid-1990s by state police in New Jersey and Maryland occurred. Based on these instances, critics of the program claim that the war on drugs promoted racial profiling. In Maryland, a notice to state troopers to watch for black men and women transporting drugs led to the stop and search of a car containing African Americans returning from a funeral. One of the travelers, Robert Wilkins, and the American Civil Liberties Union (ACLU) sued the Maryland State Police on behalf of African Americans unconstitutionally stopped in the past or the future because of the race-based drug courier profile. The state settled the suit, paid damages to the Wilkins family, issued a written policy to end stops based on race, and began to train officers on the policy and monitor their car stops. In New Jersey, Attorney General Peter Verniero issued a report concluding that racial profiling of drivers on New Jersey highways had occurred. Such evidence led in turn to the dismissal of drug and weapons charges based on evidence obtained from police stops of minorities on New Jersey highways.

At the federal level, the government put forth special efforts to stop the smuggling of drugs into the United States through airports. To discover drugs hidden in personal belongings, customs officials and police needed to search luggage carefully, but the huge numbers of international travelers passing through airports made the search of all belongings impossible. In the early 1990s, customs agents relied on a profile that, among other things, suggested that black women, often with braided hair and long fingernails, commonly served as drug couriers. Responding to pressure from media exposés and congressional hearings about the profile, the U.S. Customs Service eventually changed its policies to concentrate on behavior rather than ethnic background.

Together, actions of the government at the local, state, and federal levels led critics to call the drug war racist in its prosecution of minorities. They believed that police acted too vigorously in fighting drugs, relied on stereotypes of black and Hispanic drug users, and employed racial profiling in searching for drug traffickers. Some suggest that the media exaggerated the seriousness of the drug problem in minority communities and ignored the use of cocaine by whites in the suburbs. Those defending the actions of the police made several points in response: Crack cocaine created devastation in minority communities that far exceeded the problems of powdered cocaine use elsewhere; the high arrest rates of minority groups stemmed from their involvement in the drug trade rather than from racial profiling and discrimination; and police efforts to enforce drug laws have made minority neighborhoods better places to live.

Quality-of-Life Policing

Community policing is a general term that encompasses a wide variety of practices used to some degree by nearly all police departments. The practices in essence aim to prevent crime and improve community relations by integrating officers into the local community and having them work closely with neighborhood residents. In doing more than arrest criminals, police focus on improving the quality of life of neighborhood residents, reducing fear of crime, and increasing satisfaction of the residents with the police. They must continue to react to crimes that have already been committed but also need to try to change the conditions that generate crime.

One type of quality-of-life policing offers a solution to the problem of how to change the conditions that generate crime. The solution is to deal with types of disorderly behavior that do not violate major laws or involve serious offenses but nonetheless worsen the quality of life in a neighborhood. Such disorderly behavior involves the actions of panhandlers, drunks, addicts, rowdy teens, prostitutes, loiterers, gangs, drug sellers, and strangers. By violating informal rules of civility, these actions do much to create fear among residents. Residents fear serious crime in their neighborhoods but most face disorderly behavior more often in their daily life.

Police control of minor offenses or quality-of-life crimes makes residents less fearful and able to avoid unpleasant encounters outside their homes. Such efforts additionally have the benefit of reducing more serious crime. This occurs in part because disorderly people are more likely than others to commit more serious crime; arresting them for minor offenses prevents them from committing more serious offenses. Given the attention to minor offenses, some refer to the practices as aggressive or zero-tolerance policing.

The ability of quality-of-life policing to reduce serious crime stems from another source: Disorderly behavior signals that no one cares enough about what goes on in a community to stop the crime; stopping disorderly behavior signals that people care about preventing crime. This idea has come to be known as the"broken windows" theory. Presented in 1982 by Criminologists James Q. Wilson and George L. Kelling,[15] the theory begins with the claim that if a window in a building or home is broken and left unrepaired, the rest of the windows will soon be broken. An unrepaired window implies that no one cares and that breaking more windows costs offenders nothing.

Like a broken widow, disorder in a neighborhood signals lack of control and opportunity for crime. With disorderly people bothering them and breaking informal rules, most residents avoid coming out to public places. When they come out, they avoid contact and interaction with people. As residents stay clear of the social life in their neighborhood, it creates more opportunity for crime. As crime in turn rises, residents become even more fearful and do even more to avoid contact and interaction with people. The neighborhood loses civility and common purpose. Minor disorders thus lead to serious crime.

To deal with the problem of disorder, police need to maintain order as well as solve major crimes. They need to protect the community from disorder as well as protect individuals from crime. Quality-of-life policing deals with underlying problems in the community by focusing on stopping minor violations that promote more serious crimes and harm the quality of life of neighborhood residents. Controlling the activities of panhandlers, drunks, addicts, rowdy teens, prostitutes, loiterers, gangs, drug sellers, and strangers, before they lead to more serious crime, becomes an essential goal of policing.

Policing in New York City

Beginning in 1994, Mayor Rudolph Giuliani and Police Chief William Bratton of New York City began to implement quality-of-life policing. Their first step focused on stopping "fare-beating," or cheating the subway by jumping over the turnstile rather than paying the fare. Although the offense itself was minor, it made the subways appear lawless. Moreover, those stopped for cheating the subway might have weapons or warrants for their arrest. John Royster, Jr., for example, was found, after being apprehended for fare-beating, to have been involved in a murder and four other unsolved crimes.[16] Police soon began to detain those involved in other types of disorderly behavior, such as aggressive panhandling, sale of alcohol to minors, graffiti vandalism, public urination, unlicensed peddling, reckless bicycle riding, and making excessive noise with boom boxes.

Another component of quality-of-life policing in New York City involved stopping, questioning, and frisking suspicious persons. The police aimed to reduce the high rate of homicide in the city by getting guns off the street. Stop-and-frisk procedures might uncover those illegally carrying weapons before they were used in a killing. To make a stop without violating the rights of citizens, police would need to have a reasonable suspicion that a crime was occurring. Given concern with minor offending, they began to act on such suspicions with more frequency than in the past. In so doing, they could search for weapons.

The New York City police did more than focus on quality-of-life crimes. They also used a computerized crime mapping system (called COMPSTAT) to target resources and stop emerging crime "hot spots." The system identified busy streets or disadvantaged neighborhoods where problems appeared most serious and tracked progress in dealing with those problems. Police commanders also held weekly meetings to increase communication between precinct units and creatively work to solve neighborhood crime problems.

Remarkable changes resulted from the new procedures. Crime dropped by 12 percent in 1994, the first year of the new program, and continued to drop in the years after. The falling crime rate created a new sense of safety and satisfaction among residents. New York City experienced a renaissance in the 1990s, with cleaner streets, less disorder, greater tourism, and economic growth. Mayor Giuliani and his police chiefs received much praise for the changes, and other cities, seeing the progress against crime in the largest U.S. city, began to adopt quality-of-life policing.

However, detractors of quality-of-life policing claimed it resulted in harassment of citizens. By focusing on more common disorders and suspicious activity rather than less common, more serious crime, police gain considerable discretion in making choices about whom they should stop. With this discretion, stereotypes can excessively influence their views of what constitutes suspicious or disorderly activity. Along with dress, demeanor, location, and age, race or ethnicity may become factors that determine stops. For example, a person's presence in an area of high crime or drug activity might be seen as suspicious and a reason to stop and frisk. Yet, such neighborhoods tend to have large minority populations. Therefore, minority residents—innocent as well as guilty—will be subject to excessive searches and a form of racial profiling.

Treatment by police angered and humiliated minority residents in New York City, who accused the department of racism. Protests against police actions peaked with the 1999 killing of an unarmed black man, Amadou Diallo, who was shot 19 times after a routine stop by undercover police officers on a dark street late at night. The officers mistook Diallo's efforts to pull out his wallet for identification as going for a gun. Police claimed it was a tragic accident, but critics viewed the killing as a reflection of discriminatory police policies.

Complaints about police action in New York City came from other sources as well. Amnesty International accused New York City police of violating the human rights of African Americans and Latinos. The U.S. Civil Rights Commission determined in May 2000 that police used racial profiling in their decisions about who to stop and frisk. The commission and its head, Mary Frances Berry, criticized Mayor Giuliani and recommended the appointment of an independent prosecutor to investigate misconduct. Some members of the commission disagreed with the ruling, claiming that the evidence did not support the claim. Others believed that Amnesty International and the Civil Rights Commission, both liberal organizations, were politically motivated to embarrass the popular and conservative Mayor Giuliani. Still, the announcements affirmed the belief of many that New York City police—and perhaps other cities that follow the policing model of New York City—engaged in racial profiling.

Opponents also disputed the claim that quality-of-life policing lowered the crime rate. The crime rate had started to decline for a variety of reasons even before efforts to stop minor offenses had begun. The declining size of the youthful population most prone to crime, growth of immigrant populations with low crime rates, new educational opportunities, and a truce in gang wars did more than police efforts to reduce crime. The main result of quality-of-life policing, according to critics, has been to worsen the relations between police and the community by increasing the harassment of innocent minorities.

Despite criticism and possible reliance on racial profiling, however, quality-of-life policing remains popular. In New York City, Giuliani's successor, Mayor Michael R. Bloomberg, and Police Commissioner Raymond W. Kelly have pledged to continue the practice. Polls reveal that New Yorkers strongly support enforcing laws against graffiti-writing or aggressive panhandling.[17] African Americans, Hispanics, and Asian Americans support enforcement even more than whites. Most citizens benefit from restoration of order, but minorities living in neighborhoods with high levels of disorder, drug use, and serious crime have the most to gain from police efforts to deal with the problems. Police leaders deny they use racial profiling and argue that, with proper guidance and training for police officers, quality-of-life policing can be done without violating the civil rights of citizens.

IMMIGRATION CONTROL

Compared to most other countries, the United States has an open immigration policy. Today, the foreign-born population in the United States (including legal and illegal immigrants) has reached 33.1 million, or 11.5 percent of the population.[18] Of this total, the Census Bureau estimates 8 million to 9 million are illegal immigrants. However, since counts of this population are difficult, other estimates indicate considerably higher numbers.[19]

With existing limits on legal immigration, those desiring American jobs that pay higher than those available in their native country will try to enter or remain in the nation illegally or without proper documentation. Similarly, recently arrived immigrants, both legal and illegal, create communities in the United States with close ties to other countries. Such ties encourage more legal and illegal immigration.

Preventing illegal immigration has until recently fallen largely on the U.S. Customs Service, Border Patrol, and Immigration and Naturalization Service (beginning in March 2003, these agencies have been reorganized as part of the new U.S. Department of Homeland Security). The agencies face a daunting task given the high levels of immigration, huge numbers of persons crossing American borders, and limited resources of the government agencies. Some call for tighter border security to stop illegal immigration and even advocate using the military to patrol U.S. borders, particularly those with Mexico. They also suggest that employers do more to ensure their workers have proper documentation. Others oppose these actions, believing that immigrants contribute importantly to the U.S. economy, deserve opportunities to improve themselves outside their own countries, and represent a powerful political interest group.

Given the lack of consensus on how to deal with illegal immigration, two difficult tasks confront border and immigration officials. They must not only screen those crossing the border but must also work to apprehend illegal immigrants already in the United States. Not all persons crossing the border and certainly not all persons within the border can be thoroughly checked; other means, some involving discretion of the agents, must be used to identify those in the country illegally. Since illegal immigrants often appear physically different than the majority of citizens in skin color, ethnicity, and national origin, the potential to use racial profiling exists. Given high levels of illegal immigration from Mexico, Central America, and South

America, Latinos in particular face a special risk of being profiled as illegal immigrants.

The U.S. Supreme Court has in the past given discretion to those enforcing immigration laws to use race and ethnicity as criteria in checking for illegal immigrants. In *United States v. Martinez-Fuerte* (1976), the Court rejected the contention of a Mexican living illegally in the United States that his conviction for smuggling immigrants into the country was unconstitutional because it came from stopping people of perceived Mexican lineage at checkpoints. In *United States v. Brignoni-Ponce* (1975), the Court held that Hispanic or Mexican appearance alone does not justify stopping to check for documents but could be considered along with other factors.

More recently, legal opinions may be changing. By holding in 2000 that border agents may not consider Hispanic appearance when stopping individuals for questioning, the U.S. Ninth Circuit Court of Appeals has put new limits on the use of ethnicity by border patrol agents (see *United States v. Montero-Camargo*). The U.S. Border Patrol claimed in response to the ruling that it does not use racial profiling.

Despite such claims, many civil rights and Hispanic groups contend the opposite. For example, case files and memos of the Immigration and Naturalization Service in the New York District demonstrate that agents used skin color, a Spanish accent, and specific clothing as evidence to justify an immigration raid. Highway patrol officers in Ohio appear to have stopped Hispanic drivers to question them about immigration matters. According to civil rights groups, these actions threaten the well-being of millions of Latino citizens in the United States.

Terrorism and Immigration

With the September 11, 2001, terrorist attacks, efforts to find illegal immigrants, particularly those from the Middle East with possible terrorist ties, took on new urgency. The strikes on the two World Trade Center buildings in New York City and the Pentagon in Washington, D.C., involved the hijacking of four planes (one of which crashed in Pennsylvania before reaching a target). The hijackers, 19 Muslim Arab men, 15 of whom came from Saudi Arabia, had entered the country on valid visas but remained after the visas expired. Immigration issues now raised new concerns about terrorism and national security.

The PATRIOT Act in 2001, passed soon after the terrorist attacks, permits the attorney general of the United States to detain aliens that he certifies as threats to national security for up to seven days without bringing charges. It also increases the government's ability to use wiretaps and share secret information across agencies. Some contend that, along with violating civil rights, the act promotes racial profiling of Muslims and Arabs.

In May 2002, President George W. Bush signed another piece of legislation relating to immigration and terrorism, the Enhanced Border Security and Visa Reform Act.[20] The new law bans foreign visitors from countries deemed sponsors of terrorism and sets up procedures to track the entry and exit of all foreign visitors to the United States. Government agencies, including law enforcement agencies such as the Federal Bureau of Investigation (FBI), can also share information about immigrants. To help in these new tasks, the law supplies funds to hire new border patrol agents. Advocates believe the law will help protect homeland security, while critics believe it will increase discrimination against minorities.

Along with these new laws, other antiterrorism activities of the government have come under scrutiny. The American Civil Liberties Union (ACLU) has strongly criticized data-gathering plans of the FBI. In determining where to concentrate terrorism investigations, the agency has proposed to use demographic information on neighborhoods, including the number of mosques. This might lead agents to investigate Muslims without any information indicating terrorist activity and rely on ethnic background in identifying suspects.

A report from the U.S. government in 2003 criticized the treatment of 762 detainees, largely from Arab nations, who were jailed for immigration violations after the September 11 attacks.[21] Many had to face unduly long jail stays and harsh conditions for being in the United States illegally, despite having no connection to terrorism. Arab groups accused the Justice Department of singling out Muslims and Middle Easterners, as if coming from an Arab country signified terrorist connections. Despite criticism, the Justice Department defended the legality of its actions in regard to the illegal immigrants: "We make no apologies for finding every legal way possible to protect the American public from further terrorist attacks."[22]

ANTITERRORISM AIRPORT SCREENING

The September 11 attacks intensified not only immigration control but also screening at airports to prevent future hijackings and bombings. Given the background of the terrorists, screening in the days and weeks after September 11 focused on Muslim and Arab men—whether or not they were in the United States legally. Well-publicized instances of Arab men taken off planes because other passengers found their activities suspicious reflected bias rather than any evidence of terrorist activities. For example, Arshad Chowdhury, a U.S. citizen working toward a master's degree in business administration at Carnegie-Mellon University and the child of parents who had emigrated from Bangladesh, was prevented from boarding his flight because his name sounded like that of a suspected terrorist. After security agents investigated Chowdhury, he boarded a later flight but filed suit over the incident, claiming he was a victim of a form of racial profiling based on his Middle Eastern appearance.[23]

Since 1994, the Computer Assisted Passenger Profiling System (CAPPS) has used up to 40 pieces of information on passengers collected by the airlines to identify those who, according to the profile, warrant a more careful search. A number of randomly selected passengers are examined as well. CAPPS does not include race or ethnicity in its profile criteria. A report from the Justice Department found that the system does not discriminate on the basis of race, color, national or ethnic origin, religion, or gender.[24]

However, some worry that the items used in the profile can have disparate impact on certain groups. The criteria for screening, which remain secret, might, for example, end up selecting more persons from the Middle East or Africa than Europe. In addition, the government has, in the wake of the September 11 attacks, discussed adding additional information about travel history, buying patterns, former addresses, and other personal behavior.[25] Besides violating the privacy of travelers, the new information may do even more to select some groups rather than others for intense investigation.

Calling for more stringent airport screening, some make the case for ethnic profiling. With millions of passengers traveling through airports, any effective measure to prevent terrorism needs to use known facts to narrow the scope of inquiry. The facts relating to terrorism remain clear: Islamic anti-American terrorism almost by definition involves Muslims from the Middle East or Asia. A system of random screening that ignores this fact can easily miss potential terrorists—and threaten the safety of flyers.

If racial profiling is to be used in airports, it must rely on factors that reliably predict the likelihood of offending. Race or ethnicity alone have little predictive value but can complement behavioral factors to create a useful profile. For example, if intelligence warns that terrorists residing in Egypt have planned an attack, stopping all Egyptian visitors makes little sense. It would work, however, to give special attention to Egyptian travelers who match other characteristics of a profile. Such procedures have worked well in Israel, where screening profiles tend to select young Arab men for detailed searches, and have prevented terrorist bombings of planes for more than 30 years.

Advocates of the use of profiling in airports view the procedures as different from profiling of drug couriers on American highways. For one, failing to stop a terrorist in the airport has worse consequences than failing to catch a drug courier on the highway—the imminent death of thousands of people may result from the former, while additional drugs on the street result from the latter. For another, a stronger connection exists between Middle Eastern Muslim background and terrorism than the connection between race and drug distribution. All terrorists who have hijacked American planes for the purpose of murder have been fanatical Muslims, while the drug trade crosses all races, ethnicities, and national origin groups.

Those proposing the use of national origin profiling in airport recognize the inconvenience it would create for persons of Arab descent. In most cases, however, the extra screening does not place excessive burden on innocent travelers and can have much benefit if it prevents a terrorist act. One American woman, Fedwa Malti-Douglas, has often been detained at airports on the basis of ethnic profiling: She was born in Lebanon, travels often in the Middle East, and has an Arabic-sounding name. She nonetheless says, "Despite the inconvenience to me, I believe this scrutiny is a defensible tactic for picking out potential problem passengers. Although I am not a terrorist, others do not necessarily know it. The airline security procedures I ran into also protect me from terrorism."[26]

Opponents of racial profiling call such screening ineffective as well as immoral. Since Muslim terrorists make up only a tiny portion of all Muslims, special searches of the vast majority of law-abiding Muslims wastes resources. Moreover, terrorists come from all races, ethnic groups, and nations. Richard Reid, who tried to ignite explosives hidden in his shoes on a transatlantic flight, was a British citizen of Jamaican ancestry. Officials would do better to gain the trust and help of law-abiding Arab Americans in the terrorism fight rather than to alienate them.

Even if more effective, profiling in airports would violate the civil rights of certain groups. Opponents of racial profiling thus remain consistent in their views: Racial profiling is wrong after September 11 just as it was wrong before September 11. Protecting the public from terrorism in the air requires screening of all passengers similarly or selecting passengers at random for detailed screening.

THE CASE FOR RACIAL PROFILING

Proponents of *racial profiling* prefer not to use that term—instead, *criminal profiling*, in which race, ethnicity, or national origin serves as one component, more accurately reflects police work.[27] They argue that the use of "hard profiling" on the basis of race alone breaks the law but occurs only rarely—it is a myth, in the words of Heather Mac Donald a writer who has defended police actions.[28] In contrast, criminal profiling that includes a race, ethnic, or national-origin component is legal and appropriate under three conditions:

- The addition of race or ethnic factors to a profile should prove effective in finding the guilty. Evidence must exist to suggest that one group is more likely to participate in certain crimes than others.
- A meaningful portion of the race or ethnic group must be involved in the activity. If the percentage is small, say less than 1 percent, then the profiling brings little benefit and has much cost.
- The benefit of including race or ethnicity in a profile, such as preventing a terrorist attack or slowing the flow of drugs to cities, must be important enough to outweigh the imposition on innocent persons.[29]

In making the case for profiling, defenders suggest that police actions meet these requirements. When treating race, ethnicity, or national origin as part of a criminal profile, it does not reflect discrimination, only good investigative work. The discussion to follow provides evidence for this claim but uses the short-hand term "racial profiling" to refer to criminal profiling with a race, ethnic, or national-origin component.

INVESTIGATIVE CLUES

The case for racial profiling is easily stated: Race, ethnicity, and national origin are legitimate components of profiling because they increase the chance of discovering or preventing crime. Since certain racial, ethnic, and national origin groups statistically tend to be more involved in crime than others, police investigations by group membership does not involve discrimination in the usual sense. Rather than stemming from an irrational hatred, racial profiling stems from rational recognition of basic facts: Some race, ethnic, and national origin groups tend to be disproportionately involved in certain types of crime such as carrying, selling, or buying drugs; illegally crossing the national border; or committing terrorist acts. Police dealing with these problems will naturally focus on those groups most likely to offend in these ways.

One Los Angeles police officer puts the case thusly: "In the United States of America in the year 2000 A.D., certain ethnic groups tend to violate the law in numbers far in excess of their representation in the population. The debate may rage as to why this is so, but only after accepting the truth can honest dialogue take place."[30] The high levels of minority participation in crime reflect a variety of forces. A history of economic discrimination, low levels of skills, language problems, the lack of legitimate opportunities for success, poor schools, and generally deprived circumstances sadly contribute to higher crime among many minority groups. Still, police can do little about these larger social factors—they can focus only on preventing crime.

This may sound harsh, but most proponents of racial profiling claim they have no animus against minority groups and recognize the mistreatment they have suffered. They agree that race, ethnicity, and national origin alone do not justify making a stop, even if the group has a high rate of criminal offending. One expert states that race as the sole reason for a traffic stop is wrong, unlawful, and contrary to good police work.[31]

Instead, race can serve as one piece of a larger criminal profile of traits associated with criminal activity. These criminal profiles, which come from observation, intuition, and accumulated experience of police officers, serve as useful investigative clues and rely on behavioral characteristics as well as race, ethnicity, and national origin. When stopping suspects, police may also rely on cues such as inconsistent stories, nervous mannerisms, unlabeled packages that may hold drugs, and efforts to hide or avoid police. The key to profiling is not race itself but the association of high crime and suspicious activity with race.

If, for example, intelligence or police experience produces information that Hispanic gangs are transporting contraband in expensive cars with Florida license plates during the night over interstate highways in the Northeast, it would warrant checking drivers that fit the profile. If intelligence or police experience produces information that Russian gangs are active in dealing Ecstasy at New York City clubs, it would warrant giving special attention to men of Russian origin. If police information suggests that the burnings of black churches reflect racially motivated action, it would warrant giving special attention to white middle-aged men with bigoted attitudes.

By this logic, racial profiling applies to whites as well. Young white men driving around a minority neighborhood, particularly in areas where drugs are sold on the street, deserve special suspicion. White members of motorcycle gangs with a reputation for drug trafficking deserve suspicion as much as minority drug couriers. Suspects are stopped not only because of their race but also because the circumstances suggest they may have a possible connection to drug use, transport, or sales.

Certain types of discrimination that appear similar to racial profiling have become accepted parts of social life.[32] Based on statistical profiles, automobile insurance companies charge higher rates for younger persons than older persons and for young men than young women. Accident rates are higher for young men than young women and for younger persons than older persons. That does not mean that every young man will have an accident and that every older person will not. Rather, the discrimination relates to probabilities. The probabilities apply to crime and police efforts as well as to insurance. Police direct their attention to places where crime is high and, sadly, in American society these places tend to have many minorities.

Disproportionate Offending

Defenders of racial profiling rely on more than personal beliefs in making their claims. They cite three sources of evidence for their contention that minority groups have elevated rates of criminal participation: Data on arrest, data from victimization surveys, and data on vehicle violations.

First, the FBI reports (usually after a delay of several years) arrest figures obtained from state and local police agencies.[33] The figures for 2000, the latest available, disclose that 27.9 percent of all persons arrested are black and 69.7 percent are white. Further, of all persons arrested for weapons violations, 36.8 percent are black and 61.3 percent are white; of all persons arrested for drug abuse violations, 34.5 percent are black and 64.2 percent are white; and of all persons arrested for murder, 48.8 are black and 48.7 percent are white. Although white arrests outnumber black arrests, blacks make up about 13 percent and whites (including Hispanics) make up about 82 percent of the population. The total arrest percentages for blacks are more than two times higher than their population percentage, and murder arrests for blacks are nearly four times higher than their population percentage. The arrest rates show heavy involvement of blacks relative to whites in crime.

Second, data on crime come from the National Crime Victimization Survey. The figures do not depend on arrests by police, who may discriminate against minorities. Rather, they come from the reports of victims, who can describe the perceived race of offenders (whether or not the perpetrator was apprehended). Victim reports focus specifically on crimes of violence such as rape, robbery, and assault in which the victim can report on the characteristics of the offender; crimes such as burglary or drug sales are excluded because victims typically do not observe the offender, or both parties willingly participate. (Murder is excluded for obvious reasons.) According to the most recent survey, 64.3 percent of single offenders are white and 24.6 percent are black (nearly twice as high as their representation in the population).[34] Most of the crimes committed by blacks involve black victims rather than white victims and do not stem from false accusations by whites. For example, 83.1 percent of black victims identify their attacker as black, compared to 14.4 percent of white victims who identify their attacker as black.[35] Evidence on crimes involving multiple offenders also reveals disproportionate offending by blacks, again typically against black victims.

Third, other evidence relates to race differences in traffic violations. At least according to some reports, blacks have higher accident rates, drive more often under the influence of alcohol, and are involved in more vehicle fatalities.[36] A recent study examined 40,000 photo radar pictures of drivers going 15 miles per hour or more beyond the 65-miles-per-hour speed limit on New Jersey highways. The results indicated higher rates of speeding among blacks than whites: Blacks made up 25 percent of the speeders but only 16 percent of the drivers on the turnpike.[37] Police likely respond to traffic violations of minorities rather than to skin color alone.

Some claim in response to figures such as these that studies asking whites and blacks to self-report their criminal activity and drug use reveal few differences in offending. However, these studies are often limited to juvenile populations rather than adult populations and to minor crimes rather than major crimes. For adults and more serious crimes, supporters of racial profiling argue that self-reported crime figures, like other measures of crime, demonstrate higher offending among blacks than whites. Indeed, race differences in arrests are greatest for the most serious crimes like murder or aggravated assault—precisely the crimes in which police have the least discretion over who to investigate.

The statistics on race differences in arrest, offending, and vehicle violations thus contradict claims that police unfairly discriminate against minorities. Opponents of racial profiling often base their criticisms on the fact that the percentages of blacks stopped by police greatly exceed their percentage in the population. Yet, given race differences in offending, population size has limited relevance. If it did, one might argue that grandmothers should be represented in police stops in accordance with their population size, but in fact grandmothers rarely commit crimes. According to defenders of police, statistics that fail to consider differences across groups in criminal involvement are meaningless.

Such figures, although painful to African Americans, suggest that stopping blacks on roadways, sidewalks, and public places has a basis in fact. African Americans may recognize these facts as well as whites. In a famous 1993 quotation, Jesse Jackson stated, "There is nothing more painful to me at this stage in my life than to walk down the street and hear footsteps and start thinking about robbery. Then [I] look around and see someone white and feel relieved."[38] Many black policemen and residents of minority neighborhoods recognize the greater levels of crime committed by blacks and want police protection from risks of these crimes. Although a long history of slavery, discrimination, and poverty contribute to high African-American rates of minority crime, these unfortunate facts do not change the rates of criminal activity.

In short, some make the case that racial profiling is appropriate and fair. The disproportionate offending among blacks justifies the larger number of stops in the investigation of crime. Much the same reasoning applies to Hispanics in regard to illegal immigration and smuggling drugs across borders and to Arabs and Muslims in regard to involvement in terrorist groups. Today, most undocumented aliens are Hispanic; most of the men on the FBI's Most

Wanted Terrorists list were born in Saudi Arabia and Egypt, and all are Muslims. In these circumstances, proponents of racial profiling believe involvement in crime justifies giving special attention to minority groups.

POLICE ATTITUDE

Much of the opposition to racial profiling originates with the belief that police hold racist attitudes. Defenders of profiling reject this assertion. Except for small, marginal groups of bigots, they believe, whites today, including white police officers, do not aim to persecute minorities but would prefer equality.[39] Despite deplorable discrimination and racism in the past, attitudes across the population today favor racial equality.

A general review of research accordingly finds that officers do not discriminate in making arrests.[40] In making arrests, the actions of white police officers differ little in regard to black and white suspects and little from the actions of black officers. If racial discrimination by white police officers against blacks caused the high arrest rates, it should follow that black police officers, who lack prejudice against other blacks, would act differently than white police officers. Yet, studies find few such differences. Like white officers, black officers dispute the claim that they unfairly target minorities—as minorities themselves, they recognize that the place, time, and context of decisions are more important.

Do white officers who reject racist ideologies still use, perhaps unconsciously, unfair and inaccurate stereotypes? Again, advocates of racial profiling say no. One study of youth offenders, for example, finds that, once accounting for the seriousness of the offense, police are no more likely to arrest nonwhite than white juvenile offenders.[41] To the extent that police use stereotypes, they do so when they help in law enforcement. Although inaccurate stereotypes create problems, most stereotypes are, they claim, accurate and useful in life.[42] Rather than being used to exaggerate and discriminate, stereotypes develop on the basis of factual probabilities, and perceptions usually match objective indicators about group characteristics. When police use information on race, ethnic, and national origin, it often has a basis in fact.

If police did in fact do the opposite—stop and detain individuals based on race alone—they would face department discipline and perhaps a lawsuit. In making a stop, an officer must be able to state the reason for suspecting criminal activity. In the words of one police officer, "If the underlying reasonable suspicion is later found to be lacking, then the subsequent arrest will be ruled unlawful and the officer will be exposed to potential civil liability regardless of the factual culpability of the arrestee."[43] The evidence will not be used and the officer may be subject to a lawsuit.

If police act fairly, they nonetheless are punished for stating the obvious. Col. Carl Williams, head of the New Jersey State Police, was fired by Governor Christie Todd Whitman for suggesting that minority groups dominate the cocaine and marijuana trade. Williams stated that when U.S. officials left the country to discuss drug problems, they went to Mexico rather than Ireland. Although true, the statement led to Williams's firing because many viewed it as insensitive. "Political correctness" has, according to advocates of racial profiling, distorted issues of truth. In another instance, New Jersey state officials and the U.S. Department of Justice tried to quash a report that demonstrated higher rates of speeding by black drivers than white drivers.[44]

Some police officers are no doubt racist and act unfairly in their use of racial profiling. Stories of mistreatment of minority drivers by police officers highlight such instances. Proponents of racial profiling, however, believe that isolated examples of misuse do not characterize all police. Most officers use racial profiling appropriately, are not racist, and do well in protecting the public from crime. Accusations of racism have the unfortunate effect of diverting attention to one of the most serious problems American society faces—the high rate of crime in minority communities.

Effectiveness of Racial Profiling

Those who favor racial profiling argue that, given limited police resources, it provides an efficient means to combat crime. The alternatives needed to avoid the use of race, ethnicity, or national origin as criteria—to stop all persons, stop a random selection of persons, or use quotas in stopping—prove ineffective. If police were to stop all cars or a subset at random on a highway in the search for contraband, it would waste much time and effort on failed investigations. If police were to avoid stopping black speeders and focus on stopping white speeders in order to match racial percentages in the population, they would illegally discriminate.

The same reasoning applies to airport screening. Intensive searches of all persons would prevent the flow of travelers through an airport; intensive searches based on random selection would lead workers to carefully check elderly persons or Swedish travelers while missing young men or travelers from Egypt. One congressman reported seeing an 87-year-old woman lifted out of her wheelchair to be searched thoroughly while others passed through with only minimal checks.[45] On highways or in airports, common sense suggests checking those who have the highest risk more carefully than others.

Evidence cited by proponents in fact indicates that eliminating the use of race and ethnicity in profiling does much to harm police efforts. Worried about being second-guessed for their decisions, police would make fewer traffic stops, which would in turn lead to more vehicle violations, more crime, and less drug interdiction. For example, a 2001 report finds that Seattle police officers, who fear that their use of aggressive policing will lead to accusations of racial profiling, have cut back on the number of arrests they make. Since more offending occurs in minority neighborhoods and more calls come to the police from residents of those neighborhoods, the concerns of police officers in Seattle and elsewhere may aggravate victimization of minorities by crime.[46]

Elimination of racial profiling would hamper police in other ways as well. The ability to stop drug trafficking, which has led to high rates of violence, murder, and addiction in cities, would lessen. Efforts to rid street corners of drug dealers and to eliminate crack houses from neighborhoods, actions favored by law-abiding residents, would decline. Enforcing quality-of-life crimes, which has proven successful in making cities such as New York City more livable, would be hindered. Police would, according to the arguments of supporters, have to direct their attention away from crime if race, ethnicity, and national origin were not allowed as parts of criminal profiles.

Changes in crime in New Jersey illustrate the problems that come from eliminating racial profiling. There, the state police "no longer distribute a typical felony-offender profile to their officers" because such profiles might contribute to what the state's attorney general calls "inappropriate stereotypes" about criminals.[47] As a result, "At the height of the drug war in 1988, the [New Jersey] troopers filed 7,400 drug charges from the turnpike, most of them from consent searches; in 2000 [after ending racial profiling] they filed 370 drug charges, a number that doubtless has been dropping since then. It is unlikely that drug trafficking has dropped on New Jersey's main highway by anything like these percentages."[48] Homicide rates, which relate to drug trafficking, have at the same time risen in Newark and Camden, New Jersey.

The avoidance of racial profiling has, from the viewpoint of advocates, even more ominous implications in regard to terrorism. Failure to properly screen people in airports can result in something as horrible as the September 11 attacks. An FBI official in Phoenix reported to superiors that many Arab men had enrolled in U.S. flight schools. The *New York Times* reported that "FBI officials said there was reluctance at the time to mount such a major review [of Arabs enrolled in the flight schools] because of a concern that the bureau would be criticized for ethnic profiling of foreigners."[49] Perhaps some form of profiling could have prevented the September 11 tragedy. In any case, ignoring the likelihood that members of some groups are more likely to attempt terrorist attacks than others puts all flyers at risk.

If use of profiling to deal with drug couriers, street criminals, and terrorists sometimes results in stopping innocent men and women, the benefits in protecting citizens from crime outweigh this cost. Typically the cost is small, as innocent persons are inconvenienced only briefly by a stop. As one African-American man states, "Sooner or later we all have to make a sacrifice in order to maintain law and order, to keep people under control. That's something I am willing to sacrifice, but I'm not sure how far I'm willing to take it. I don't have anything to hide, so if it takes searching my car, or searching every car cops come across that they think is suspect, then go ahead and do it."[50]

THE CASE AGAINST RACIAL PROFILING

Politicians with diverse political views offer near-unanimous opposition to racial profiling. President Bill Clinton called racial profiling a "morally indefensible, deeply corrosive practice . . . the opposite of good police work, where actions are based on hard facts, not stereotypes. It is wrong, it is destructive, and it must stop."[51] In his 2001 State of the Union address, President George W. Bush said of racial profiling, "It's wrong, and we will end it in America."[52]

Former Republican senator from Missouri and current (as of 2003) attorney general of the United States John Ashcroft stated in a Senate hearing on alleged instances of racial profiling that "The mere fact that these allegations exist troubles me greatly. It troubles me not only for the constitutional implications that it raises, but also for the extraordinary destructive effect that such allegations would have on the confidence of people in the Government."[53] Ashcroft's Democratic colleague in the Senate hearing, Russell Feingold of Wisconsin, makes an equally strong statement against racial profiling:

> *Victims of racial profiling are forced to endure an incredibly humiliating experience, sometimes even a physically threatening one, on roadsides or in the back seat of police cruisers. Why? Because of the color of their skin. Not just African Americans and Latinos, but all Americans should feel threatened when any one of us is denied our personal liberty in such an insidious and humiliating way. In 21st century America, racial profiling is not only indefensible, it is an affront to our Nation's fundamental principles of justice, liberty, and equality.*[54]

Like most politicians, critics of racial profiling oppose the use of race, ethnicity, or national origin as criteria in any form—even when only part of a larger criminal profile. They believe that it is unfair, based on flawed reasoning, ineffective for police, and harmful to society.

Unfairness

The unfairness of racial profiling comes from making judgments about individuals on the basis of membership in race, ethnic, and national-origin groups rather than on their behavior. In essence, racial profiling relies on the use of stereotypes. A stereotype inflexibly generalizes all members of a group based on the behavior or traits of some members. Stereotypes may in some cases have validity: Ex-convicts must report to parole officers because some return to crime immediately on release from prison. However, stereotypes applied to race, ethnic, and national-origin groups rely on appearance rather than behavior, rarely, if ever, have validity, and violate American principles of individuality.

If some African Americans are involved in the drug trade, if some Hispanics are illegal aliens, and if some Arab Muslims are terrorists, it should not cast suspicion on all African Americans, Hispanics, and Arab Muslims. That the United States has higher homicide rates than other high-income nations does not imply that all Americans are criminals. Nor should the behavior of some minorities imply that all members of the groups are criminals. In assuming that all members of a group are alike, such reasoning, although reflected in racial profiling according to critics, is oversimplified, inaccurate, and prejudiced.

Most people realize intellectually that they should not make generalizations about race, ethnic, and national-origin groups. Still, even the most well-meaning find it hard to avoid using stereotypes—they may not even be consciously aware of their thinking. Certain beliefs—such as the high involvement of minorities in crime—become so widely accepted that people cannot help but act on them. Indeed, the depiction of crime in the media may promote these beliefs. The resulting discrimination is informal rather than formal, appears in subtle rather than obvious ways, and differs from the legally mandated discrimination in the past. Still, the discrimination remains immoral and unfair.

To illustrate the continued existence of discrimination, the television show *ABC News Prime Time Live* filmed an experiment. Two friends, identical in nearly all respects but one—John is white and Glen is black—tried to rent an apartment, respond to job advertisements, and purchase a car. Using a hidden camera, the show compared people's reactions to the two men. In both white and racially mixed communities, John generally received more positive treatment than did Glen. The different responses related not to the actions of the men but to largely unconscious stereotypes about the races. In similarly unfair ways, people may wrongly use the distinctive dress of some African-American youth as indication of gang membership, the accent of Hispanic Americans as indication of illegal immigration, and Middle Eastern names and dress as indication of hatred of the United States.

Like others in society, police use unfair stereotypes. Some police officers may have individual prejudices against minorities, hold racist beliefs, use insulting slang, or tell belittling jokes. However, police need not be evil or corrupt to misuse stereotypes in racial profiling. Even those who work hard, value honesty, and perform with bravery can, given the society in which they live and work, act unfairly. *Institutional racism*, a term refers to that day-to-day practices that have harmful effects on minorities, can promote discrimination much as individual racism does. With institutional racism, a double standard—one for the majority and one for the minority—is built into the system. Individual police officers may not have motives to harm minorities, but the practices they implement have that effect. Racial profiling represents one practice that reflects institutional racism and the unequal positions of race, ethnic, and national-origin groups in the United States.

Consider some examples of institutional racism cited by critics of racial profiling. If police come to define use of crack cocaine, used primarily by minorities, as a more serious problem than the use of powdered cocaine or Ecstasy, used more often by whites, it has the effect of focusing police attention on minorities. If police define street crime as more serious than white-collar crime, the impact falls on the minorities who tend in U.S. society to most often be victims of poverty. If police define groups with different ways of acting, speaking, and dressing as abnormal or inappropriate, it leads them to view innocent behavior with suspicion. In these ways, widely accepted beliefs, policies, and definitions that on the surface do not involve racism still have discriminatory effects.

Racial profiling reflects institutional racism in another way. Differences in power between minority and majority groups inevitably produce unequal interaction. Non-Hispanic whites have higher incomes, better education, and more prestigious jobs than most minorities; dominate culture, media, and scholarship, and enjoy political, economic, and social power. With police representing the established power structure and enforcing its values and beliefs, and with minorities subject to domination by the majority, conflict results. Police have difficulty implementing laws in a color-blind way and come to rely unfairly on perceived group differences in their actions. Such problems in group relations and majority-minority interaction have become commonplace in U.S. society.

The unfairness of racial profiling should, according to opponents, trouble both liberals and conservatives. Because of their traditional concern with inequality and support for disadvantaged groups, liberals worry about the power of police. Use of racial profiling, in their view, works to reinforce the power of advantaged groups and threaten the civil rights of the less powerful. For different reasons, some conservatives also worry about the potential for police abuse inherent in racial profiling. Reflecting their concern about the potential for government tyranny, they believe that racial profiling violates values of individual liberty, personal responsibility, and freedom from government power.

RACE DIFFERENCES IN CRIME

Statistics reveal higher arrest rates of blacks than whites, leading some to suggest that crime and drug use reach higher levels among blacks than whites and justify racial profiling. However, opponents of racial profiling contend that race statistics on arrests say virtually nothing about real behavior. Nor do other statistics or informal experiences of police officers with members of race, ethnic, and national-origin minorities excuse racial profiling in making stops. Such information has fundamental and serious flaws.

Arrest statistics are flawed because they reflect the behavior of police as much as the behavior of those arrested. If police rely on stereotypes about race, ethnic, and national-origin groups in their investigations, they will focus more on minorities. Since there is a strong relationship between looking for things and finding them, racial profiling will lead police to find illegal activity among minorities. If police stop excessive numbers of black drivers, they will find evidence of excess black crime. This represents a self-fulfilling prophecy according to David A. Harris, a law professor and critic of racial profiling: "More blacks are arrested, so more blacks are criminals, so to catch more criminals, police stop more blacks, which leads to more blacks arrested."[55] Similarly, discriminatory laws that make penalties more severe for crack cocaine than for powdered cocaine lead police to look for, find, and arrest more black than white drug users.

Victim reports of the race of offenders reflect a different sort of bias—they miss drug offenses, one of the central crimes justifying racial profiling. Most victims of assault, rape, or robbery naturally report the crime to police. However, drug crimes involving the sale, use, or transport of illegal substances do not involve a victim in the same way—those involved willingly participate. Victimization surveys neglect such crime, and the data they provide do not merit giving special attention to minorities in the search for drugs.

More helpful data come from national surveys of drug use. A report from the National Household Survey of Drug Abuse for persons ages 12 and over states, "Rates of current illicit drug use among the major racial/ethnic groups in 2001 were 7.2 percent for whites, 6.4 percent for Hispanics, and 7.4 percent for blacks."[56] Such small differences between blacks and whites, and the low rates among Hispanics, do not justify racial profiling in the war on drugs.

The similar rates of drug use across race and ethnic groups are revealed in what officials call "hit rates"—the percentage of searches in which drugs are found. In one study, the hit rates for vehicles stopped on interstate highways were nearly identical for blacks and whites.[57] Similarly, a study of U.S. customs searches found that nationwide hit rates were 6.7 percent for whites, 6.2 percent for blacks, and 2.8 percent for Hispanics.[58] Again, the figures belie claims, used to defend racial profiling, of excessive smuggling among minorities.

Perhaps racial profiling contributed to the decline in crime rates in the United States and in several large cities during the 1990s. Again, however, a careful look at the statistics suggests otherwise according to those critical of racial profiling. Crime rates fell in New York City, where police appear to have used racial profiling as part of their emphasis on quality-of-life crimes. Yet, crime rates fell just as much in San Diego and Boston, where police avoided zero-tolerance tactics and racial profiling. These two cities instead used community policing methods that involved cooperation with residents of minority neighborhoods.

In short, those making the case against racial profiling argue that the facts about crime do not excuse the practice. Given similarities in black, white, and Hispanic criminal behavior, police attention to race follows from inappropriate stereotypes and discrimination.

Flaws in Profiling

Critics of racial profiling suggest that the guidelines for profiling are so vague, even contradictory, as to be ineffective. They have over the years become so broad as to potentially include nearly everyone. At one time or another, for example, driving new and expensive cars, old and inexpensive cars, or rented cars were part of profiles of drug couriers, as were having too much or too little luggage. Under these circumstances, police have much discretion over whom they decide to stop. Race—whether or not officers admit it—easily can become the key characteristic in a decision to stop someone.[59]

Broadening of profiles is to be expected: If drug couriers try to confuse police by doing the opposite expected of them, then profiles will come to include a behavior and its opposite. Religious belongings in a car might be used to confuse police who expect drug smugglers to be nonreligious; dressing like a professional might likewise be used to confuse police who expect stereotypical gang clothing. Indications of religiousness and a professional job can, ironically, become part of a profile of a drug courier.

Law professor David Cole summarizes the problem: "In theory, it simply compiles the collective wisdom and judgment of a given agency's officials. . . . In practice, the drug courier profile is a scattershot hodgepodge of traits and characteristics so expansive that it potentially justifies stopping anybody and everybody."[60] Illustrative of this are some of the traits listed as part of a profile in regard to air travel:

- arrived late at night, arrived early in the morning, arrived in the afternoon;
- one of the first to deplane, one of the last to deplane, deplaned in the middle;
- purchased ticket at airport, made reservation on short notice, bought coach ticket, bought first-class ticket;
- carried no luggage, carried brand-new luggage, carried a small bag, carried a medium-sized bag, carried two bulky garment bags, carried two heavy suitcases, carried four pieces of luggage;
- walked quickly through airport, walked slowly through airport, walked aimlessly through airport;
- left airport by taxi, left airport by limousine, left airport by private car, left airport by hotel courtesy van; and
- dressed casually, wore expensive clothing with gold jewelry.

Such lists provide too much discretion to officers in making choices, discretion that may lead to reliance on race, ethnicity, or national origin rather than true clues of drug smuggling or transporting.

Profiles may in other circumstances entail similarly doubtful inferences. Police may view loitering on street corners as suspicious activity. However, given small apartments, the expense of going to restaurants or clubs, and the lack of public meeting places for minorities in poor neighborhoods, talking on street corners makes sense. Police may look for nervous behavior and efforts to evade them as suspicious activity. Yet, innocent minorities accustomed to mistreatment of residents of their neighborhood by police may act nervously and evasively. Police may view minorities in white neighborhoods with suspicion, even though minority groups by definition will more often be "out of place" than majority groups: With most areas being dominant white, much legitimate travel by minorities will put them "out of place." These instances of simple and innocent conduct by minorities may, under racial profiling practices, subject them to unfair monitoring by police.

Ultimately, then, opponents maintain that racial profiling efforts will fail because they are ineffective as well as unjust. Most racial profiling traits have only a weak association with criminal behavior, and statistical averages based on race, ethnicity, or national origin rarely help predict the behavior of individual group members. Even if a racial profile trait has some validity based on past experience, offenders will develop new ways to get around the profiling. If profiling has a place in criminal investigation, it cannot include race, ethnic, or national-origin characteristics.

COSTS OF PROFILING

Racial profiling has serious psychological costs. Innocent victims first experience fear, humiliation, and degradation, and ultimately anger, indignation, and feelings of injustice. Minorities feel harassed, intimidated, and violated—the emotional distress is so great that some victims compare it to a physical assault. As with an assault, victims of racial profiling are subject to the demands of the police—however unfair they are—and have little control over the situation. Christopher Darden, one of the prosecutors in the O. J. Simpson case, has, he believes, been stopped by police because he is black. He says: "It is so demeaning. It undermines and calls into question everything you've accomplished in your life, everything you have worked for. No matter how hard you've worked, no matter what you do, no matter how diligently [you've] pursued the American dream, you're treated like a common criminal."[61]

The harm of racial profiling can, according to some experts, last for long periods. One psychologist has compared the experience of blacks and minorities in dealing with racism in general, including experiences such as those resulting from racial profiling, "as a form of emotional . . . and psychological trauma."[62] In this way, the humiliation of being unfairly stopped by police can be similar to post-traumatic stress syndrome. Post-traumatic stress syndrome is often diagnosed in Vietnam War veterans, victims of rape, and survivors of a natural disaster such as a flood. The traumatic event causes continued stress through re-experiencing the event in thoughts and dreams, avoiding situations that symbolize the event, and becoming unresponsive in social relationships. Some may view an unwarranted stop of minorities by police as a minor inconvenience, but others see the consequences as more serious.

Personal costs come in other ways. Because they worry about police pulling them over, minorities may avoid traveling certain routes or into certain neighborhoods, buying luxury cars that might be perceived as stolen or financed by illicit earnings, and dressing in ways that might attract attention. Even while shopping, minorities may feel uncomfortable because the practice of racial profiling leads store employees to wrongly monitor and confront them about shoplifting. More than a brief annoyance, racial profiling requires minorities to attend to their daily activities with the fear of being stopped.

The costs of racial profiling extend beyond the individual victims. In a larger sense, racial profiling harms all members of society by weakening the civil rights that protect citizens from the power of the government. If minorities are subject to profiling, profiling may extend to majority groups in the future. It threatens the idea of "innocent until proven guilty" by assuming that certain actions or characteristics imply guilt. Most Americans disapprove of racial profiling, so if the police continue to use it, they will lose legitimacy in the eyes of the public. Not surprisingly, those who have had personal experiences with profiling have a lower opinion of local and state police.

Ultimately, racial profiling weakens law enforcement rather than improves it. In the short run, use of race to investigate subjects may catch criminals, but in the long run it will make law enforcement harder. If minority groups view the actions of police as illegitimate, they will do less to cooperate: They will report crime less often and do less to stop crime. While effective policing requires the cooperation and trust of the public, racial profiling breeds cynicism. Minority jurors as well may distrust police testimony in trials and acquit guilty defendants.

Even in the short run, discovery of crime using racial profiling may not produce a conviction. Evidence obtained in ways that violate the civil rights of offenders is excluded from trials. Thus, courts in New Jersey overturned the convictions of drug offenders because the evidence of possession came from the use of racial profiling procedures. New Jersey prosecutors have as a result dropped charges against many other persons arrested on highways where the state police used racial profiling.

In some cases, use of racial profiling has led to litigation. The state of Maryland paid damages to settle a suit brought by an African-American man stopped and searched when driving through the state. After facing a suit from the federal government, the New Jersey State Police signed a consent decree that managed the way the department would work and lost much of its independence in regard to making vehicle stops. Other police departments may be vulnerable to litigation claims that they failed to train officers to avoid actions based on race. In these ways, the use of racial profiling ultimately harms police departments.

Perhaps most important, racial profiling contributes to race, ethnic, and national-origin segregation. If minorities believe they will receive undesired attention from police when they travel in predominately white areas, they may avoid those areas. Informal travel restrictions may prevent more inner-city minorities from taking jobs located in suburbs, affluent areas, and white neighborhoods. In the end, racial profiling serves to reinforce existing neighborhood segregation and makes interaction across race and ethnic groups more difficult. Laws may not prevent integrated neighborhoods, but police actions can have the same effect. Some even suggest that police use of racial profiling to stop minorities in white neighborhoods is comparable to preventing noncitizens from crossing into U.S. borders—it treats minorities as foreigners in their own country.

The reliance on stereotypes in the use of racial profiling further harms relationships between race and ethnic groups. It tends to exaggerate racial stereotypes and widen social distances. Police stops of minorities, even if unwarranted, may lead whites to develop negative views of other groups. Minorities in turn tend to view whites as making unfair judgments about them. With racial relations such a serious problem in the United States, anything to worsen them must be avoided.

In sum, opponents of racial profiling see these costs as real and serious. Even if racial profiling has some benefit for reducing crime—a claim disputed by critics of the practice—these benefits would not outweigh the harm. In the words of national columnist Marilyn vos Savant, writing about racial profiling, "The history of blacks in our country is too troubled to bear worsening the feelings of alienation that have contributed to the higher rate of crime in the first place."[63]

EXTENT OF THE PRACTICE

Disputes over racial profiling focus not only on whether the procedure is fair and effective but also on whether it is common. Proponents argue that the wrongful use of race, ethnicity, and national origin in criminal profiles seldom occurs. To the extent that police use these traits, they do so appropriately, to apprehend criminals. Opponents argue that racial profiling of innocent minorities has become widespread. Two types of evidence, anecdotal and statistical, serve to support opposing sides of the argument. The evidence thus far does not provide a simple answer to debates over the extent of racial profiling. It does, however, give a sense of the complexity of the issues involved in proving claims on either side.

ANECDOTAL EVIDENCE

Stories told by members of minority groups illustrate the existence and harm of racial profiling. Many tell of being stopped by police for no apparent reason and sometimes abused for protesting their treatment. A few stories do not by themselves demonstrate widespread use of the practice, but the stories are common enough to make it difficult to dismiss them as exceptions. In working on a book about racial profiling, David Harris, a vocal critic of the practice, says, "Almost every African American or Latino I talked to had either had this experience [of being subject to racial profiling] personally or had a family member or close friend who had."[64]

Even if the stories do not provide a strong scientific basis for reaching conclusions about the extent of racial profiling, they have another purpose:

The mistreatment apparent in the stories reveals what critics see as the injustice of racial profiling. To illustrate this kind of evidence, this section summarizes several published stories.

Instances of Racial Profiling

Master Sergeant Rossano Gerald, an African-American, decorated war veteran who had served in the armed forces for 18 years, was driving across the country with his 12-year-old son. On entering the state of Oklahoma, he noticed a patrol car and made sure he followed the speed limit. After being stopped once anyway, for the stated reason that he had followed another car too closely, he was stopped again. This time the officer questioned Gerald about being nervous. Along with writing a warning ticket, the trooper then asked if he could search Gerald's car. When Gerald declined, the trooper claimed he had the right to search the car anyway and called for a drug-sniffing dog. Without any apparent alert from the dog, the trooper nonetheless claimed it had smelled something, which justified a full search of the car.

The full search involved using a drill to explore underneath the carpet. Mistaking a footrest in the car as a hiding place, the officers handcuffed Gerald and placed him in the patrol car. His son was placed in another car, where questions from the police and barking of the dog frightened him. The officers also removed and searched Gerald's luggage but found nothing illegal in either the car or luggage. After two hours, the troopers left the scene with the luggage unpacked and $1,000 worth of damage to the car floor. Gerald immediately called his commanding officer and drove to a nearby army base to see if drugs had been planted in his car. An army-certified drug-sniffing dog found no drugs of any kind.

In reflecting on the experience, Gerald described the reaction of his son, who cried over the interrogation about his father's supposed drug trafficking and became physically sick from sitting in a hot patrol car. Gerald said, "I was very humiliated by this experience. I was embarrassed. I was ashamed that people driving by would think I had committed a crime. It was particularly hard to be treated like a criminal in front of my impressionable young son." Having never had a traffic ticket, an arrest, or trouble in the army, Gerald filed a lawsuit over the incident.[65]

Larry Sykes, an African American who worked as a bank vice-president and headed the local school board in Toledo, Ohio, had traveled as part of a delegation to an economic development conference in Cleveland. After spending the day at the conference, he left to drive back to Toledo. Near his hometown, an Ohio Highway Patrol officer pulled him over. Although Sykes was not speeding, he noticed that a white person driving nearby and going over the limit was not stopped. The officer informed Sykes that he had been pulled over because he did not have a front license plate and requested to see his driver's license, registration, and insurance papers.

Despite having all his papers in order, Sykes was then asked by the trooper, without giving a reason, to step out of the car and walk back toward the patrol car. Saying that Sykes might have a gun, the trooper began a frisk and asked further questions about carrying drugs. Next, the trooper asked him to lean on the flashing patrol car with his legs spread and arms out. It made no sense to Sykes that missing a front license plate would warrant this kind of treatment, and he asked the trooper why he was suspected of having a weapon or drugs but received no explanation. Most humiliating, while Sykes stood against the patrol car in the search position, a bus drove by filled with his colleagues who had attended the conference in Cleveland. Although he did not receive a ticket and eventually was allowed to leave, it looked to those in the bus as if Sykes was being arrested.[66]

The experience of Curtis V. Rodriguez, a Latino attorney in California, illustrates the use of ethnic profiling ("driving while brown"). While traveling on a highway to San Jose, Rodriguez and his passenger noticed that five cars carrying dark-skinned Hispanics had been pulled over and searched during a 10–15 minute span. Although carefully following the speed limit, Rodriguez was soon pulled over by the California Highway Patrol. The trooper said the car touched the line along the side of the road, which Rodriguez denies.

After viewing documents and asking (without any justification) about weapons in the car, the trooper said he needed to search the car because the passenger had made suspicious movements. Rodriguez and his passenger waited outside the car during the search and then waited inside the car during a discussion between the trooper and an agent from the Narcotics Enforcement Bureau. A dog was then brought to sniff outside the car for drug odors. Finding no evidence of drugs, the trooper told Rodriguez that he could go and apologized for the delay. Since the officers knew the car occupants were criminal attorneys, they appeared very serious and careful, but the pattern of using racial profiling—without any other indication of suspicious activity—was apparent.[67]

Stories also come from celebrities who claim they have been stopped by police for no reason—other than their skin color—on suspicion of being involved in crime. A list of famous African-American men who have been stopped by police includes Joe Morgan, the Hall of Fame baseball player and announcer for ESPN; LeVar Burton, the actor from *Star Trek: The Next Generation* and host of the children's show *Reading Rainbow;* Johnnie Cochran, defense attorney for O. J. Simpson; Christopher Darden, the district attorney who prosecuted O. J. Simpson; Wesley Snipes, the actor who appeared in *Blade*, *Major League*, and *White Men Can't Jump;* Wynton Marsalis, the jazz musician; Tony Dungy, the head football coach of the Indianapolis Colts; Michael McCrary, a singer in Boyz II Men; and Will Smith, the star of the movies *Independence Day*, *Men in Black*, and *Ali.*[68]

Joe Morgan tells the story of waiting in the Los Angeles International Airport for a flight to Tucson, Arizona. While making a telephone call, Morgan was approached by a police officer, asked for identification, and accused of traveling with a suspected drug dealer. Morgan objected, but when he moved to get identification from his luggage, "the officer grabbed him from behind, handcuffed him, put his hand over Morgan's mouth and nose, and led him off to a small room, where the police ascertained that Morgan was not traveling with the suspected drug dealer after all."[69] The police accused Morgan of being hostile and swinging his arms but had little reason to stop him, except that they were on the lookout for a black man.

Stories also illustrate how Asian Americans, although statistically less involved in crime than other race and ethnic groups, must deal with profiling. In 1992, C. Vang, a 14-year-old living in Madison, Wisconsin, and from a family of Laotian refugees, was in a car one night with some friends. Police ordered the car to pull over, and when the driver did so, eight to 10 officers surrounded the car with guns drawn. The occupants were ordered out of the car and required to lie on the ground while the police searched the car for weapons. They found nothing and let the boys go. Given the respect of the boys for authority figures, they did not at first report the incident, but, according to many anecdotal reports, police stop Asian youth on suspicion of belonging to gangs.[70]

Alternative Views

Proponents of racial profiling rarely challenge the truth of the stories, and they admit that in isolated instances racial profiling can be misused. They argue, however, that anecdotes fail to demonstrate widespread abuse of the practice. Countering stories of racial profiling, advocates cite stories of the experiences of black police in dealing with crime, the appreciation of minority residents for the protection from crime that police provide, and the horrible victimization of decent citizens in minority neighborhoods by criminals.

For example, one writer interviewed African-American police officers. In the interviews, the officers denied unfairly targeting minorities and criticize what they view as antipolice propaganda. Lieutenant Tony Barksdale of the Baltimore Police Department says about racial profiling, "We're so afraid to tell the truth. Often the entire neighborhood is black, so of course you're going to be stopping blacks—based on their behavior."[71] Barksdale worries that accusations of racial profiling may inhibit officers from stopping criminals.

In Arlington, Virginia, residents of a minority neighborhood came to the police chief, Ed Flynn, to request more aggressive policing in their part of town. To disrupt drug dealing, the police began to stop cars with cracked windshields, darkened windows, expired tags, and excessive speed. They also cracked down on quality-of-life crimes such as public urination. The effort successfully eliminated drug-dealing hot spots in the neighborhood, and the police received thanks in the community newsletter.

In a review of newspaper stories, an article chronicles all murders reported in the *New York Daily News* for a randomly chosen week in May 2001. Among the 11 murders reported are the following: A 65-year-old black man was killed in Harlem when he was caught in the crossfire between two drug gangs; a 54-year-old black man in the Bronx shot and killed a 37-year-old black vagrant when he found him vandalizing his car; an 80-year-old white woman in Greenwich Village was stabbed to death by a 28-year-old black drug addict whom the older woman had befriended and helped; a black Brooklyn teenager was fatally stabbed during a street argument; and a white woman and two white men were shot execution style in the woman's Manhattan apartment during a drug robbery by two ex-convicts. During the same week, a young woman complained that she had been racially profiled after being stopped for a traffic violation. The contrast between the seriousness of the homicides and the minor inconvenience of the stop for a traffic violation highlights the importance of stopping the rising tide of violence, argues the author of this article.[72]

Statistical Evidence

Methodological Problems

Although stories of racial profiling may have a powerful emotional impact, they alone do not provide the kind of evidence needed to make public policy. More scientific data are needed to evaluate allegations of racial profiling. A review of the literature found more than 20 published reports on millions of police stops and hundreds of law enforcement agencies. The vast majority of these studies, however, are flawed. In the words of the government report, "The most common pattern is to collect data on traffic stops in a city, and to compare the percentage of minority stops to the percentage of minorities in the entire city. This type of approach is far too simplistic, and it fails to incorporate information on police operational procedures."[73]

An example of such a study comes from the U.S. Bureau of Justice Statistics, which did a national survey on contacts between the police and the public. The study found that 12.3 percent of blacks reported that they had been stopped at least once, and 10.4 percent of whites reported they had been stopped at least once.[74] A higher percentage of blacks also reports having been stopped more than once. Yet the survey contains no information on the behaviors of the respondents that might have led to the stops. Critics of such statistics note that income tends to be lower, crime tends to be higher, and police activity tends to be more common in minority neighborhoods. This will lead to more stops of minority residents not because of racial bias or profiling but because police appropriately respond to crime and community problems.

Similarly, comparing minority stops to minority population size ignores the possibility that minorities are more involved in crime. Say, for example, that 25 percent of motorists stopped on a highway are Hispanic—a percentage that suggests discrimination because it is more than twice the percentage of Hispanics in the population. Yet, if 25 percent of those violating traffic rules on the highway are Hispanic, the stops are appropriate. If only 10 percent of those violating traffic rules are Hispanic, it would likely reflect racial profiling. In any case, the size of the population does not offer an appropriate comparison.

Some assert that this problem has an inadequate benchmark, or base rate. To know if police have stopped too many persons in a race or ethnic group, researchers need to know the extent of lawbreaking in that group. In other words, they need some measure of the expected rate of minority stops if racial profiling played no role. One type of benchmark would measure the racial breakdown of offenders in a city or on a highway. However, to allow meaningful comparisons, the benchmark data on offending must match the other data on the place, time, and type of patrol of stops; comparing stops on one highway to traffic violations on another would distort the results. Another type of benchmark would compare the "hit rates" of stops, or the percentage of searches that find contraband. Obtaining data on appropriate benchmarks proves more difficult than obtaining data on police stops.

No studies thus far fully meet the requirements for scientific accuracy. Yet, several studies of racial profiling do better than most to define valid benchmarks and comparisons.

Key Studies

First, a study of police stops and arrests in New Jersey led by Professor John Lamberth of Temple University has played an important role in legal proceedings involving racial profiling. The researchers in the study used binoculars while standing beside the road to observe the race of the driver and speed of the car at randomly selected times and parts of the New Jersey

Turnpike. Based on the observations, an African American drove or occupied 14 percent of the cars. Next, the researchers drove along the highway at 60 miles per hour (five miles per hour over the speed limit) and recorded the race of any driver or passenger who passed them. The 15 percent of the speeders who were African American closely matched the percentage of all drivers who were African American.

The researchers lastly examined the records of the New Jersey State Police on the race of drivers stopped and arrested after a stop. These records lack complete information, as patrol logs listed the race of persons stopped in only one-third of the cases. For the completed logs, 35 percent of all drivers stopped were African American and 73 percent of those arrested were African American. These figures greatly exceed the figures for African-American drivers and speeders, and led the authors to conclude that the New Jersey State Police used racial profiling.

Critics of the study, however, point out some flaws. Classifying all drivers going six miles or more above the speed limit does not distinguish the seriousness of the traffic violation. As a result, nearly all observed drivers on the highway—about 98 percent—violated at least one traffic law. No wonder minority speeders comprised about the same percentage as minority drivers—speeders and drivers were nearly classified identically. The police claim that the minorities they stop drive well above the limit. Further, the patrol logs appear more likely to include information on race when the driver was black. This has the effect of exaggerating the percentage of black drivers stopped. The patrol log data on racial stops and arrests also covered a period some two years earlier than the observations on drivers and speeders. A government report on racial profiling studies concludes, "Because of several limitations in the study's methodology, this study does not provide clear evidence of racial profiling of African American drivers."[75]

Second, another analysis of racial profiling by Professor Lamberth examined stops by Maryland State Police officers on an interstate highway in northeastern Maryland. In this study, researchers drove the speed limit over randomly selected parts of the highway during randomly selected times and again observed the race of drivers who passed them. The observations disclosed that 17 percent of the cars had African-American drivers. Data on police stops, searches, and drug arrests for the highway under study were also gathered from police records. They showed that 29 percent of vehicles stopped had African-American drivers, and 71 percent of the searches involved cars with African-American drivers. Interestingly, although blacks were stopped and searched more often than whites, about 28 percent of blacks and 29 percent of whites—statistically identical figures—were found to be carrying contraband. The researchers concluded that blacks did not carry illegal products more than whites.

Again, however, critics note that driving the speed limit and observing drivers going only one mile or more over the speed limit does little to distinguish between the races of more serious traffic offenders. Nor does the research consider reasons other than speeding for stopping cars, which may affect minorities more than others. Along with inconsistencies in the time periods covered by the speeding data and stop data, these methodology problems again led evaluators to determine that the study does not provide clear evidence of racial profiling.

Others point out a flaw in the conclusions reached by the study about "hit rates." The similarity of hit rates across races may in fact contradict rather than support claims of racial profiling.[76] If police had discriminated against black drivers and had stopped more innocent black drivers, it would show in lower hit rates. That police were equally effective in finding contraband in vehicles with black and with white drivers show they appropriately targeted drivers to maximize the potential for success in finding drugs.

Third, a study commissioned by the New Jersey attorney general and carried out by the Public Service Research Institute of Maryland involved taking photos with a high-speed camera and measuring the speed with a radar gun of more than 40,000 drivers on the New Jersey Turnpike. A team of three evaluators independently identified the race of the driver from the photos, and the researchers linked race to speeding violations (at least 15 miles per hour over the posted 65-miles-per-hour speed limit). According to the results, black drivers made up 16 percent of the drivers but 25 percent of the speeders. This result justifies police stopping blacks more often than whites on the turnpike and contradicts claims of racial profiling.

The U.S. Department of Justice tried to block the release of the study because in about one-third of the photos, the driver's race could not be determined. Defenders of the report point out that if cameras cannot determine the race of speeders, neither could the police in determining who to stop. Still, the New Jersey attorney general, David Samson, agreed with the Department of Justice about the problems of the study. He stated that the study "does not alter the past or undermine the evidence that profiling was real."[77] The results were eventually reported by a New Jersey newspaper and the report placed on the Internet.

Fourth, a recent study of stop and search records of the Washington State Patrol examined more than 2 million traffic stops during a 30-month period.[78] According to the analysis, the race of the driver had little influence on being stopped, which supports the contention that police do not use racial profiling. However, once stopped, blacks, Latinos, and Native Americans were more likely than whites to be searched. The most important determinant of a search was the seriousness of the traffic offense and the number of violations of the motorist. Still, that race and ethnicity had some influence offers evidence on one aspect of racial profiling.

Fifth, another study approaches the issue in a different way and comes up with mixed findings. In examining data collected by the police department in Richmond, Virginia, researchers focused on police stops in black and in white neighborhoods. In addition, the study considered the crime, poverty, and unemployment rates of the neighborhoods. The results demonstrate that the crime rate in the neighborhood influences the rate of police stops, but the racial composition of the neighborhood does not. In other words, given the same crime rates, police make no more stops in black neighborhoods than in white neighborhoods. However, racial differences emerged in relation to searches: More stops resulted in searches in black neighborhoods than in white neighborhoods. The authors thus conclude that racial profiling does not appear early in the crime detection process but may emerge after the initial stop.[79]

The Richmond study, although considering crime differences across neighborhoods as a source of stops, also has limitations. Most seriously, the data do not provide information on the characteristics of individual drivers but only measure the characteristics of neighborhoods in which the stops occurred. Ideally, studies should examine both the race of the drivers stopped and the characteristics of the neighborhood where the stop occurred. In addition, the fact that the results come from a single city over a period from January 17 to March 31, 2002, limits the generality of the findings.

Neither advocates nor critics of racial profiling can yet accurately claim that the evidence on racial profiling best supports their views. Although both sides in the dispute tend to cite only the data that fit their arguments, the studies have enough limitations to require more data gathering and statistical analysis.

PUBLIC OPINION POLLS

PERCEPTIONS OF VICTIMIZATION

Regardless of the statistical evidence, most members of minority groups see racial profiling as a serious problem. A survey by the Harris polling organization asked respondents, "Do you think the police in your community treat all races fairly, or do they tend to treat one or more of these groups unfairly?" Among whites, 20 percent believed police treat some groups unfairly, while among blacks 60 percent believed police treat some groups unfairly.[80] Such attitudes reflect greater distrust of the criminal justice system in general and police in particular by blacks than whites.

Polls asking questions about police use of racial profiling obtain similar findings. In a Gallup poll, 77 percent of African-American respondents thought racial profiling was widespread. The same poll asked African Americans if they had been stopped because of their race. More than 40 percent said yes, and 72 percent of those aged 18–34 said yes. Among those saying they were stopped unfairly, most said it had occurred several times. Even most white respondents, 56 percent, agreed that the use of racial profiling was widespread, even though only 6 percent believe they personally had been stopped because of their race.[81]

Another poll done in 2001 by the *Washington Post*, the Henry J. Kaiser Foundation, and Harvard University found that 37 percent of blacks said they were unfairly stopped by police because of their race.[82] For black men, the figure reached 52 percent and for black women it reached 25 percent. For Latinos and Asian Americans, the figure was 20 percent, lower than for blacks but still high enough to generate concern.

Blacks do more than complain about racial profiling to interviewers—they tell their children about the problem. Saul Green, the U.S. attorney for eastern Michigan, an African American, and a top federal law enforcement official, met with U.S. Attorney General Janet Reno and other law enforcement officials, academics, and representatives of advocacy groups to discuss racial profiling. Responding to some claims of police that they did not use the practice, Green said he had warned his 16-year-old son on receiving his driver's license that he would likely be stopped because he was black.[83] Other African Americans and Hispanics tell their children much the same.

Perceptions of racial profiling, like the anecdotes about personal experiences, do not prove the practice is common. The public may have mistaken or biased views about controversial issues like racial profiling. They may not fully understand the reasons for police actions and may accept certain notions based on media publicity rather than the real facts. Still, the perceptions of unjustified racial profiling, even if not based on scientific facts, indicate the seriousness of the problem.

DISAPPROVAL OF RACIAL PROFILING

Along with believing that racial profiling is common, the public has—until recently—opposed the practice. In a 1999 Gallup poll, 81 percent of respondents said they disapprove of racial profiling.[84] The opposition likely relates to publicity about highway stops of innocent minority drivers.

However, the terrorist attacks of September 11, 2001, have produced changes in the public's opposition to the practice. A few days after the attacks, a poll in Los Angeles found that 68 percent of those questioned would approve of law enforcement officers "randomly stopping people who may fit the profile of suspected terrorists."[85] A national poll also found that most Americans support requiring people of Arab descent to "undergo special, more intensive security checks before boarding airplanes in the U.S."[86] Even 60 percent of black Americans favored a policy of special scrutiny for Arab Americans at airport security.

Consistent with changes after September 11, a survey done online and by phone in February 2002 found that a majority of Americans favor racial profiling.[87] In response to the statement, "I oppose any form of racial profiling," 48 percent agreed, leaving 52 percent willing to approve some forms of racial profiling. Large differences exist across races in the answers, with 64 percent of blacks, 51 percent of Hispanics, and 44 percent of whites objecting to racial profiling. For minorities, younger people more than older people and men more than women oppose profiling.

The importance of terrorism to attitudes about racial profiling emerges in another question. When asked in the same 2002 poll about the statement "I believe that racial profiling has select uses, such as in cases of suspected terrorism or national security threats," a large portion of the population agreed. Specifically, 61 percent of blacks, 76 percent of Hispanics, and 77 percent of whites approved of the statement. These results reveal wide support for use of racial profiling in relation to terrorism and national security.[88]

The change toward greater acceptance of racial profiling may reflect a short-term response to the tragedy of the September 11 attacks and may wane in the future. However, if more terrorist attacks occur in the United States in the future, support for the practice may increase. Certainly, the public more willingly accepts profiling in the fight against foreign terrorism in airports and at the borders than it does of profiling of African Americans on highways and streets.

EFFORTS TO END RACIAL PROFILING

Efforts to end racial profiling come from those who not only oppose the practice but believe it is widespread. The strategies they recommend include passing new legislation and implementing antiprofiling government policies (see Chapter 2, The Law and Racial Profiling). Even in the absence of federal and state measures, however, police agencies and private citizens have taken certain actions. This section reviews these actions as well as arguments made in opposition to them by advocates of racial profiling.

DATA COLLECTION

Opponents of racial profiling believe that recording the race and ethnicity of every driver stopped by police can help eradicate the practice. Collecting such data will reveal the extent of race-based stops, make officers more aware of unconscious tendencies to use race or ethnicity, and offer a baseline on which to improve. By 2002, 16 states had required state law enforcement agencies to record race information, and the federal government has since the Clinton administration encouraged similar record-keeping.

The federal government has sponsored several reports that make recommendations to law enforcement agencies about how to best reach their data collection goals. The reports suggest employing laptop computers in police vehicles to easily record the information and minimize the burden on the law enforcement system. For each stop, the officer should record the date, time, and location of the stop, license plate number, state, and type of vehicle stopped, length of stop, officers involved in the stop, age, race, ethnicity, and gender of driver stopped, reason for the stop, and outcome of the stop (such as issuance of a warning or citation, search, or arrest). Whatever information the forms include, the recording procedures need to ensure that officers supply accurate reports.

After collating and analyzing the data, police departments can determine if they need to take corrective steps. However, any conclusions also must recognize the complexities and weaknesses of the racial profiling data. Different rates of stopping minorities cannot by themselves prove the use of racial profiling, and disagreements over measurement issues will limit the value of the data. Accepted benchmarks to compare stops to offending remain to be developed. Nonetheless, federal and state governments have promoted data gathering, as have several police groups, such as the San Diego Police Department, the National Black Police Association, and the Hispanic American Police Command Officers.

Installing audiovisual technology in police vehicles represents another approach to stopping racial profiling. With cameras and microphones attached to the dashboard, grill, or roof, police vehicles can record all stops. Ideally, the videotapes can depict the violation justifying the stop, the actions of the police officer, the circumstances of a search or detention, and the behavior of the suspects. Although videotaping cannot record actions outside the range of the camera or hidden by a car, it can capture much objective evidence.

Both advocates and opponents of racial profiling agree on the usefulness of audiovisual technology. Opponents believe that it will, much like other data collection methods, prohibit the unwarranted use of racial profiling. When their actions are recorded, officers will likely avoid discriminatory behavior. Cameras alone will not end the problem—other forms of data gathering are still needed—but they can help. Proponents view cameras as a way to protect police against unfounded complaints. In one New Jersey case, an officer sued by a driver for allegedly using racial profiling and mistreatment used videotape evidence that the driver had been going 92 miles per hour and been treated courteously by the officer.[89] Charges were brought against the complainant for fraud. If police do not use racial profiling, then audiovisual technology will support their case that the stops they make are warranted.

A major problem in use of audiovisual technology comes from the expense. The cameras are expensive, last only a few years, and require costs for maintenance, tapes, and tape storage. The federal government has provided more than $15 million in grants to equip police cars, and some states, such as Texas, have put aside funds for this goal. Still, lack of police department funds may prevent installing the equipment in all police cars.

Police Training and Procedure

Law enforcement agencies can set their own policies to eliminate racial bias. The key is to train and require officers to focus on behavior rather than appearance.

As a first step, police policies can require that officers treat citizens with respect and courtesy in any contact they have. This may entail police officers introducing themselves with names and affiliations, clearly stating the reason for the stop, addressing the citizen politely, answering any questions clearly, and apologizing for any inconvenience. Politeness and respect can do much to defuse hostility and counter perceptions of mistreatment and racial profiling. Police agencies also can do much to eliminate racial profiling by improving community relations. Continual contact of police with neighborhood merchants, leaders, pastors, and civic groups would encourage communication about policies in stopping vehicles and pedestrians. It would also make police aware of community concerns about their procedures.

More controversially, policies to bar pretext stops and consent searches would help eliminate racial profiling. Although the U.S. Supreme Court has ruled that these practices are constitutional, critics suggest that they allow too much police discretion and encourage racial profiling. Law enforcement agencies therefore do not have to use them. They might limit police actions during a traffic stop to the traffic violation only (rather than using the violation as a reason to search for other criminal activity). They might allow for investigation of nontraffic offenses only when there is a clearly stated and reasonable suspicion that a crime has occurred. Similarly, police might also be required to have a clearly stated and reasonable suspicion to ask for permission to make a search and should have written consent of the driver. To ensure that these guidelines are not violated, policies could further require that the police file a written report that explains the reason for any action involving something more than a traffic violation.

These anti–racial profiling procedures may not have much influence without appropriate training of officers. Recognizing the importance of police training, the Community Oriented Policing Services (COPS) of the U.S. Department of Justice has produced a training video and lesson plan for police officers.[90] The video and plan aim to increase mutual respect in policing and explore the misleading assumptions officers may hold about the persons they stop. One lesson involves discussing the proper grounds for probable cause and reasonable suspicion. Another addresses the components of good criminal investigation and the inappropriateness of using racial profiling in investigations.

Other training programs attend to cultural and lifestyle differences across race, ethnic, and national-origin groups. Multicultural or cultural sensitivity training can increase the awareness of officers about differences in normal behavior of particular race and ethnic groups and the potential to misuse stereotypes. For example, loud talk may be an innocent style of communication rather than a means to threaten, failing to make eye contact may be a way of showing respect rather than evasiveness, and wariness of police may reflect unfamiliarity with American culture rather than hostility. Understanding the special behaviors of minority groups can help police understand the subtle ways race and ethnicity affect their interpretations—and take special effort to avoid misinterpretations.

Regardless of the policies and training procedures they adopt, police agencies can further help diminish racial profiling by hiring officers from minority groups and with high education. Minority officers bring diverse perspectives to the police force and more understanding of minority concerns. Educated officers also seem less prone to rely on race, ethnicity, and national origin in their actions.

Private Litigation

The alleged use of racial profiling has spawned numerous lawsuits. The first successful such suit came from Robert Wilkins, whose car had been stopped in Maryland when he and family members were returning late at night from a funeral out of state. Wilkins sued the Maryland State Police for violating his civil rights. In 1995, the state settled the suit by paying damages to the Wilkins family, agreeing to change their traffic stop policies, and maintaining records on traffic stops.

Another highly publicized case in 1998 involved four young African-American men driving through New Jersey in a rented van after they had attended a basketball camp in North Carolina. The police stopped the van for speeding, but when they approached, the driver accidentally put the automatic shift into reverse. Fearing for their lives when the van began to move backward, the officers opened fire. Three of the four passengers were wounded by the 11 shots fired. Represented by Johnnie Cochran, O. J. Simpson's former defense counsel, the young men sued, claiming they had not been speeding and were stopped because of racial profiling. The state of New Jersey paid nearly $13 million in damages to settle the suit and prosecuted the police officers who fired the shots.

In Eagle County, Colorado, seven African Americans and Latinos stopped by sheriff's deputies filed a class-action suit on behalf of 400 individuals who had been investigated on the basis of a drug courier profile that included race and ethnicity. The county settled by paying $800,000 to the plaintiffs.

Press releases from the American Civil Liberties Union list several other suits:

- Motorists who were victims of racial profiling received more than $775,000 from the state of New Jersey in a settlement;
- the state of Maryland approved a settlement in response to a class-action racial profiling lawsuit;
- three African-American high school students stopped in Illinois sued the state for unlawful detention and search;
- a lawsuit accused the Transportation Security Administration of detention and arrest of airline passengers on the basis of skin color and national origin; and
- three African-American students filed suit against the city of Charleston, West Virginia, and its law enforcement officers for being racially profiled.

In regard to racial profiling by airlines after the September 11 terrorist attacks, five men removed from planes for stated reasons of security filed lawsuits against American, Continental, Northwest, and United Airlines. The men, all of Middle Eastern or Asian descent, were prevented from flying because of their ethnic appearance. In some cases, the removal from the plane came after other passengers, airline employees, or pilots complained—unfairly, according to the plaintiffs—of suspicious behavior.

Recently, lawsuits against racial profiling have moved from the arena of police action and vehicle stops to businesses and consumer discrimination. In the first half of 2003, minorities filed suits against Dillard's, Macy's, and J. C. Penney department stores, claiming, among other things, that the stores used profiles based on race to monitor and search customers for stolen items. Calling the phenomenon "shopping while black," lawyers for the plaintiffs argued that a large number of minorities have had their civil rights violated by this practice. Since the September 11 attacks, Arabs and Muslims have filed similar suits.

With litigation employed as a means to end racial profiling, the American Civil Liberties Union solicits information from those believing they were victims of racial discrimination (the U.S. Department of Justice also solicits complaints). One book tells victims of racial profiling what to do if they are unfairly stopped: Do not argue, take names, and take legal action.[91] If federal and state legislation do not outlaw racial profiling, opponents hope that court victories will make the practice too expensive for law enforcement agencies to continue.

OPPOSITION

Opposition exists to anti–racial profiling data collection, changes in police policies, and litigation. The opponents deny that police—except in rare instances—use race, ethnicity, or national origin alone in deciding to stop drivers or pedestrians. If they use these group characteristics as part of a larger criminal profile, it implies good police work rather than discrimination. Not only would new data collection procedures, policies, and litigation address a nonexistent problem, they would also create problems, opponents say.

Gathering data creates a paperwork burden on officers who should devote as much time as possible to preventing and fighting crime. In addition, it can place officers in a difficult situation. They must identify the race, ethnicity, or national origin of drivers just by looking at them. Appearances do not always reveal group memberships, but asking people about their race, ethnicity, or national origin would create hostility and resistance.

Even if information can be accurately recorded, gathering data creates the potential for misinterpretation. Advocates of racial profiling contend that figures on racial percentages of stops, particularly when compared to the composition of the population, are flawed. Race differences in stops make sense only when compared to race differences in criminal involvement. For example, when a study of stops in San Jose, California, found that a high percentage involved minority drivers, the police simply noted that they get more calls about problems and crimes from residents of minority neighborhoods.[92] However, because of the complexity of determining a benchmark for proper comparisons, simple figures would invariably lead to false accusations of racial profiling.

Although the numbers by themselves would prove little, police advocates worry that they would provide ammunition for critics of police and worsen relationships between police and minorities. Despite the flaws, traffic stop data would encourage frivolous lawsuits against well-intentioned police officers. Threat of a lawsuit or discipline might then force police to respond by making stops not on behavior and criminal profiles but on quotas. If they have already stopped a percentage of minority drivers equal to their proportion in the population, they would feel obliged to stop only whites. Data collection would, in the end, damage the effectiveness of policing and make minorities, elderly persons, and others more vulnerable to victimization by criminals.

Perhaps more seriously, concern about accusations of racial profiling in airport screening could inhibit effective antiterrorist measures. Here, errors in identifying potential criminals can have terrible consequences for public safety, more immediately serious than those errors in drug enforcement and community policing.

What about the few police officers (or security screeners) who abuse racial profiling? Under existing constitutional law, judges will exclude from trials any evidence obtained improperly by police. Moreover, those who use improper procedure will face departmental discipline and perhaps even lawsuits from citizens. The U.S. Department of Justice currently has the authority to investigate abuses and has in fact forced the New Jersey State Police and the police departments of Los Angeles and Pittsburgh to change their procedures. With these measures already on hand, new data collection, training, and litigation procedures are unnecessary, according to supporters of profiling.

Policing has become a difficult task, one that low pay, high crime, accusations, and outside control make all the more difficult. Although not always well publicized, police departments are facing a personnel crisis because of these problems. The attrition rate among police has risen, recruitment of new officers has fallen, officers are increasingly unwilling to accept senior positions, and hiring police chiefs has become more difficult.[93] False accusations of racial profiling and the misuse of data to support these accusations may contribute to this problem. With worries about lawsuits and discipline, and restrictions on the actions they can take, police may feel too intimidated to fully enforce the law.

If new regulations or policies restricting police action are to be implemented, advocates of racial profiling support changes at the local rather than the federal or state level. Given that the problems faced by law enforcement agencies differ greatly across localities, no law or policy will apply equally well to these diverse circumstances. Rules that make sense in one jurisdiction may not make sense in another; ways to collect meaningful data in one place may produce distortions in another; and punishments that seem appropriate in one area may seem too harsh or lenient in others. Local police agencies can thus determine best how to approach the issue of racial profiling.

---

[1] Deborah Ramirez, Jack McDevitt, and Amy Farrell, *A Resource Guide on Racial Profiling Data Collection Systems: Promising Practices and Lessons Learned.* Washington, D.C.: U.S. Department of Justice, 2000, p. 3.

[2] Heather Mac Donald, *Are Cops Racist?* Chicago: Ivan R. Dee, 2003, p. 15.

[3] Jonathan Turley, "Aviation Security and Passenger Profiling at United States Airports," in *Profiling for Public Safety: Rational or Racist, Hearing before the Subcommittee on Aviation of the Committee on Transportation and Infrastructure, House of Representatives, One Hundred Seventh Congress, Second Session.* Washington, D.C.: U.S. Government Printing Office, 2002, p. 72.

[4] David Cole, *No Equal Justice: Race and Class in the American Criminal Justice System.* New York: The New Press, 1999, p. 6.

[5] Cole, *No Equal Justice*, p. 39.

[6] Homer Hawkins and Richard Thomas, "White Policing of Black Populations: A History of Race and Social Control in America," in Ellis Cashmore and Eugene McLaughlin, eds., *Out of Order? Policing Black People.* London: Routledge, 1991, pp. 67–68.

[7] Sandra Bass, "Out of Place: Petit Apartheid and the Police," in Dragan Milovanovic and Katheryn K. Russell, eds., *Petit Apartheid in the U.S. Criminal Justice System.* Durham, N.C.: Carolina Academic Press, 2001, p. 44; Hawkins and Thomas, "White Policing of Black Populations," pp. 67–74.

[8] Howard N. Rabinowitz, "The Conflict between Blacks and the Police in the Urban South, 1865–1900," in Donald G. Nieman, ed., *Black Southerners and the Law*, 1865–1900. New York: Garland Publishing, 1994, p. 297.

[9] Katheryn K. Russell, *The Color of Crime: Racial Hoaxes, White Fear, Black Protectionism, Police Harassment, and Other Macroaggressions.* New York: New York University Press, 1998, p. 35.

[10] David A. Harris, "Driving While Black: Racial Profiling on Our Nation's Highways," American Civil Liberties Union Special Report. Available online. URL: http://archive.aclu.org/profiling/report. Posted in June 1999.

[11] *Frontline*, "Thirty Years of America's Drug War: A Chronology," PBS Online. Available online. URL: http://www.pbs.org/wgbh/pages/frontline/shows/drugs/cron. Posted in October 2000.

[12] Jeanette Covington, "Round up the Usual Suspects: Racial Profiling and the War on Drugs," in Milovanovic and Russell, *Petit Apartheid in the U.S. Criminal Justice System*, p. 34.

[13] The Sentencing Project, "Report Summary: Young Black Americans and the Criminal Justice System: Five Years Later," The Sentencing Project Online. Available online. URL: http://www.sentencingproject.org/pdfs/9070smy.pdf. Posted in 1995.

[14] U.S. Drug Enforcement Administration, "Operation Pipeline and Convoy," Drug Enforcement Administration Online. Available online. URL: http://www.usdoj.gov/dea/programs/pipecon.htm, Downloaded in June 2003.

[15] James Q. Wilson and George L. Kelling, "Broken Windows," *The Atlantic Monthly*, March 1992, pp. 29–38. Available online. URL: http://www.theatlantic.com/politics/crime/windows.htm, Downloaded in July 2003.

[16] Andrew Golub, et al., "Quality-of-Life Policing, Net Widening, and Crime Specialization," National Criminal Justice Reference Service. Available online. URL: http://www.ncjrs.org/pdffiles1/nij/grants/196674.pdf. Posted on October 3, 2002.

[17] George L. Kelling, "A Policing Strategy New Yorkers Like," *New York Times*, January 3, 2002, p. A23.

[18] Center for Immigration Studies, "Current Numbers," Center for Immigration Studies Online. Available online. URL: http://www.cis.org/topics/currentnumbers.html. Downloaded in June 2003.

[19] Center for Immigration Studies, "Illegal Immigration," Center for Immigration Studies Online. Available online. URL: http://www.cis.org/topics/illegalimmigration.html. Downloaded in June 2003.

[20] Sergio Bustos, "New Law Will Mean Closer Monitoring of Foreign Visitors," Gannett News Service. Available online. URL: http://www.gannettonline.com/gns/911/feature1.htm. Downloaded in June 2003.

[21] Eric Lichtblau, "U.S. Report Faults the Roundup of Illegal Immigrants after 9/11," *New York Times*, June 3, 2002, p. A1.

[22] Lichtblau, "U.S. Report Faults the Roundup of Illegal Immigrants after 9/11," p. A1.

[23] Leela Jacinto, "Flying While Arab," ABCNews.com. Available online. URL: http://abcnews.go.com/sections/world/DailyNews/visa020814.html. Posted on August 14, 2002.

[24] Department of Justice, "Report by the Department of Justice to the Department of Transportation on the Civil Rights Review of the Proposed Automated Passenger Screening System," in *Profiling for Public Safety: Rational or Racist, Hearing before the Subcommittee on Aviation of the Committee on Transportation and Infrastructure House of Representatives, One Hundred Seventh Congress, Second Session.* Washington, D.C.: U.S. Government Printing Office, 2002, p. 87–97.

[25] Katie Corrigan, "Air Passenger Profiling," in *Profiling for Public Safety: Rational or Racist, Hearing before the Subcommittee on Aviation of the Committee on Transportation and Infrastructure House of Representatives, One Hundred Seventh Congress, Second Session.* Washington, D.C.: U.S. Government Printing Office, 2002, pp. 45–46.

[26] Fedwa Malti-Douglas, "Let Them Profile Me," *New York Times*, February 6, 2002, p. A21.

[27] Johnny L. Hughes, "Statement," in *Racial Profiling within Law Enforcement Agencies, Hearing before the Subcommittee on the Constitution, Federalism, and Property Rights of the Committee on the Judiciary, United States Senate, One Hundred Sixth Congress, Second Session.* Washington, D.C.: U.S. Government Printing Office, 2000, pp. 43–44.

[28] Mac Donald, *Are Cops Racist?*, p. 9–27.

[29] Robert A. Levy, "Ethnic Profiling: A Rational and Moral Framework," Cato Institute. Available online. URL: http://www.cato.org/current/terrorism/pubs/levy-011002.html. Posted on October 2, 2001.

[30] Jack Dunphy, "Racial Profiling," National Review Online. Available online. URL: http://www.nationalreview.com/comment/comment101600b.shtml. Posted on October 16, 2000.

[31] James T. O'Reilly, *Police Traffic Stops and Racial Profiling: Resolving Management, Labor and Civil Rights Conflicts.* Springfield, Ill.: Charles C. Thomas, 2002, p. 5.

[32] Dinesh D'Souza, "Sometimes Discrimination Can Make Sense," *USA Today*, June 2, 1999, p. 15 A. Available online. URL: http://www-hoover.stanford.edu/publications/digest/994/dsouza.html. Posted on June 2, 1999.

[33] Federal Bureau of Investigation, "Crime in the United States 2000," Uniform Crime Reports. Available online. URL: http://www.fbi.gov/ucr/cius_00/contents.pdf. Posted in 2002.

[34] U.S. Department of Justice, "Criminal Victimization in the United States, 2001 Statistical Tables," Office of Justice Programs, Bureau of Justice Statistics. Available online. URL: http://www.ojp.usdoj.gov/bjs/pub/pdf/cvus0102.pdf. Posted on January 1, 2003.

[35] U.S. Department of Justice, "Criminal Victimization in the United States," p. 30.

[36] Mac Donald, *Are Cops Racist?*, p. 15.

[37] Mac Donald, *Are Cops Racist?*, p. 31.

[38] Stuart Taylor, Jr. "Cabbies, Cops, Pizza Deliveries, and Racial Profiling," The Atlantic Online. Available online. URL: http://www.theatlantic.com/politics/nj/taylor2000-06-02.htm. Posted on June 20, 2000.

[39] John Derbyshire, "Defending Racial Profiling—Again," National Review Online. Available online. URL: http://nationalreview.com/Derbyshire/derbyshire020901.shtml. Posted on February 9, 2001.

[40] William Wilbanks, *The Myth of a Racist Criminal Justice System*. Monterey, Calif.: Brooks-Cole, 1987. p. 69.

[41] Carl E. Pope and Howard N. Snyder, "Race as a Factor in Juvenile Arrests," *Juvenile Justice Bulletin*. Office of Juvenile Justice and Delinquency Prevention, April 2003, pp. 1–8.

[42] Yueh-Ting Lee, Lee J. Jussim, and Clark R. McCauley, eds., *Stereotype Accuracy: Toward Appreciating Group Differences*. Washington, D.C.: American Psychological Association, 1995, pp. 5–6.

[43] Jack Dunphy, "Ending Law Enforcement as We Know It," National Review Online. Available online. URL: http://www.nationalreview.com/dunphy/dunphy030501.shtml. Posted on March 5, 2001.

[44] Chris Weinkopf, "Shifting Gears on Racial Profiling," FrontPageMagazine.com. Available online. URL: http://www.frontpagemag.com/articles/printable.asp?ID=806. Posted on April 3, 2002.

[45] Peter A. DeFazio, "Comments," in *Profiling for Public Safety: Rational or Racist, Hearing before the Subcommittee on Aviation of the Committee on Transportation and Infrastructure, House of Representatives, One Hundred Seventh Congress, Second Session*. Washington, D.C.: U.S. Government Printing Office, 2002, p. 3.

[46] Jonathan Serrie, "Seattle Cops, Wary of Race-Profiling Accusations, Cutting Back on Minority Arrests," in *S. 989: The End of Racial Profiling Act of 2001, Hearing before the Subcommittee on the Constitution, Federalism, and Property Rights of the Committee on the Judiciary, United States Senate, One Hundred Seventh Congress, First Session*. Washington, D.C.: U.S. Government Printing Office, 2001, p. 123.

[47] Mac Donald, *Are Cops Racist?*, p. 25.

[48] Mac Donald, *Are Cops Racist?*, p. 30.

[49] James Risen, "FBI Told of Worry over Flight Lessons before Sept. 11," *New York Times*, May 4, 2002, p. A10.

[50] Quoted in Kenneth Meeks, *Driving While Black*. New York: Broadway Books, 2000, p. 59.

[51] Bill Clinton, "Remarks by the President on Civil Rights Law Enforcement," White House, Office of the President. Available online. URL: http://clinton3.nara.gov/WH/New/html/19990609.html. Posted on June 9, 1999.

[52] "Text of Bush's Address to Congress," Washingtonpost.com On Politics. Available online. URL: http://www.washingtonpost.com/wp-srv/onpolitics/transcripts/bushtext022701.htm. Posted on February 27, 2001.

[53] John Ashcroft, "Comments," in *Racial Profiling within Law Enforcement Agencies, Hearing before the Subcommittee on the Constitution, Federalism, and Property Rights of the Committee on the Judiciary, United States Senate, One Hundred Sixth Congress, Second Session.* Washington, D.C.: U.S. Government Printing Office, 2000, p. 2.

[54] Russell D. Feingold, "Comments," in *Racial Profiling within Law Enforcement Agencies, Hearing before the Subcommittee on the Constitution, Federalism, and Property Rights of the Committee on the Judiciary, United States Senate, One Hundred Sixth Congress, Second Session.* Washington, D.C.: U.S. Government Printing Office, 2000, pp. 4–5.

[55] David A. Harris, "Profiling—A Self-Fulfilling Racist Policy," Media Awareness Project. Available online. URL: http://www.mapinc.org/letters/1999/03/lte86.html. Posted on March 19, 1999.

[56] Substance Abuse and Mental Health Services Association, "2001 National Household Survey on Drug Abuse (NHSDA)," SAMHSA Public Information. Available online. URL: http://www.samhsa.gov/oas/nhsda/2k1nhsda/vol1/chapter2.htm#2.race. Updated on May 10, 2003.

[57] David A. Harris, *Profiles in Injustice: Why Racial Profiling Cannot Work*. New York: The New Press, 2002, p. 80.

[58] Harris, *Profiles in Injustice*, p. 84.

[59] Covington, "Round Up the Usual Suspects," p. 40.

[60] Cole, *No Equal Justice*, p. 47.

[61] Christopher Darden, quoted in Harris, *Profiles in Injustice*, p. 96.

[62] Quoted in Harris, *Profiles in Injustice*, p. 97.

[63] Marilyn vos Savant, "Ask Marilyn," *Parade Magazine*, June 8, 2003, p. 21.

[64] Harris, *Profiles in Injustice*, p. ix.

[65] Rossano Gerald, "Testimony," in *Racial Profiling within Law Enforcement Agencies, Hearing before the Subcommittee on the Constitution, Federalism, and Property Rights of the Committee on the Judiciary, United States Senate, One Hundred Sixth Congress, Second Session.* Washington, D.C.: U.S. Government Printing Office, 2000, pp. 11–15.

[66] Harris, *Profiles in Injustice*, pp. 91–93.

[67] Curtis V. Rodriquez, "Testimony," in *Racial Profiling within Law Enforcement Agencies, Hearing before the Subcommittee on the Constitution, Federalism, and Property Rights of the Committee on the Judiciary, United States Senate, One Hundred Sixth Congress, Second Session.* Washington, D.C.: U.S. Government Printing Office, 2000, pp. 21–25.

[68] Russell, *The Color of Crime*, p. 36.
[69] Cole, *No Equal Justice*, p. 25.
[70] Kabzuag Vaj, "Statement," in *S. 989: The End of Racial Profiling Act of 2001, Hearing before the Subcommittee on the Constitution, Federalism, and Property Rights of the Committee on the Judiciary, United States Senate, One Hundred Seventh Congress, First Session.* Washington, D.C.: U.S. Government Printing Office, 2001, p. 87.
[71] Tony Barksdale, quoted in Mac Donald, *Are Cops Racist?*, p. 90.
[72] William Tucker, "The Tragedy of Racial Profiling: It's Unjust—and It Works," in *S. 989: The End of Racial Profiling Act of 2001, Hearing before the Subcommittee on the Constitution, Federalism, and Property Rights of the Committee on the Judiciary, United States Senate, One Hundred Seventh Congress, First Session.* Washington, D.C.: U.S. Government Printing Office, 2001, pp. 125–29.
[73] Joyce McMahon et al., *How to Correctly Collect and Analyze Racial Profiling Data: Your Reputation Depends On It.* Washington, D.C.: Office of Community Oriented Policing Services, U.S. Department of Justice, 2002, p. 7.
[74] Harris, *Profiles in Injustice*, p. 100.
[75] U.S. General Accounting Office, *Racial Profiling: Limited Data Available on Motorist Stops.* Washington, D.C.: U.S. General Accounting Office, 2000, p. 26.
[76] John Knowles, Nicola Persico, and Petra Todd, "Racial Bias in Motor Vehicle Searches: Theory and Evidence," *Journal of Political Economy*, vol. 109, no. 11, 2001, pp. 203–29.
[77] David Sampson, quoted in Weinkopf, "Shifting Gears on Racial Profiling."
[78] Warren Cornwall, "Study Disputes Bias Claims in Stops by Troopers," *Seattle Times*, June 20, 2003, p. B-1. Available online. URL: http://seattletimes.nwsource.com/html/localnews/135039859_statepatrol20e.html. Posted on June 20, 2003.
[79] Matthew Petrocelli, Alex R. Piquero, and Michael R. Smith, "Conflict Theory and Racial Profiling: An Empirical Analysis of Police Traffic Stop Data," *Journal of Criminal Justice*, vol. 31, January/February 2003, pp. 1–11.
[80] Harris, *Profiles in Injustice*, p. 119.
[81] Ramirez, McDevitt, and Farrell, *A Resource Guide on Racial Profiling Data Collection Systems*, p. 4.
[82] Richard Morin and Michael H. Cottman, "Discrimination's Lingering Sting; Minorities Tell of Profiling, Other Bias," *Washington Post*, June 22, 2001, p. A1.
[83] Harris, *Profiles in Injustice*, pp. 108–10.
[84] Gallup Organization, "Racial Profiling Is Seen as Widespread, Particularly Among Young Black Men," Gallup Poll News Service. Available online. URL: http://www.gallup.com/subscription/?m=f&c_id=10343. Posted on December 9, 1999.
[85] Harvey Weinstein, Michael Finnegan, and Teresa Watanabe, "Racial Profiling Gains Support as Search Tactic," *Los Angeles Times*, September 24, 2001, p. A1. Available online. URL: http://www.latimes.com/news/nationworld/nation/la-092401racial.story. Posted on September 24, 2001.
[86] Jacinto, "Flying While Arab."
[87] John Fetto, "The Usual Suspects," *American Demographics*, vol. 24, June 2002, p. 14.

[88] Fetto, "The Usual Suspects," p. 14.

[89] Charles Dunbar, Jr., "Testimony,"in *The Benefits of Audio-Visual Technology in Addressing Racial Profiling, Hearing before the Committee on Government Reform, House of Representatives, One Hundred Seventh Congress, First Session.* Washington, D.C.: U.S. Government Printing Office, July 19, 2001, pp. 71–72.

[90] Community Oriented Policing Services, U.S. Department of Justice, *Mutual Respect in Policing: Lesson Plan.* Washington, D.C.: Community Oriented Policing Services, U.S. Department of Justice, 2001, pp. 5–24.

[91] Meeks, *Driving While Black*, pp. 142–143.

[92] Ramirez, *A Resource Guide on Racial Profiling Data Collection Systems*, pp. 21–22.

[93] Fox Butterfield, "City Police Work Losing Its Appeal and Its Veterans," *New York Times*, July 30, 2001, p. A1.

CHAPTER 2

THE LAW AND RACIAL PROFILING

Except in a few states, racial profiling in its more limited form remains legal. When race, ethnicity, or national origin is the sole basis for a decision to stop and detain someone, it violates constitutional guarantees against unreasonable search and seizure (Fourth Amendment) and selective enforcement of the law (Fourteenth Amendment). When race, ethnicity, or national origin is one part of a larger criminal profile, courts have not, with some exceptions, forbidden the practice. Federal, state, and local legislative bodies could, however, pass legislation to outlaw or limit the practice.

LEGISLATION

Federal Statutes

At the federal level, Congress has failed in several legislative attempts to deal with the issue of racial profiling. The Traffic Stops Statistics Study Act of 2000 would have required the attorney general to collect data on racial profiling from police departments that voluntarily agree to participate. With data on a nationwide sample of police jurisdictions, supporters of the legislation hoped the seriousness of the problem and the need for corrective action would become apparent. Although the bill passed in the House of Representatives, it did not pass in the Senate.

Another bill, the End Racial Profiling Act of 2001, went further than the earlier one. It would ban racial profiling and allow the U.S. Department of Justice or individuals to file suit against those practicing racial profiling. To help law enforcement agencies adopt effective complaint, disciplinary, and data collection procedures, the bill would also provide federal funds to state and local agencies. As of January 2004, this bill has not passed either the Senate or House, in large part because the events of September 11, 2001, have dominated the attention of legislators.

Despite the absence of legislation specific to racial profiling, the federal government has used other laws to end the practice. Section 14141 of Title 42, U.S. Code, states that it is unlawful to deprive persons of civil rights. The Department of Justice has the authority to investigate and sue any agency engaging in a pattern of misconduct that deprives individuals of their constitutional rights. The statute makes no reference to racial profiling, but the Department of Justice has interpreted racial profiling as a form of police misconduct that violates civil rights.[1]

After investigating accusations of the use of racial profiling by New Jersey state troopers, the U.S. Department of Justice in 1999 used Section 14141 of the U.S. Code to file a complaint against the state. To end the litigation, the New Jersey state attorney general, under pressure and over his initial opposition, signed a consent decree (a binding agreement that does not require admission of guilt). The decree does not represent federal law but illustrates the kinds of controls the federal government can force on states seen as using racial profiling to violate civil rights. In this case, the decree includes the following provisions:

1. State troopers may not rely to any degree on the race, ethnicity, or national origin of motorists in selecting vehicles for traffic stops.
2. State troopers engaged in patrol activities will document the race, ethnic origin, and gender of all motor vehicle drivers who are the subject of a traffic stop.
3. Supervisors regularly will review trooper reports concerning stop enforcement actions and procedures to ensure that troopers are employing appropriate practices and procedures.
4. The state will develop an early warning system to assist state police supervisors to identify and modify potentially problematic behavior.
5. The state police will make complaint forms available, institute a toll-free hotline number, and publicize the procedures for making complaints. Where misconduct allegations are substantiated, discipline shall be imposed.
6. The state police will continue to implement measures to improve training in matters such as communication skills, cultural diversity, and the nondiscrimination requirements of the decree.
7. The state attorney general's office will have special responsibility for ensuring implementation of the decree. The office will conduct various audits of state police performance, which will include contacting samples of persons who were the subject of a state police traffic stop.

8. The state police will issue semiannual public reports containing aggregate statistics on certain law enforcement activities, including traffic stop statistics.
9. An independent monitor serving as an agent of the court will monitor and report on the state's implementation of the decree.
10. The basic term of the decree will be five years, however, based on the state's record of substantial compliance for two years, the term may be shortened.

Federal Administrative Policies

The executive branch has taken action in other ways against racial profiling. In the absence of congressional legislation, the president can set policies to guide federal law enforcement agencies. President Bill Clinton in 1999 ordered the U.S. attorney general to begin collecting and reporting data on the race, ethnic, and national-origin characteristics of persons stopped. In response to the executive action, reports from the Department of Justice have made recommendations about the appropriate means to collect and use such data. Other government offices have funded data-gathering efforts of state and local police departments.[2]

Specific agencies within the federal government have developed their own policies. A report by the General Accounting Office analyzed data on searches made by the U.S. Customs Service. Figures showed that, of those searched while going through customs, 46 percent were black women and 23 percent were white women.[3] After congressional hearings on the problem and a class-action suit brought by nearly 90 African-American women, the new head of Customs, Raymond W. Kelly, revised policies to eliminate racial bias in searches. Personal searches would require a supervisor's approval rather than an agent's discretion, unless there was clear evidence of wrongdoing. Agents must limit the criteria to select someone for a personal search for drugs to factors such as nervous sweating, an unusual walk or bulge in clothing, inconsistent answers to questions, outside intelligence, or an alert from a drug-sniffing dog. The new policies led to fewer searches but an increase in the percentage of searches that discovered contraband, from 3.5 to 5.8 percent.[4]

After the September 11 terrorist attacks, the U.S. Department of Transportation took action against racial profiling at airports. After several well-publicized incidents of passengers with Middle Eastern or Asian appearance being removed from planes or prevented from boarding, Transportation Secretary Norman Mineta informed the airlines about the department's opposition to racial profiling. Mineta, who as an 11-year-old was a victim of a form of racial profiling when he and his Japanese-American family were interned at a camp in Wyoming during World War II, received praise for the action from Arab-American groups. Energy Secretary Spencer Abraham, a descendant of Arab immigrants, also sent a memo to department employees stating his opposition to racial profiling.

More recently, President George W. Bush announced guidelines barring agents in 70 federal law enforcement agencies from using race or ethnicity in routine investigations. According to a spokesman, the guidelines will prevent the use of race or ethnicity as a proxy for certain types of criminal activities and do more than required by the courts to eliminate racial profiling.[5] However, President Bush allowed, to the extent permitted by the Constitution and laws, for the use of race and ethnicity in some circumstances to identify potential terrorists and protect national borders. Opponents of racial profiling believe this exception weakens the benefits of the new guidelines and criticize the president for not specifying detailed enforcement procedures. Still, an administrative order from the president carries considerable weight and will affect the way federal law enforcement officers carry out their investigations.

State Statutes

At least six states have enacted statutes that prohibit law enforcement officers from engaging in racial profiling: California, Connecticut, Kentucky, New Jersey, Oklahoma, and Rhode Island.

In California, the 2001 penal code states that "(1) Racial profiling is a practice that presents a great danger to the fundamental principles of a democratic society. It is abhorrent and cannot be tolerated. (2) Motorists who have been stopped by the police for no reason other than the color of their skin or their apparent nationality or ethnicity are the victim of discriminatory practices." Racial profiling is defined more specifically as detaining a suspect based on a broad set of criteria that casts suspicion on an entire class of people without any individualized suspicion of the particular person being stopped. To ensure that law enforcement officers do not engage in this practice, the state recommends expanded training of new officers and refresher courses every year for experienced officers.

In Connecticut, a 1999 measure makes racial profiling illegal by requiring police agencies to record the race and ethnicity of every motorist stopped for traffic violations. Any police agency found to practice racial profiling will lose state funding. However, rather than specify antiprofiling policies itself, the legislation required police agencies to adopt their own written policies.

In Kentucky, a 2001 law states that "No state law enforcement agency or official shall stop, detain, or search any person when the action is solely motivated by considerations of race, color, or ethnicity, and the action would constitute a violation of the civil rights of the person." The policy in written form should be disseminated and followed by all sheriffs and local law enforcement officials, and each administrative unit shall adopt actions to take when officers violate the policy. All officers must also receive training related to racial profiling and the policy.

In New Jersey, Governor James E. McGreevey signed a law on March 14, 2003, to make racial profiling illegal. The law specifies a penalty of jail for up to five years for use of racial profiling by police and public officials and up to 10 years if someone is injured during a profiling incident. It also punishes officers guilty of forging or covering up information on racial stops. However, a person must commit the prohibited action twice to be found guilty.

In Oklahoma, a 2001 statute specifies that "No officer of any municipal, county or state law enforcement agency shall engage in racial profiling," where *racial profiling* "means the detention, interdiction or other disparate treatment of an individual solely on the basis of the racial or ethnic status of such individual. . . . A violation shall be a misdemeanor . . . [and] a person believed to be stopped or arrested in violation of the act can file a complaint with Oklahoma Human Rights Commission and the appropriate county district attorney."

In Rhode Island, the legislature in 2000 enacted a law relating to motor and other vehicles. It states that racial profiling as the sole reason for stopping or searching motorists on public highways is against public policy and violates the civil rights of the motorists. *Racial profiling* here refers to disparate treatment solely on the basis of racial or ethnic status. The act does not specify punishment but focuses on requirements for collecting data. The data collected are to be used, according to the act, for research or statistical purposes rather than in any legal or administrative proceeding.

States more commonly have mandated data collection procedures rather than passed laws to prohibit racial profiling. Of the 49 state police agencies (Hawaii and the District of Columbia do not have such agencies), 16 require officers to collect race or ethnicity data for all traffic stops. These states are California, Connecticut, Florida, Iowa, Massachusetts, Michigan, Missouri, New Jersey, North Carolina, Ohio, Oregon, Rhode Island, South Carolina, Texas, Virginia, and Washington. Another 23 states require collection of data under more limited circumstances, such as when an arrest occurs or force is used. A few states require collection of data only on special units, such as those involved in criminal interdiction. In total, 39 of the 49 state agencies require some form of data collection on race and ethnic distribution of traffic stops. Ten state police agencies do not require traffic patrol officers to collect race data for any stops. These states are Arizona, Arkansas, Idaho, Illinois, Minnesota, Montana, New Mexico, North Dakota, Oklahoma, and Utah.

COURT CASES

Because racial profiling typically involves stops by police of members of minority groups, many of the court cases relevant to the issue involve interpretations of the allowable grounds for making a stop. The cases address constitutional issues over the meaning of the Fourth Amendment, which protects citizens from unreasonable search and seizure, and the Fourteenth Amendment, which protects citizens from selective enforcement of the law. This section describes some of the important cases that relate to the allowable grounds for police to stop someone and the use of race, ethnicity, and national origin as part of those grounds.

Supreme Court Decisions

U.S. Supreme Court decisions have addressed issues that relate indirectly to racial profiling: the use of reasonable suspicion versus probable cause for making stops, requests by police for consent to make a search, and pretext stops to check for more serious crimes. These decisions all concern the limits on police discretion (and the ability to employ racial profiling). Otherwise, the Court has examined issues relating more directly to racial profiling by prohibiting use of race or ethnicity alone but allowing use of profiles in general. The cases suggest that racial profiling in a limited sense would be constitutional.

TERRY V. OHIO, 392 U.S. 1 (1968)

Background

In 1963, a plainclothes police officer patrolling his beat in Cleveland, Ohio, noticed two men, Terry and Chilton, whom he had never seen before. On his beat, the officer, Detective Martin McFadden, had developed the habit of looking for shoplifters and pickpockets, often by watching people walk the streets. In this case, something did not look right to the officer about the two men, so he began to watch them from a distance. He saw one of the men walk a short distance, look into a store window, and walk back to his companion, and confer. The second man then did the same thing. The two men repeated these actions five or six times until a third man, Katz, approached, conversed, and then left. Soon after, the first two men followed the third.

These actions raised the suspicion of Officer McFadden that the men were "casing a job, a stick-up" and might have a weapon. When he saw the three men meet in front of a store, he confronted them by identifying himself as a policeman and asking their names. When the men "mumbled something" in response, the officer spun Terry around and patted down the outside of his clothing and felt a pistol. He then ordered the men into the store, where he removed Terry's weapon, ordered the three men against the wall, searched more thoroughly for weapons, and removed one more weapon from Chilton. He then took Terry and Chilton to the police station, where he charged them with carrying a concealed weapon.

During their trial, Terry and Chilton moved to have evidence of the gun suppressed. They argued that the gun had been discovered during an unlawful search, one without the officer having probable cause for an arrest. The trial court rejected the motion, and the defendants were found guilty. The court of appeals affirmed the conviction, and the Ohio State Supreme Court dismissed another appeal. In 1968, the Supreme Court considered the case and delivered its opinion.

Legal Issues

The legal issues involve the grounds for search and seizure under the constitutional guarantees of the Fourth Amendment. Is it reasonable for police to seize and subject a person to a search, in this case for weapons, when no probable cause exists for an arrest? On one side, the state of Ohio, representing the police, claimed that, because Terry was never really seized during the quick search, the Fourth Amendment does not apply to the case. A frisk of outside clothing differs from a full-fledged search in the inconvenience faced and time lost by the suspect and does not raise constitutional issues. Even if the search involved a seizure as specified in the Fourth Amendment, it was reasonable. Although the officer did not have probable cause for an arrest, he did have reason to believe the defendants were acting suspiciously and deserved some investigation. Given the need for an investigation and protection from the suspects, the police officer acted properly in checking for weapons.

On the other side, the petitioner claimed that the search involved a seizure—Terry was restrained in his freedom of action by the officer. The indignity and threat to personal integrity of a search, even a brief one, is serious enough to warrant protection by the Fourth Amendment. Further, the search lacked probable cause or clear evidence that the suspect had committed a crime. Lacking a warrant, the officer had no authority to search Terry.

Decision

The Supreme Court agreed that the search of Terry raised constitutional issues involving the Fourth Amendment. However, it rejected the claim of the defendants to exclude evidence from the trial based on the search and affirmed the conviction. The decision, written by Chief Justice Earl Warren, held that, whenever practical, police must obtain advanced judicial approval for searches and seizures in the form of a warrant. However, in some cases, on-the-spot observations by police may require swift action that would preclude obtaining a warrant. If, for example, officers have reason to believe that their safety or the safety of others is in immediate jeopardy, they may not be able to wait for a judge to approve making a stop and search. In such circumstances, the government's interest in preventing harm outweighs concerns about the invasion of a person's privacy.

In this particular case, the Court concluded that the facts confronting Officer McFadden would lead a reasonably prudent person to conclude that Terry was armed and presented a danger. This conclusion—that the defendant was preparing to rob a store, and such a crime would likely include the use of a weapon—allowed for a limited search, one minimally necessary for the goal of insuring the safety of the officer. The circumstances did not justify a general search for any evidence of a crime, but the officer appropriately limited his search to the concern about being protected from a weapon. Since the officer kept the search brief and checked only for a weapon, he did not violate the rights of the defendant. The evidence obtained from the search was rightly admitted into evidence against Terry.

In summary terms, the decision states, "We merely hold today that where a police officer observes unusual conduct which leads him reasonably to conclude in light of his experience that criminal activity may be afoot and that the persons with whom he is dealing may be armed and presently dangerous, . . . he is entitled for the protection of himself and others in the area to conduct a carefully limited search." Such a search is reasonable under the Fourth Amendment and allows for the introduction of obtained evidence.

In dissenting, Justice William O. Douglas maintained that unless the officer had probable cause for believing a crime was being committed, he had no right to make a seizure and conduct a search. He noted that a judge in these circumstances would not have enough evidence to deliver a warrant for a search, and so the decision gives police authority to make a search that a judge would not have. In the end, according to Douglas, the decision extends increasing power to police over individuals and their constitutional rights.

Impact

In making brief stops and restricted searches permissible on grounds of reasonable suspicion rather than probable cause, this decision justified the "stop and frisk" procedures used by police on the street. Police can stop individuals for suspicious activity, including minor offenses, and then search suspects for weapons if they feel the suspects present a danger. In other words, the decision allows police to deal with circumstances that likely will lead directly to a crime rather than reacting to the occurrence of the crime. The procedures have had much apparent success in New York City. Stop-and-frisk measures there have removed many weapons from the street and contributed to the decline in homicide. Not having to wait for stronger evidence of a crime before taking action with a quick stop and frisk means police can do more to prevent crime.

This and following decisions have reaffirmed the validity of taking action on reasonable suspicion. Police need more than a simple hunch or vague feeling—they must be able to offer clearly stated facts to justify the reasonable suspicion. They also must limit their actions so as not to detain or inconvenience subjects for more than a short time. More comprehensive searches and longer stops require probable cause and perhaps a warrant. Within these limits, the Court has reaffirmed the need for society to balance the dual goals of protecting citizens from crime and upholding their civil rights.

Critics of the decision believe it gives the police too much discretion in deciding whom to stop and search and the courts too little control over the motives used to make a stop. The broad grounds for reasonable suspicion might, among other things, encourage racial profiling. For example, an innocent individual simply walking in a high-risk area inhabited by minorities may create a reasonable suspicion in the mind of a police officer. In a similar way, evading the police can create a suspicion that a crime is afoot, but, since minorities often fear police mistreatment, their innocent actions may lead to improper stops. Minorities will, in the end, face racial profiling and police stops without real facts of guilt. Some thus object to the potential for abuse of stop-and-frisk police tactics allowed by the Terry decision.

UNITED STATES V. BRIGNONI-PONCE, 422 U.S. 873 (1975)

Background

Two U.S. Border Patrol agents were observing traffic traveling north (away from Mexico) as they parked on the side of an interstate highway between San Diego and Los Angeles, California. They noticed that the occupants of one car appeared to be of Mexican descent, pursued the car, and stopped it. On questioning the occupants about their citizenship, the patrol agents found the two vehicle passengers lacked documentation and had entered the country illegally. The driver, Brignoni-Ponce, was charged with knowingly transporting illegal aliens and was convicted on both counts. The trial judge rejected a motion to suppress evidence based on the claim that it came from an illegal stop and seizure. The court of appeals reversed, holding that the stop was not based on reasonable suspicion and therefore the evidence should have been excluded. The U.S. Supreme Court agreed to hear an appeal from the government over the reversal.

Legal Issues

Although the stop raised issues involving the ability of roving border patrols to stop cars distant from the U.S. border, another legal dispute concerned the Supreme Court. The Court addressed the question of whether or not a vehicle and occupants can be stopped near the border when the occupants' apparent Mexican ancestry defined the only ground for suspicion of illegal activity. The government held that it has two grounds for stopping cars on this basis. First, the Immigration and Naturalization Act authorizes officers or employees of the Immigration and Naturalization Service to question any person believed to be an alien about his or her right to be or remain in the United States. Near the Mexican border, the appearance of Mexican ancestry allows questioning under the statute. Second, another statute grants agents the authority to stop moving vehicles and question the occupants about their citizenship anywhere within 100 miles of the border, even without reason to believe the occupants are aliens.

In addition, the government asserted that the public interest demands effective means to prevent illegal immigration. Illegal immigration in the United States had by the 1970s reached high levels, thus creating competition with citizens for jobs, increasing demand and costs for social services, and raising concerns about exploitation by employers. Since most illegal immigrants come from Mexico, where they can slip into the United States away from border patrol checkpoints or enter on a valid visa yet remain after it expires, the best way to apprehend illegal immigrants comes from stops inside the border. A stop creates only a minor inconvenience to citizens and legal immigrants—they merely have to answer a few brief questions. Such a stop properly balances the public's interest in controlling illegal immigration with an individual's right to be free from arbitrary police interference.

Responding to these claims, the defendants stressed that existing statutes cannot authorize patrol agents to violate the Constitution and the Fourth Amendment protection against unreasonable search and seizure. Although the government has an interest in preventing illegal immigration and the stops represent only a modest inconvenience, agents must, under previous court decisions, have a reasonable suspicion to justify a stop. Physical appearance by itself does not meet the standard of reasonable suspicion. Because the agents relied only on ethnic appearance, they did not have reasonable suspicion of a crime and acted unconstitutionally in making a stop.

Decision

The Supreme Court affirmed the ruling of the court of appeals. The trial court had erred by allowing introduction of evidence from the stop of Brignoni-Ponce and in convicting the defendant. In addition to determining that the evidence had been obtained illegally, the Court also helped set standards for making a vehicle stop. The decision gave the border control authority to briefly stop vehicles with minimal intrusion in order to prevent illegal immigration. However, a vehicle cannot be stopped without reason to suspect that the occupants have violated the law.

To have a reasonable suspicion, agents may consider a number of factors other than ethnic appearance. Information on recent illegal border crossings, experience with immigration traffic in the area, erratic or evasive driving, and use of vans and trucks well-suited for smuggling immigrants might qualify as defining suspicious activity. Agents may also consider factors such as mode of dress and haircut, which may appear characteristic of those who live outside the United States. However, relying on a single factor, the appearance of Mexican ancestry, does not meet the standard of reasonable suspicion.

Even if authorized by existing statutes, stopping cars inside the border without such suspicion would have significant negative consequences. It would disrupt traffic involving large numbers of citizens who live or work near the border and intrude on the rights of U.S. citizens to be free from undue government interference. Native-born and naturalized Hispanic Americans, who make up a substantial part of the population in parts of Texas, New Mexico, and California, have the same appearance of Mexican ancestry as illegal immigrants. Based on appearance alone, they might be mistaken for illegal immigrants and commonly stopped by border patrol agents. Avoiding this problem requires a standard of reasonable suspicion rather than appearance alone to justify a stop.

A last line in the body of the decision also has important implications: "The likelihood that any given person of Mexican ancestry is an alien is high enough to make Mexican appearance a relevant factor, but standing alone does not justify stopping all Mexican-Americans to ask if they are aliens." Although not fully discussed, this point suggests that ethnic profiling in a limited form meets constitutional requirements.

Impact

This decision clearly established that the use of race, ethnicity, or national origin as the sole factor in making a stop violates constitutional protections. Although the case applies specifically to immigration, its implications can be extended to the use of racial profiling for drug interdiction, neighborhood crime, and terrorism. The decision prevents the worst excesses of racial profiling and leads opponents of racial profiling to claim the practice is illegal. However, the decision does not rule out altogether the use of race, ethnicity, or national origin as one relevant factor in a larger profile. In a more restricted form, then, racial profiling remains legal.

UNITED STATES V. MARTINEZ-FUERTE ET AL., 74–1560 (1976)

Background

Amado Martinez-Fuerte approached a border patrol checkpoint while driving a vehicle with two women who had entered the United States illegally from Mexico. The checkpoint is located 66 miles north of the Mexican border on the principal California highway connecting San Diego and Los Angeles. About one mile before the checkpoint, a sign informed drivers of the forthcoming need to stop. As the traffic proceeds slowly through the checkpoint area, border patrol agents look at drivers and passengers, allowing most to pass through but stopping some for further inquiry. On being stopped, Martinez-Fuerte produced proper papers, but the passengers admitted to having come into the country illegally. Martinez-Fuerte was charged and convicted on two counts of illegally transporting aliens. Before the trial, the defendant moved to suppress the evidence because it had been obtained from a stop that violated his Fourth Amendment rights, but the judge denied the motion. The appeals court reversed the decision, as it had recently affirmed some other decisions to suppress evidence obtained in similar circumstances. To clarify the proper grounds for a stop and search, the Supreme Court considered the case.

Legal Issues

The case raised two major issues to address. First, did routine checkpoint stops infringe on the rights against unreasonable search and seizure required by the Fourth Amendment? The defendants argued that, because they do not rely on reasonable suspicion or probable cause, the stops are unconstitutional. The government argued that brief questioning at the checkpoint does not amount to search or seizure, does not require reasonable suspicion, and is consistent with constitutional provisions. Second, does selecting some motorists rather than others at the checkpoint violate the Fourteenth Amendment by inappropriately using race and ethnicity? The defendants argued that the selection relied on ethnicity, while the government argued that it relied on other factors in addition to Mexican ancestry.

Decision

In a 7-2 majority decision that combined several cases besides the one involving Martinez-Fuerte, the Supreme Court sided with the government and overturned the appeals court. It concluded that checkpoints for illegal immigration are constitutional. The government has important interests in using checkpoints to deal with problems of illegal immigration, while drivers, whose cars are not searched without appropriate evidence, face only minimal intrusion. Even those drivers selected for additional inspection merely need to answer a few questions before proceeding. As Justice Powell stated in the written opinion, the selection process is constitutional: "Even if it be assumed that such referrals are made largely on the basis of apparent Mexican ancestry, we perceive no constitutional violation . . . the intrusion here is sufficiently minimal that no particularized reason need exist to justify it." Moreover, the selection of a smaller portion of the drivers than the proportion of Mexican Americans in the population suggests that the agents used factors other than ethnicity in their decisions.

Impact

This decision affirms the legality of using ethnicity as one factor in a larger profile. In this case, the profile involved the judgments of border patrol agents in selecting vehicle occupants for brief questioning. The agents do not stop the vehicles for a long duration or search them—unless answers to questions present reasons for suspicion—and use multiple criteria in the selection process. They can therefore continue their checkpoint procedures. Critics view the decision as contributing to the potential for misuse of race, ethnicity, and national origin in the selection process.

United States v. Sokolow, 87–1295 (1989)

Background

In 1984, Andrew Sokolow purchased two round-trip tickets to Miami at the Honolulu Airport under the names of "Andrew Kray" and "Janet Norian." He paid $2,100 in cash for the tickets, taking the money from a large roll of

$20 bills. Dressed in a black jumpsuit, with much gold jewelry, he appeared nervous and did not check any of the four pieces of luggage he and his companion carried. Informed by the ticket agent of the two passengers, a member of the Honolulu Police Department found that the phone number Sokolow gave in buying the tickets did not match the names he gave, and the officer informed the Drug Enforcement Administration about the travelers. On returning three days after they left, Sokolow and his companion were stopped and brought to a special room where a drug-sniffing dog alerted the police of drugs in the luggage. Obtaining a search warrant, the agents eventually discovered cocaine in the luggage.

Charged on possession of cocaine with intent to distribute, the defendant moved to suppress the evidence as illegally obtained. Although the trial judge ruled that the drug agents had reasonable suspicion for stopping Sokolow at the airport, the appeals court reversed the conviction. The reversal held that the agents did not have reasonable suspicion. Given the importance of the enforcement of federal narcotics laws and controversy over the appropriateness of searches, the Supreme Court granted certiorari to review the appeals court decision.

Legal Issues

In representing the drug enforcement agents, the government argued that six factors created reasonable suspicion to stop the defendant: (1) cash payment for tickets, (2) traveling under a name that did not match the given phone number, (3) a destination known as a source of illegal drugs, (4) a stay in Miami of only 48 hours when the round-trip flight took 20 hours, (5) a nervous demeanor, and (6) not checking luggage. These characteristics fit a profile of a drug trafficker closely enough to instigate a brief stop and a check of the luggage by a drug-sniffing dog. The alert from the dog gave the officers probable cause to obtain a warrant for a more detailed search.

In arguing for suppression of the evidence, the defendant contended that the search did not meet the standards required by the Fourth Amendment. Specifically, none of the factors used by the drug agents involves evidence of ongoing criminal behavior such as trying to evade the agents. Without such evidence, other factors relating to the characteristics of the respondent do not define reasonable suspicion. By themselves, factors such as appearing nervous, not checking luggage, or paying cash could be explained as normal actions of those afraid of flying, not wanting to wait for luggage to be delivered, and preferring not to use credit cards. Because he fit the behavior of innocent persons as well as drug couriers, the defendant should not have been stopped by the agents.

Decision

In a 7-2 majority decision written by Chief Justice William Rehnquist, the Supreme Court ruled that the agents had reasonable suspicion to believe the defendant was transporting illegal drugs and justification for stopping him. Since reasonable suspicion requires a minimal level of objective evidence rather than certainty, factors that have a likely association with crime rather than a clear indication of crime become relevant. Although paying in cash, using an alias, and staying only briefly in Miami can be consistent with innocent travel, they together amount to reasonable suspicion that criminal conduct was afoot. Therefore, the agents had justification for a restricted search.

In specifying standards for a permissible stop and search, the Court emphasized the importance of considering the totality of circumstances. Each factor individually may appear innocent, but the factors combined may lead to suspicion. Since a drug courier profile lists a series of characteristics rather than a single one, the decision affirms the appropriateness of using profiles in investigation. Moreover, such profiles need not include specific evidence of criminal behavior.

Impact

Although it does not directly address the issue of racial profiling, this decision endorses the use of general profiling as constitutional. When employing the standard of reasonable suspicion, law enforcement agents need not have evidence of criminal conduct but may rely on characteristics of a profile that have a likely association with criminal conduct. In this case, the profile characteristics do not include skin color or ethnicity, and other decisions make clear that race or ethnicity alone cannot justify a stop. However, given the legality of using profiles and the connection of race, ethnicity, and national origin to certain types of offending, the Sokolow ruling may indirectly permit use of racial profiling in a restricted sense (that is, as one relevant factor in a larger profile).

FLORIDA V. BOSTICK, 89-1717 501 U.S. 429 (1991)

Background

In 1985, Terrance Bostick, a 28-year-old black man traveling on a bus from Miami to Atlanta, was sleeping as the bus made a brief stop in Fort Lauderdale. Two officers with badges, insignia, and pouches containing pistols boarded the bus to check for drugs. They noticed Bostick asleep in the back row, woke him up, and asked to see his ticket and identification. With the ticket and the identification in order, the officers had no reasonable suspicion that Bostick was involved in any crime. Yet, they explained to him that they were narcotics agents on the lookout for illegal drugs and asked if they could search his luggage. In legal terms, they asked for a consent search.

The officers and defendant dispute the facts at this point. The officers said Bostick agreed to allow the search after being told he had the right to refuse. Bostick said he was not informed of his right to refuse, felt intimidated by the weapons carried by the officers, and agreed to a search of one bag but not another. In any case, one piece of luggage contained cocaine, which led to the arrest and later conviction of the defendant for trafficking in cocaine. During the trial, the defendant moved to suppress the cocaine evidence on the grounds that it had been obtained illegally. When the judge rejected the motion, Bostick entered a guilty plea while reserving the right to appeal.

The Florida District Court of Appeals affirmed the decision to allow the evidence, but the Florida Supreme Court also considered the issue, finding that the search violated the Fourth Amendment. It also ruled that the police could not randomly board buses as a means of interdicting the movement of drugs. The Supreme Court then heard the case.

Legal Issues

The officers did not have reasonable suspicion or probable cause to justify the search. The legal issues hence relate to the question of whether the encounter on the bus amounted to an unlawful seizure prohibited by the Fourth Amendment. On one side, the government pointed to precedents that a consensual encounter does not raise Fourth Amendment issues about search and seizure. Officers may ask questions of individuals, including asking permission to make a search, without having reasonable suspicion or probable cause. As long as the officers do not imply that the individual must comply, the encounter remains voluntary. Given the voluntary nature of the contact with the police, Bostick could at any time have declined to answer any more questions and refused to allow a search.

On the other side, the defendant maintained that he did not feel free to avoid the questioning or decline the officer's requests. Since he had paid for a ticket and had not completed the journey, he could not exit the bus. And with police in front of him, he felt pressured to agree to the search. Knowing he had drugs in his luggage, the defendant would agree to the search only if he felt forced to do so. According to the motion to suppress, then, the encounter between the police and Bostick involved a type of search and seizure prohibited by the Fourth Amendment. Not based on reasonable suspicion, the search did not meet the standard laid down by the Supreme Court in *Terry v. Ohio*.

Decision

In a 6-3 majority decision authored by Justice Sandra Day O'Connor, the Court reversed the decision of the Florida Supreme Court. The decision concluded that the search was legal, remanded the case to Florida, and required the proceedings to continue in a way consistent with the opinion. The Court reasoned that, even though it took place on a bus, the encounter was consensual, not coercive. Therefore, the search did not require reasonable suspicion or raise Fourth Amendment issues.

A key point in the ruling noted that, for the encounter to be consensual, the individual being questioned did not need to be free to physically leave. He only needed to feel free to decline a request for a search. In *Terry v. Ohio*, the Court stated, "Obviously, not all personal intercourse between policemen and citizens involves 'seizures' of persons. Only when the officer, by means of physical force or show of authority, has in some way restrained the liberty of a citizen may we conclude that a 'seizure' has occurred." Similarly, "even when officers have no basis for suspecting a particular individual, they may generally ask questions of that individual, ask to examine the individual's identification, and request to search his or her luggage—as long as police do not convey a message that compliance with their request is required." Since the officers did not point guns at Bostick, threaten him, or imply he could not refuse, a seizure did not occur.

The decision recognizes circumstances in which police intimidation may make any agreement to a search coercive and unconstitutional. The appropriate standard is that a reasonable person would not have felt free to decline the officer's request. In this case, the encounter with police on the bus did not meet the standard. The decision also rejects the claim of the defendant that no reasonable person would consent to a search of luggage that contains drugs. Based on precedent, the reasonableness of a request for search must be judged from the perspective of an innocent person. Otherwise, all consent searches that find contraband would by definition involve coercion regardless of the circumstances of the request.

Impact

The decision gives police the opportunity to ask simple questions of individuals in their efforts to prevent drug trafficking and other crimes. As long as they do not coerce or intimidate, police can ask for consent to make a search, even if they do not have reasonable suspicion of a crime having been committed. Law enforcement officers have used this technique successfully, as many people, even those carrying contraband, agree to the search.

Critics of the decision believe that it gives the police too much power. They say that people in daily life will not feel free to refuse requests of police for a search. Minorities in particular will worry that a refusal will anger police and lead them to make an even more thorough search. Many people may in fact not realize they have the right to refuse. In these instances, the coercion is subtle rather than obvious, but it still exists. Critics also believe the decision gives the police too much discretion. Even without evidence of any sort that a crime has occurred, they can approach anyone they want to ask questions. This heightens the potential for police to violate the Fourth Amendment rights of citizens.

By increasing police power and discretion, the ruling can encourage racial profiling. According to critics, more disadvantaged, less powerful members of minority communities will feel unable to refuse requests. Given historical conflict between minorities and police and well-publicized instances of police brutality, few members of a minority group will feel free to ignore or walk away from, say, a drug interdiction team. In turn, if police have more success in receiving consent to search from minorities than others, they will target minorities. The *Bostick* decision may thus indirectly promote racial profiling and discrimination.

Michael A. Whren and James L. Brown v. United States, 95-5841 (1995)

Background

In 1993, police patrolling an area in Washington, D.C., known for drug use observed a Pathfinder truck waiting at a stop sign. The truck contained young men and bore temporary license plates and seemed to remain stopped at the intersection for an unusually long time—more than 20 seconds. When the police turned their unmarked car around, the truck quickly turned right and sped off at an unreasonable speed. The police followed and eventually pulled alongside the truck at a red light. One officer then stepped out, identified himself, and asked the driver to pull over. He then noticed that one passenger, Whren, held two bags of cocaine, and arrested the suspects for possession of illegal drugs.

After being charged with violating federal drug laws, the defendants moved in a pretrial hearing to suppress the evidence on the grounds that the stop and seizure was illegal. They argued that the police did not have probable cause or even reasonable suspicion that the occupants of the car had been involved in illegal drug activity. The police responded that they approached the car on the basis of something other than a search for drugs. They had probable cause to stop the car for traffic violations—turning without signaling and driving at an unreasonable speed—and then observed the drugs. The district court denied the motion, the petitioners were convicted on all counts, and the court of appeals affirmed the conviction. On further appeal, the Supreme Court agreed to hear the case.

Legal Issues

The legal issues revolve around the use of a traffic stop as a pretext to search for other criminal violations. In defending the stop and the use of the drug evidence, the government argued that the police, since they observed violations of traffic laws, had probable cause to make the traffic stop. Once the police stopped the vehicle for the traffic violations, the drugs were in plain sight, which gave the police probable cause for an arrest. Although they discovered drugs during the stop, the police claimed they did not need reasonable suspicion or probable cause of drug distribution to make the traffic stop.

The defendants argued that drivers can never comply totally with traffic laws, which gives the police almost unlimited opportunity to stop nearly any motorist on a technical violation. This opportunity permits police officers to use grounds such as the race of drivers (in this case, all occupants of the car were African Americans) in making a stop. It also permits officers to use the stop as a means to investigate other law violations without having reasonable suspicion or probable cause for their actions. Police may have observed the car stopped at an intersection longer than normal, but this does not provide grounds for suspicion of drug possession. In short, use of a traffic stop as a pretext to check for other violations of the law constitutes unreasonable search and seizure.

The key to making the stop should not, according to the defendants' appeal, be probable cause that a traffic violation has occurred but probable cause that a reasonable officer would make the stop for the reason given. In this case, the defendants might have committed minor traffic offenses, but a reasonable officer would not have bothered to make a stop for the offense. Unlike traffic cops patrolling for the specific purpose of enforcing traffic laws, the officers in this case were in plain clothes and an unmarked car. The stop served no other purpose than to search for drugs. To prevent the use of ulterior motives in traffic stops, the defendants urged the Court to adopt the reasonable officer standard.

Decision

The Supreme Court ruled unanimously that the officers did not act unconstitutionally when they made the stop. The evidence of drug possession discovered during the stop was therefore correctly admitted by the court of appeals. The ruling reasoned that the fairness of a stop does not depend on the motive of the officers. Trying to establish whether an officer had the proper state of mind in making a stop would present a difficult, if not impossible, task for courts. Although issues of subjectivity might relate to violations of the Fourteenth Amendment—selective enforcement of the law—they do not appear relevant to violations of the Fourth Amendment for search and seizure protection. Instead, the factor to consider is the objective reasonableness of the stop. In this case, objective evidence of violating traffic laws made the stop reasonable.

The Court rejected the defendants' claim that the legality of a stop should depend on the actions of a reasonable officer in the same circumstances. If it is difficult to determine the subjective intent of an officer in making a stop, it is even more difficult to determine the subjective intent of a hypothetical reasonable officer. Reliance on a reasonable officer would make the standard subject to variations in police habits across time and place rather than to written law.

The Court also rejected the claim that, because the traffic laws are so broad and difficult to obey that virtually everyone is guilty of something, the police should not be permitted to make certain stops. Although police have some discretion in enforcing the law, no legal principle exists to determine when the law becomes so expansive that the police should no longer enforce it. In short, the police can use the laws as objectively written in making a stop. If the stop serves as a pretext for other concerns of the police, it does not violate the Fourth Amendment as long as probable cause exists for at least one violation.

Impact

The *Whren* decision provides legal justification for the common police strategy of making pretext stops for minor violations to check for more serious violations. On highways, police can stop cars for speeding, not using turn signals, having a light burned out, and other minor traffic violations. They can then check the license plate numbers, observe the passengers, and view the contents of the vehicle for evidence of a crime that would allow for a fuller search of the vehicle, or they can ask for consent to search the car. On the street, stopping someone for jaywalking or loitering can allow the police to ask questions about and look for evidence of other crimes, such as carrying a weapon. These practices have become part of most police procedures.

By removing issues of the subjective intent of officers in making a stop, the decision also makes it hard to prove that a stop involved inappropriate considerations such as race. With breaking a traffic law as sufficient justification for making a stop, other motivations, such as the belief that minorities are more likely to carry drugs, can remain hidden. Many traffic violations, such as changing lanes too quickly or weaving across lines, are difficult to disprove, which furthers the discretion of police.

For these reasons, opponents of racial profiling harshly criticize the decision. They believe that allowing officers to create pretext for a stop permits dishonest police work. Police can always find a reason for a stop, no matter how petty, which has the effect of masking the real reasons for the stop—including those relating to the skin color of the suspect. Critics contend that the ruling thus frees police to target members of minority groups. Even evidence that a particular officer had a history of stopping disproportionate numbers of minorities would prove irrelevant as long as the officer had some evidence of a traffic violation.

UNITED STATES V. ARMSTRONG ET AL., 95–157 (1996)

Background

In 1992, a California federal district attorney indicted Christopher Lee Armstrong and several others on charges of conspiring to possess cocaine with intent to distribute and violating federal firearm laws. The charges came after federal and local agents from Inglewood, California, had obtained information from confidential informants about the defendants. The informants had infiltrated the cocaine distribution ring, made purchases of substantial amounts of crack, and observed the defendants carrying illegal firearms. In a sting operation, the agents videotaped a drug exchange, searched the hotel room where the sale had taken place, arrested the suspects, and found more crack and a loaded gun. Other members of the ring were arrested later.

The defendants, all African Americans, filed a motion for discovery or dismissal of the charges on the grounds that prosecutors discriminated in the selection of their cases. They offered evidence that all of 24 cases handled by the public defender in 1991 involved African-American defendants. The government opposed the motion, arguing that the defendants provided no evidence of the failure of police to prosecute defendants of other races. The district court granted the motion by ordering the government to allow for discovery (that is, to give the defendants statistics on the race of defendants in all drug and firearm cases over the last three years). The government refused to provide the data, effectively causing dismissal of the charges. The court of appeals reversed the district court decision, after which the Supreme Court granted certiorari.

Legal Issues

The legal issues involve the kind of evidence needed to demonstrate the use of racial profiling in prosecutor decision making. The defendants, believing that racial profiling led to their investigation and prosecution, did not have the data and figures needed to prove their belief. They had preliminary and incomplete information that was sufficient, in their view, to justify discovery or more complete access to government data. With discovery, they could properly present a defense based on selective enforcement of the law, racial profiling, and discrimination. Their motion thus requested accesses to race data on the defendants in other government cases.

In denying racial profiling had any role in the investigation or prosecution, the government opposed the motion. Prosecutors claimed that, rather than race, the large amounts of cocaine involved in the ring, the videotaped evidence of the illegal sale, the defendants' history of drug involvement, and the seriousness of firearms possession led to the charges and trial. The government also offered figures on the involvement of African Americans in the distribution of crack. This involvement supported their view that prosecution of African Americans did not stem from racism but criminal behavior.

Decision

The Supreme Court ruled that the defendants did not provide sufficient evidence of racial profiling to justify discovery. To establish discrimination based on race, the defendants needed to show that the government declined to prosecute similarly situated suspects of other races. In this case, the amount of drugs involved, the dangerousness of the weapons carried, and the strength of the videotaped evidence made for a strong case. Proof of discrimination would come from demonstrating that whites who distributed similar amounts of cocaine, owned as many illegal weapons, and were caught on tape making sales were not prosecuted. Without information on the circumstances involved in other cases, statistics on the race of defendants would not establish discriminatory intent on the part of prosecutors.

Impact

In one sense, the decision involves a narrow ruling on the threshold needed for entitlement to discovery. In another sense, it provides some guidelines for evidence needed to demonstrate the use of racial profiling by police and prosecutors. As specified by the Supreme Court, discrimination should appear in the different treatment of suspects who are of different races but similar in other circumstances. Figures on the proportion of minority defendants (or of vehicles stopped with minority drivers) would by themselves not show discrimination. These types of figures have only limited legal value because they do not consider if the actions of police and prosecutors differ toward minorities and whites. This raises the bar for evidence of racial profiling.

Federal Appeals Court Decisions

Given that the Supreme Court has left some room for interpretation in the use of race, ethnicity, or national origin as part of criminal profiles, the decisions of lower courts about the issue have sometimes reached contrasting conclusions. As summarized in the following two cases, one decision allows use of ethnicity in questioning persons in airports who are suspected of transporting drugs, while another forbids the use of ethnicity altogether in stopping possible illegal immigrants on highways near the national border.

UNITED STATES V. TRAVIS, 94-5771 (1995) SIXTH CIRCUIT COURT OF APPEALS

Background

In 1992, Mike Evans, a detective working in the Cincinnati/Northern Kentucky Airport, decided to check a flight from Los Angeles for drug couriers. This flight had produced many drug arrests in the past, particularly among passengers connecting to flights for Cleveland or New York City. Reviewing the passenger list, he looked for names that, because they sounded like an alias, might indicate drug smuggling. One name, Angel Chavez, appeared suspicious because it included a common Hispanic surname and an unusual first name. Evans denied he picked the name because of the Hispanic surname alone and pointed out that he had chosen not to investigate two other passengers with the surnames Diaz and Del Negro.

Asking for more information on the passenger, Evans found out that she had purchased a one-way ticket to Cleveland five hours before the flight at the Inglewood Travel Agency. Drug couriers often purchased one-way tickets at the last minute and, in the detective's experience, often used this particular travel agency. These facts led the detective to decide to question Chavez when she left the plane. However, looking for a Hispanic woman, he missed the suspect, who was in fact African American. Going to the boarding area for the connecting Cleveland flight, he noticed two women standing alone, one of whom turned out to be Chavez. Evans sat next to the suspect, showed her his badge, and asked if he could speak to her. The suspect agreed and showed her airline ticket and drivers license. Noting that the ticket listed the name Angela Chavez, and the license listed the name Angela Travis, Evans next asked for consent to search her bags. Obtaining consent, he found cocaine and arrested the suspect.

In a pretrial hearing, the defendant moved to suppress the evidence because the detective had discriminated against her on the basis of race. The district court denied the motion to suppress, after which Travis entered a conditional guilty plea with the reservation that she could appeal the denial of the motion. The Sixth Circuit Court of Appeals then considered the issue.

Legal Issues

The legal issue raised by the defendant does not involve unreasonable search and seizure. She had agreed to the questioning and the search without any evidence of coercion—the consensual encounter did not require reasonable suspicion on the part of the detectives. Rather, the appeal focused on whether the detective violated the defendant's equal protection rights when he selected her for a consensual interview. Did the officer select her solely on the basis of race?

If race was the sole basis for the consensual encounter, it would involve selective enforcement of the law and violate the Fourteenth Amendment. In the absence of discrimination, only a rationale based on something more than race would permit selection of the suspect for questioning. Generally, the burden of proof falls on the defendant to prove the officers relied solely on race. Appropriate evidence might include instances involving others of different races who were not chosen for an airport interview. In this case, the defendant argued that incident reports filed by the Airport Police Task Force disclosed questioning of a disproportionate number of minorities.

If the officers had reasons other than race to justify the interview, then it would not violate constitutional protections. Even if race serves as one relevant characteristic, the existence of other legitimate reasons would mean the contact falls within constitutional limits. The government claimed that the detective, who in fact did not realize the suspect was African American until he approached her, relied on several reasons independent of race to question the defendant.

Decision

The appeals court ruled that the detective had gathered sufficient information at the precontact stage to justify approaching the suspect. The action of purchasing a one-way airline ticket five hours before the flight at a travel agency known to assist drug couriers appropriately raised suspicion without relating to race. In addition, the suspicious name turned out, as suspected, to be an alias. That the detective did not investigate other passengers with Hispanic surnames indicates that the detective did not inappropriately rely on ethnicity. This evidence counters the claim that the defendant was approached solely on the basis of race.

The ruling also rejected the validity of evidence on the disproportionate number of interviews of minorities presented by the defendant. The court viewed the figures as flawed by the lack of information on contacts that did not result in an arrest.

Impact

Like the Supreme Court decision in the *United States v. Brignoni-Ponce* concerning immigration and the Fourth Amendment, this court decision in regard to transporting drugs and the Fourteenth Amendment rejected the use of race alone by police in approaching persons for a consensual interview. However, again like the earlier Supreme Court ruling, this decision permits consideration of race along with other legitimate factors that raise suspicion. It thus appears consistent with racial profiling in the more limited sense of including race with other behavioral characteristics in a criminal profile.

UNITED STATES V. MONTERO-CAMARGO ET AL., 97-50643 (2000) NINTH CIRCUIT COURT OF APPEALS

Background

The defendants, German Espinoza Montero-Camargo and Lorenzo Sanchez-Guillen, were driving two vehicles north on a highway in California in 1996. Just before reaching a border patrol checkpoint in El Centro, California, about 50 miles from the border, they made U-turns. On receiving a tip about the U-turns, agents headed south to investigate. They saw two cars with Mexican license plates pulled over to a spot often used as a drop-off and pick-up point for undocumented aliens and contraband. Seeing these actions as a basis for reasonable suspicion, agents stopped the two cars. The agents said that, as they pulled behind one car, they noticed that both the driver and passenger appeared to be Hispanic, which further aroused their suspicions. So did the actions of the driver to check the rearview mirror and a passenger to pick up a newspaper.

After detaining the cars, the agents searched the trunk of one and found two large bags of marijuana. Montero-Camargo and the passengers were charged with conspiracy to possess marijuana with the intent to distribute. The defendants filed a pre-trial motion to suppress the evidence on the grounds that agents did not have reasonable suspicion for the stop. The district court denied the motion to suppress, a decision which the defendants appealed.

Legal Issues

The legal issues centered on the question of whether the border patrol agents had reasonable suspicion to stop Montero-Camargo. In supporting the stop, the government argued that numerous factors create reasonable suspicion of criminal activity. A vehicle with Mexican license plates making a U-turn before a border patrol checkpoint demonstrates evasive action; a stop at a place notorious for illegal activities implies wrongdoing; drivers who appeared to be of Hispanic descent suggests they may be illegal immigrants; and actions such as checking the rearview mirror and picking up a newspaper as the patrol car approached indicate excessive concern about being stopped by the police.

The defendants argued that none of these factors represents criminal behavior that would warrant the stop. Making a U-turn and stopping on the highway might reflect missing a turnoff and checking for directions. Similarly, looking in the rearview mirror and picking up a newspaper say little about criminal activity. Focusing on Mexican license plates and Hispanic appearance reflects discrimination based on ethnicity and national origin rather than criminal behavior. The patrol agents therefore violated the defendants' rights against unreasonable search and seizure. Based on evidence uncovered during an unconstitutional stop, the conviction based on that evidence should be overturned.

Decision

The Ninth Circuit Court of Appeals affirmed the lower court's decision on the legality of the stop, the correctness of employing the evidence in the trial, and the earlier conviction of the defendants. However, the court also determined that the agents used some inappropriate criteria in making the case for having reasonable suspicion. The U-turn before a checkpoint and a stop in the place where illegal activities occur created reasonable suspicion. However, Hispanic appearance did not.

As stated by Circuit Judge Reinhardt in the written opinion, the court reasoned as follows: "Stops based on race or ethnic appearance send the underlying message to all our citizens that those who are not white are judged by the color of the skin alone. Such stops also send a clear message that those who are not white enjoy a lesser degree of constitutional protection—that they are in effect assumed to be potential criminals first and individuals second." Use of Hispanic appearance in making stops, according to the ruling, has particularly negative consequences in areas like Southern California that have a substantial Hispanic population (73 percent in Imperial County, the location of the checkpoint). The potential for stopping innocent drivers makes Hispanic appearance irrelevant to assigning reasonable suspicion.

Impact

In one sense, the decision has little impact on the actions of the border control. A representative of the Immigration and Naturalization Service stated that it does not stop people based on their race, and that the decision was consistent with current operations.[6] In another sense, however, the decision has a potentially huge impact. In 1975, the Supreme Court implied that race or ethnicity could serve as one of many relevant factors in determining reasonable suspicion (*United States v. Brignoni-Ponce*). Circuit Judge Reinhardt's opinion takes exception to that point by stating, "Brignoni-Ponce was handed down in 1975, some 25 years ago. Current demographic data demonstrate that the statistical premises on which the dictum relies are no longer applicable." In other words, the presence of large numbers of Hispanic citizens in the population makes invalid the use of ethnic appearance as a clue for identifying undocumented aliens.

The decision falls short of outlawing use of race, ethnicity, or national origin altogether, but more than any previous decision, it makes suspect the use of these criteria in any form. It may have the effect of changing police procedures for making stops in California, the West, and perhaps in other parts of the country. At minimum, law enforcement agencies following the guidelines of the decision would have to show a strong statistical basis or intelligence information to use race, ethnicity, or national origin as part of a profile for suspicious behavior.

State Court Cases

Cases in two states, Maryland and New Jersey, have received the most attention: the first because it led to the nation's first settlement for racial profiling, and the second because a court declared that police had used illegal racial profiling. A third case, however, led to dismissal of a suit to obtain damages for racial profiling.

WILKINS V. MARYLAND STATE POLICE, 93-468 (1996) DISTRICT COURT OF MARYLAND

Background

After attending his grandfather's funeral, Robert L. Wilkins, a black Washington, D.C., criminal defense attorney, was traveling with family members late at night on a highway near Cumberland, Maryland. A Maryland state trooper stopped the car and informed the driver that he had been speeding. After a brief wait, the officer next notified the occupants that he wanted to search the car and produced a consent form to sign. Having identified himself as an attorney, Wilkins said they would not sign the form. The officer said they would then have to wait for a drug-sniffing dog to check the car.

When the dog came, the passengers were forced to get out of the car and wait in the rain. The dog found nothing, and the officer wrote a speeding ticket before allowing Wilkins and his party to leave.

Wilkins decided to take legal action, and gained the support of the Maryland chapter of the American Civil Liberties Union (ACLU) and a Washington, D.C., law firm. The class-action suit represented not only Wilkins but also other minority motorists treated in the same way.

Legal Issues

The suit alleged that the Maryland State Police violated the Fourteenth Amendment when using profiles that included racial characteristics. As part of the legal process, the plaintiffs received a criminal intelligence report from the Maryland State Police. The report advised troopers that drug couriers, most of them black, were traveling through Maryland in rental cars with Virginia license plates. In addition, the defendants hired an expert to analyze data on Maryland traffic. The results of the data analysis disclosed few differences in speeding by race but huge race differences in stops made by police. The Maryland State Police argued that stopping black drivers resulted from sound police work rather than racial discrimination and any data to the contrary were flawed.

Decision

The parties to the suit agreed to a settlement. The settlement included modest damages of $50,000 for the occupants of the car and $46,000 in attorney's fees. More important, it required the Maryland State Police to prohibit the use of race-based drug courier profiles in stopping, detaining, or searching motorists, train all troopers on the content of the policy, maintain records on the race of all drivers stopped and searched, and discipline troopers who violate the policy. The settlement also specified measures to monitor the performance of the state police in following the new requirements.

Impact

The settlement led to the first state action against racial profiling but, because the state of Maryland agreed before trial to eliminate racial profiling, it did not produce a legal precedent. In terms of stopping the practice, Wilkins reports that the settlement has had less success. Figures on stops showed more than 70 percent of drivers stopped on Interstate 95 in Maryland were African American, while only 17 percent of total drivers were African American. For each car searched with a white driver, Wilkins reports that four black drivers were searched. Another suit was filed for violations of the settlement agreement, and a new class-action suit was filed for new drivers stopped under racial profiling procedures.

NEW JERSEY V. PEDRO SOTO, ET AL. 324 (1996) N.J. SUPERIOR COURT

Background

Seventeen defendants of African-American background who had been stopped and arrested on the New Jersey Turnpike between 1988 and 1991 brought suit against the New Jersey State Police. They accused the agency of discriminatory enforcement of the law and moved to suppress the evidence based on the stops. The claim of discrimination relied on statistical evidence of disparity in stops and arrests by race.

Legal Issues

The legal issues involved in the case centered on the quality of statistical evidence relating to racial differences in police stops and traffic offenses. The judge noted that the Fourteenth Amendment of the U.S. Constitution and the New Jersey Constitution firmly supported the right to be free from government discrimination. If stops of African Americans involved selective enforcement of traffic laws by police officers, it would indeed violate the rights of the drivers and allow for suppression of evidence obtained during the stop. Typically, courts determine the constitutionality of a stop not by exploring the motives of the officers but by evaluating the objective facts. In addition, however, discriminatory intent may also be inferred from statistical evidence. A comparison of the racial composition of traffic law violators with the racial composition of those arrested can, for example, demonstrate discrimination.

The defendants provided several types of evidence to support their claim of racial profiling. First, a study of speeders supervised by Professor John Lamberth of Temple University found irregularities. The percentage of stops of black drivers (46.2 percent) on the highways greatly exceeded the percentage of black drivers who sped (13.5 percent). Expert witnesses testified to the scientific validity of the study. Second, another study compared speeding tickets based on use of radar with speeding tickets based on officer observations. That minorities less often received tickets based on the radar, which removes police discretion, than on officer observations again indicated the influence of race in high-discretion police stops. Third, two troopers testified that they had been trained and coached to make profile stops in attempting to interdict drug transport. Fourth, testimony indicated that the state police changed their procedures after a television exposé of racial profiling.

The state did not present its own data to rebut the claims of the defendants. It did, however, criticize the defendants' evidence. Expert witnesses noted that the defense study did not distinguish the racial makeup of those going over the speed limit by large amounts (15 miles per hour) from those going over the speed limit by small amounts (6 miles per hour). Since police are more likely to stop excessive speeding than mild speeding, the racial figures based on minor speeding violations are flawed. The state also presented its own police representatives, who denied that the agency ever promoted or allowed use of race in making stops.

Decision

In comparing the statistical evidence, the judge favored the case made by the defense. Given the evidence of selective enforcement, the judge stated that "the State must introduce specific evidence that either there are actually defects which bias the results or the missing factors, when properly organized and accounted for, eliminate or explain the disparity." Merely calling attention to possible flaws or unmeasured factors is not sufficient, he reasoned, because it is based only on denials and conjectures. The ruling concluded, then, that the facts demonstrated selective enforcement, the state police leaders failed to monitor and control efforts to stop drug trafficking, and the police discriminated against African Americans in their use of racial profiling.

Impact

The decision gave opponents of racial profiling legitimacy in their criticisms of the New Jersey State Police. It led to the dismissal of charges against not only the 17 defendants but more than 100 other minority defendants arrested on the highway. It also led to changes in police procedures. The New Jersey state attorney general settled a U.S. Department of Justice lawsuit by signing a consent decree that allowed the federal government to supervise efforts to eliminate use of race in highway stops. The decision represents a major victory for opponents to racial profiling.

PESO CHAVEZ ET AL. V. ILLINOIS STATE POLICE, 99–3691 (2001) SEVENTH CIRCUIT COURT OF APPEALS

Background

Peso Chavez, a Hispanic private investigator, was hired by a defense attorney to obtain information on police behavior. The plan was for Chavez to drive on Illinois highways while another person followed behind in a separate car to observe police behavior. During one trip, a state trooper did indeed follow and eventually stop Chavez after determining from a license check that the car was rented. The officer claimed that Chavez acted nervously during the encounter, had used air freshener in the car, and had maps open. After giving him a warning ticket, the policeman asked Chavez to allow a search of the car. When Chavez said he wanted to go, the officer called in a drug-sniffing dog, claimed the dog gave a drug alert, and searched the car. No drugs were found and Chavez was able to leave after about 35–55 minutes.

Chavez filed a class-action suit in 1994 on the basis of the stop, claiming that the search (and others like it) stemmed from racial profiling and violated his civil rights. His case was dismissed but then reconsidered on appeal.

Legal Issues

Under the usual standard, a claim of discrimination must show that the defendant's actions had a discriminatory effect and were motivated by a discriminatory intent. The plaintiff argued that the use of racial profiling meets both conditions. Disproportionate stops of minorities as part of a special drug interdiction program certainly had disparate impact on minorities as well as demonstrated intent to stop more minorities. The police maintained that the officers were trained to make stops only for traffic violations, not on the skin color or appearance of the driver. After the stop, they can, according to Supreme Court decisions, look for indications of drug activity and request a search only when they have reasonable suspicion of a crime.

Decision

After addressing a variety of procedural issues, the appeals court ruled against the plaintiffs and affirmed the lower court decision to dismiss. Despite recognizing the harm of racial and ethnic profiling, the ruling concluded that the plaintiffs did not prove that officers of the Illinois State Police stop, detain, and search African-American and Hispanic motorists on the basis of race and ethnic profiling. Flaws in the statistics make them inadequate for showing discriminatory impact. The lack of information on white drivers in similar circumstances who were treated differently meant the plaintiffs did not meet the burden of establishing the discriminatory intent of the police.

Impact

The lack of a strong statistical study in the Chavez case, such as existed in the De Soto case in New Jersey, limited the ability of the plaintiffs to prove racial profiling. The standard for proof of discrimination indicates the attention courts give to valid data in racial profiling cases.

---

[1] James T. O'Reilly, *Police Traffic Stops and Racial Profiling: Resolving Management, Labor and Civil Rights Conflicts.* Springfield, Ill.: Charles C. Thomas, 2002, p. 91.

[2] Viet Dinh, "Testimony," in *The Benefits of Audio-Visual Technology in Addressing Racial Profiling, Hearing before the Committee on Government Reform, House of Representatives, One Hundred Seventh Congress, First Session.* Washington, D.C.: U.S. Government Printing Office, July 19, 2001, pp. 28–45.

[3] Kenneth Meeks, *Driving While Black.* New York: Broadway Books, 2000, p. 120.

[4] David A. Harris, *Profiles in Injustice: Why Racial Profiling Cannot Work.* New York: The New Press, 2002, p. 221.

[5] Eric Lichtblau, "Bush Issues Racial Profiling Ban but Exempts Security Inquiries," *New York Times,* June 17, 2003, p. A1.

[6] U.S. Visa News, "Court Rules Against Border Racial Profiling at U.S.-Mexican Border," U.S. Visa News Headlines. Available online. URL: http://www.usvisanews.com/memo953.html. Posted on April 24, 2000.

CHAPTER 3

CHRONOLOGY

This chapter presents a chronology of significant events in the recent history of racial profiling. Although discrimination by those in power against other race, ethnic, and national-origin groups has occurred throughout history, the controversy over racial profiling in the United States is recent. The chronology thus begins with events in the 1940s and highlights those in the last decade.

1942–1946

- The government interns 120,000 Japanese Americans in special camps and confiscates their property over concerns that they may aid Japan, America's enemy during World War II.

1964

- President Lyndon Johnson signs the Civil Rights Act of 1964, which outlaws discrimination in public accommodations and in most business employment.

1964–1967

- Long-standing tensions between African Americans and police result in rioting in the Harlem area of New York City, the Watts area of Los Angeles, and Detroit, Michigan; in each case, the riots are precipitated by police actions.

1968

- In *Terry v. Ohio*, the Supreme Court rules that police can, if they have reasonable suspicion that crime is afoot, stop and briefly search persons.

1969

- The U.S. government, in an attempt to reduce drug smuggling from Mexico, subjects every vehicle to a three-minute inspection. Although disrupting the flow of traffic, the two-week procedure does little to slow the flow of drugs into the country and indicates the need for more selective searches.

1971

- President Richard Nixon names drug abuse as the number one public enemy in the United States and begins the war on drugs.

1973

- The Drug Enforcement Agency (DEA) is founded to handle all aspects of the drug problem. The agency will be accused in years to come of employing methods that violate Fourth Amendment protection against unreasonable search and seizure.

1975

- In the *United States v. Brignoni-Ponce*, the Supreme Court holds that Hispanic appearance alone does not justify stopping to check for immigration documents but can be considered along with other factors.

1976

- In *United States v. Martinez-Fuerte*, the Supreme Court rejects the contention that stopping vehicles at a checkpoint and selecting people of apparent Mexican lineage for more questioning is unconstitutional. The decision allows the Immigration and Naturalization Service (INS) to continue using checkpoints inside national borders.

1979

- A deadly shootout between Colombian drug traffickers in broad daylight in a Miami mall brings the problem of cocaine trafficking to the attention of U.S. law enforcement agencies and the public.

1982

- James Q. Wilson and George L. Kelling publish an article that claims that if a broken window in a building or home is left unrepaired, the rest of the windows on the block will soon be broken. The "broken window" argument in years to follow will help justify police efforts to maintain order by stopping minor, quality-of-life offenses.
- Responding to outrage over drug violence in Miami, President Ronald Reagan creates a cabinet-level task force headed by Vice President

George H. W. Bush to mobilize law enforcement agencies to stop drug trafficking in South Florida. The taskforce will, among other things, develop a highway drug interdiction program.

1984

- The Drug Enforcement Agency (DEA) founds Operation Pipeline, a nationwide highway interdiction program that focuses on private motor vehicles. The program trains officers across the United States in the law, drug trafficking trends, and key characteristics shared by drug couriers. Critics accuse the program of using racial profiling in their operations.

1985

- Use of crack, a potent form of cocaine that is smoked rather than snuffed, explodes in New York City. Crack's low price and high potential for addiction make it particularly destructive in inner-city neighborhoods.

1986

- President Ronald Reagan signs the Anti–Drug Abuse Act of 1986. The act provides more funds for prisons, drug education, and drug treatment, and specifies minimum mandatory sentences for drug possession. Because the minimum sentence is more severe for crack cocaine than powdered cocaine, critics view the act as discrimination against minorities and a motivation to use racial profiling.
- Len Bias, a basketball star from the University of Maryland signed to a rich contract with the Boston Celtics of the National Basketball Association (NBA), dies from a cocaine overdose. The publicity over his death heightens concern about cocaine abuse.

1987

- The New York City Taxi and Limousine Commission and the Human Rights Commission bring attention to the problem of racial profiling by cabbies in picking up riders. They sponsor a study that finds cabbies failed to pick up black decoys almost 50 percent more often than they failed to pick up white decoys. The commissions also begins a formal hearing on a complaint against a driver accused of refusing service on the basis of race.

1989

- In a settlement reached in federal district court, the Immigration and Naturalization Service (INS) agrees not to single out Hispanic-looking people in their search for illegal immigrants but also does not admit to having done so in the past. The settlement stems from a suit filed in 1981 on behalf of Hispanic people in southwestern Michigan who were stopped for interrogations and searches.

- President George H. W. Bush establishes the new Office of National Drug Control Policy under the leadership of "drug czar" William Bennett. Using an approach he calls denormalization, Bennett aims to reduce the demand for drugs by making their use socially unacceptable. The focus on lowering demand complements the focus on lowering supply through drug interdiction efforts.

1991

- ***March 2:*** After being ordered off an airplane and questioned for three hours, an Iranian-born American citizen files a discrimination suit against Pan American Airlines. The plaintiff, Mohammad Ghonoudian, says he was singled out for this treatment on the basis of his national origin. The airlines had been in a state of high alert after the start of the Persian Gulf War against Iraq, but Pan Am said the suit was without merit.

1992

- ***May 8:*** Robert Wilkins, an African-American lawyer driving with his family through Maryland after attending a funeral in Chicago, is stopped on the highway by a state trooper and his car is searched. Wilkins sues the state on behalf of African Americans unconstitutionally stopped in the past or the future because of a race-based drug-courier profile.

1993

- ***August 7:*** Worried that accusations of racial profiling would make convictions difficult, prosecutors in Middlesex County, New Jersey, drop charges for drug and weapon possession against drivers stopped on the New Jersey Turnpike. A judge had ruled in April that evidence of use of racial profiling by troopers was insufficient to prove discrimination. Prosecutors worry, however, that the suspects' claims they had been stopped illegally would make convictions unlikely.
- ***September 11:*** The president of a college in rural upstate New York, State University of New York's College at Oneonta, apologizes to 125 African-American students whose names were given to the police investigating an assault case. The assailant was described as a black man with a cut on his hand, but use of the list treated all African Americans in the town as suspects.

1994

- The Computer Assisted Passenger Profiling System (CAPPS) is developed. It uses 40 pieces of information collected by airlines to identify passengers who, according to the profile, warrant a more careful search. The system also chooses a number of randomly selected passengers for examination. CAPPS does not include race or ethnicity in its profile criteria.
- Mayor Rudolph Giuliani and Police Chief William Bratton of New York City begin to implement quality-of-life policing. By concentrating on stopping minor offenses, this policing style aims to prevent more serious crime and restore order. Although crime rates fall dramatically, representatives of minority groups claim the policing procedure leads to harassment of innocent citizens and encourages racial profiling.
- ***September 4:*** The American Civil Liberties Union (ACLU) files a federal lawsuit on behalf of black and Hispanic drivers stopped by Illinois state troopers searching for drugs. To obtain proof of racial profiling, a Hispanic private investigator, Peso Chavez of Santa Fe, New Mexico, was hired to drive on Interstate 80 in Illinois. He was stopped for an illegal lane change and had his car searched for drugs without his consent or a warrant.

1995

- ***January:*** The state of Maryland settles the suit brought by the Wilkins family over racial profiling. In the settlement, the state issues a written policy to end stops based on race, begins to train officers on the policy, and starts to monitor car stops.
- ***May:*** The U.S. Sentencing Commission calls attention in a report to racial disparities in sentencing for cocaine versus crack use. Despite a recommendation to end the disparities with changes in sentencing laws, Congress leaves sentencing laws unchanged.
- ***December 7:*** *Investigative Reports,* a television show on the cable channel A&E examines police enforcement of anti–drug trafficking laws. The police stop drivers, usually black or Hispanic, for minor offenses, such as changing lanes without signaling, and use the stop to ask for consent to search. They can take significant cash found in the search if it appears to involve drug trafficking. The show questions whether the police use the practice to stop drug traffic or increase their funds.

1996

- ***March 6:*** Army general Barry McCaffrey begins his appointment as President Bill Clinton's director of the Office of National Drug Control Policy (or "drug czar").

- ***June 26:*** Amnesty International accuses New York City police of brutality and violating the human rights of African Americans and Latinos. The organization is critical of quality-of-life policing and use of racial profiling, but Mayor Rudolph Giuliani and police reject the accusations.
- ***November 17:*** Based on data collected on the race and ethnicity of drivers stopped by Maryland troopers, the American Civil Liberties Union (ACLU) brings suit against the state on behalf of minorities stopped on Interstate 95. The suit asserts that disproportional stopping of minorities reflects racial profiling and violates the 1995 settlement of an earlier racial profiling suit. Maryland police deny race played any role in the stops.
- ***November 27:*** An ABC *Prime Time Live* television show, using film taken by a hidden camera of three New Jersey police officers who stopped and interrogated a vehicle with three black men, calls the stop illegal and the officers racist. The police later sue the network, but a court rules the statements were not defamatory.

1997

- ***October 1:*** A report from the Justice Department finds that the CAPPS system for selecting air passengers for special searches does not discriminate on the basis of race, color, national origin, ethnicity, religion, or gender.

1998

- ***April 23:*** After stopping a van with four young black men, two New Jersey troopers shoot 11 bullets into the van when it moves in reverse toward the officers. The shots wound three of the four passengers, two seriously. Johnnie L. Cochran, Jr., who will represent the young men in a suit against the state of New Jersey, claims the stop was based on racial profiling. The police officers answer that the van was speeding and, after the stop, they feared the van was trying to run them over.
- ***June 4:*** African-American police officers from New York and New Jersey report on their efforts to patrol the New Jersey Turnpike over the Memorial Day weekend to check for the use of racial profiling in making stops. They announce that they found no evidence of profiling, in part because of their efforts. The action was organized by the New Jersey Black Police Organization, 100 Blacks in Law Enforcement, and the Grand Guardians Council.
- ***August 1:*** In response to allegations that an all-white police department in Trumbull, Connecticut, engaged in racial profiling by singling out black and Hispanic drivers on traffic charges, the FBI begins an investigation.

- ***September 17:*** African-American activists criticize a report of President Bill Clinton's advisory board on race relations for not considering restrictions on racial profiling. The report recommends creating a permanent board on racial issues and working with schools, business, and youth to deal with problems but makes no specific recommendations about racial profiling.

1999

- ***February 4:*** An unarmed black man, Amadou Diallo, is shot multiple times after a routine stop by undercover police officers in New York City. The officers mistook Diallo's efforts to pull out his wallet to show identification as going for a gun. Police claim it was a tragic accident, but critics viewed the killing as a reflection on police policies of racial profiling and brutality against minorities.
- ***March 1:*** Carl A. Williams, head of the New Jersey State Police, is fired by Governor Christie Todd Whitman after making comments about racial profiling and the involvement of African Americans and Hispanics in drug trafficking. After protest by civil rights leaders, she fires Williams on the grounds that the remarks were insensitive and harmed the credibility of the state police, who had for some time been fighting accusations of racial profiling.
- ***May 21:*** A house panel hears witnesses who accuse the U.S. Customs Service of racial profiling in selecting them for drug searches. Customs commissioner Raymond Kelly says in response, "In no instances will we allow racial bias to be tolerated as a substitute for good law enforcement." After ordering an independent panel to investigate the issue, he makes changes in procedures to eliminate any racial profiling and protect the rights of those searched.
- ***June 9:*** President Bill Clinton issues an executive memorandum requiring federal law enforcement agencies to collect information on the race, ethnicity, and gender of all persons they detain. Clinton calls racial profiling a "morally indefensible, deeply corrosive practice . . . the opposite of good police work, where actions are based on hard facts, not stereotypes. It is wrong, it is destructive, and it must stop."
- ***December 30:*** The U.S. Justice Department and the state of New Jersey sign a consent decree to end litigation brought by the federal government over use of racial profiling by the New Jersey State Police officers in stopping motorists on its highways. The decree mandates elimination of racial profiling, collection of data on the race and ethnic background of all drivers stopped, independent monitoring of police activities, and a number of other provisions that limit the independence of state police.

2000

- ***January 14:*** Montgomery County, Maryland, signs a "Memorandum of Agreement" with the U.S. Department of Justice to collect data on the race of drivers stopped and to eliminate racial profiling.
- ***March 30:*** The Subcommittee on the Constitution, Federalism, and Property Rights of the Committee on the Judiciary, U.S. Senate, 106th Congress, Second Session, holds hearings on "Racial Profiling within Law Enforcement Agencies." The hearing discusses legislation to require police agencies to collect statistics on the race of drivers stopped by officers.
- ***April 11:*** In holding that border agents may not stop individuals for questioning based on their Hispanic appearance, the U.S. Ninth Circuit Court of Appeals in *United States v. Montero-Comargo* puts limits on the search for illegal immigrants. The U.S. Border Patrol maintains that it does not use racial profiling, but the decision limits use of race more than previous court decisions have.
- ***June 16:*** The U.S. Civil Rights Commission releases a report accusing the New York City police of racial profiling. The report further recommends appointing an independent prosecutor to investigate misconduct. Some members of the commission disagree with the ruling, claiming that the evidence does not support the accusations. Others believe the report is politically motivated.
- ***September 13:*** Wen Ho Lee, a former nuclear weapons scientist at the Los Alamos National Laboratory, leaves prison after 279 days in solitary confinement. Arrested in 1999 on suspicion of spying for China, he consistently denied all accusations. Asian groups had accused the government of relying on racial profiling in their actions against Lee. A weak case against the scientist and a plea bargain that dismissed all charges but a minor one gave credence to the claims.

2001

- ***February 27:*** In his State of the Union Address to Congress, President George W. Bush declares his opposition to racial profiling. He states, "Earlier today, I asked John Ashcroft, the attorney general, to develop specific recommendations to end racial profiling. It's wrong, and we will end it in America. In so doing, we will not hinder the work of our nation's bravest police officers. They protect us every day, often at great risk. But by stopping the abuses of a few, we will add to the public confidence our police officers earn and deserve."
- ***April 16:*** Spencer Abraham, head of the Department of Energy, sends a memorandum to all department employees, many of whom play an

important role in protecting national security, with a statement of the policy against racial profiling. The memo specifies that any practice of racial profiling be eliminated and prevented.

- ***May 1:*** A review by the *New York Times* of case files and memos from the Immigration and Naturalization Service (INS) in the New York District reveals that agents used skin color, Spanish accent, and clothing as evidence to justify an immigration raid. Critics say this proves the agency uses racial profiling.
- ***July 19:*** The Committee on Government Reform, House of Representatives, 107th Congress, First Session, holds hearings on "The Benefits of Audio-Visual Technology in Addressing Racial Profiling." The hearings explore the potential and problems in videotaping contacts of police officers with the public. Ideally, the videotapes can prevent and prove instances of racial profiling.
- ***July 27:*** Seattle police officers, who fear their use of aggressive police tactics will lead to accusations of racial profiling, claim to be cutting back on the number of arrests they make. Since more criminal offending occurs in poor and minority neighborhoods in Seattle and more calls come to the police from those same neighborhoods, the actions of police officers may worsen crime problems among disadvantaged groups.
- ***August 1:*** The Subcommittee on the Constitution, Federalism, and Property Rights of the Committee on the Judiciary, U.S. Senate, 107th Congress, Second Session, holds hearings on "The End Racial Profiling Act of 2001." The proposed legislation will ban the practice and require federal, state, and local law enforcement agencies to take steps to implement the law. However, events in the next month will lead Congress to focus on other matters.
- ***September 11:*** Terrorist attacks on the World Trade Center buildings in New York City and the Pentagon in Washington, D.C. and the crash of a hijacked plane in Pennsylvania before reaching a target, kills more than 3,000 people. The 19 Muslim Arab men behind the attack, most from Saudi Arabia, had entered the United States on valid visas but remained after the visas expired. Immigration issues now raise new concerns about terrorism and national security.
- ***September 21:*** Airlines investigate five incidents after the September 11 terrorist attacks involving men of Arab descent being removed from flights because they were considered security risks. The airlines claim authority to remove passengers who appear threatening but also note that they do not consider skin color, ethnicity, or national origin in their decisions. However, the travelers appear to have no links to terrorist activities.
- ***October 26:*** President George W. Bush signs the USA PATRIOT Act, legislation that permits the attorney general to detain aliens he certifies

as threats to national security for up to seven days without bringing charges. It also increases the government's ability to use wiretaps and share secret information across agencies. Critics contend that along with violating the civil rights of immigrants, the act will promote racial profiling.

- ***November 21:*** Responding to requests from the Department of Justice to help in interviewing Middle Eastern men, police chiefs across the United States express concerns that the plan involves racial profiling. Ironically, the Department of Justice has criticized local police departments in the past for use of racial profiling, but the efforts of the federal government to protect the nation from further terrorist attacks such as occurred on September 11 has reversed the positions.
- ***December 22:*** Richard Reid, a British citizen on an American Airlines flight from Paris to Miami, tries to ignite explosives hidden in his shoes. He is subdued before he can do so and arrested. (He is later sentenced to life imprisonment.) Reid's British citizenship and Caucasian appearance lead some to suggest that profiling on the basis of national origin will be ineffective.
- ***December 26:*** Based on the request of the pilot, an Arab-American Secret Service agent who serves on President George W. Bush's security detail is removed from an American Airlines flight for more security checks. The airline says the incident did not involve racial profiling and stemmed from questions about the agent's credentials to carry a gun on board. However, the Council on Arab-Islamic Relations claims the removal from the plane resulted from racial and ethnic profiling.

2002

- ***January 24:*** A federal review suggests that reforms of the New Jersey State Police have eliminated evidence of the use of racial profiling. A monitoring team reviewed 175 motor vehicle stops and concluded that they were made for serious violations of criminal or motor vehicle law. The troopers used consent searches less often than in the past but had more success in discovering drugs.
- ***February 27:*** The Subcommittee on Aviation of the Committee on Transportation and Infrastructure of House of Representatives, 107th Congress, Second Session, holds hearings on "Profiling for Public Safety: Rational or Racist?" Many House representatives and presenters oppose the use of race, ethnicity, or national origin altogether in screening, while others believe such factors should play some role in airport procedures.
- ***March 14:*** New York City police commissioner Raymond W. Kelly issues an order against the use of racial profiling in law enforcement actions.

Although the department has never acknowledged using racial profiling, concerns in the minority community about the practice led to the written order. The order does not specify procedures other than self-inspection to monitor possible use of the practice, but critics of racial profiling generally welcome the announcement.

- *March 31:* The New Jersey state attorney general, David Sampson, decides to release the findings of a disputed study that relates to issues of racial profiling. The study, which found that black drivers were twice as likely to speed as white drivers, had been heavily criticized by civil rights organizations and state officials. The attorney general stated that releasing the report would not undermine past evidence that racial profiling was real.
- *April 4:* To reduce racial profiling and excessive use of force by police patrolling the streets, several groups in Cincinnati—city leaders, police groups, the Ohio office of the American Civil Liberties Union, and African Americans—reach an agreement to change the Cincinnati Police Department's procedures in dealing with the public. The changes are intended to improve police-community relations after the shooting of a young black man by police led to four days of rioting. A court-appointed monitor will oversee the changes.
- *April 19:* New Jersey state prosecutors dismiss criminal charges or convictions against 86 persons for possession of drugs, weapons, or contraband because the cases appear to involve use of racial profiling by state troopers. State troopers call the dismissals a dangerous mistake, while prosecutors call them movement toward justice.
- *May 3:* FBI officials say that they were reluctant to mount a major review of Arabs enrolled in U.S. flight schools because of a concern that the bureau would be criticized for ethnic profiling of foreigners. An FBI agent in Phoenix had told counterterrorism officials at the bureau's headquarters before the September 11 attacks of an alarming pattern of Arab men with possible ties to terrorism taking aviation training courses. The agency did not act on the information.
- *May 8:* To combat what they view as racial profiling, black New Jersey ministers announce the "Just Say No" campaign to inform minority drivers that they have the right to refuse to submit to consent searches. Even if police have no reason for suspicion, they can ask to search a vehicle. The ministers hope that the campaign will prevent unfounded searches.
- *May 14:* President George W. Bush signs the Enhanced Border Security and Visa Reform Act. The new law bans foreigners from countries deemed sponsors of terrorism and sets up procedures to track the entry

and exit of all foreign visitors to the United States. Government agencies, including law enforcement agencies such as the FBI, can also share information about immigrants. Advocates believe the law will do more to protect homeland security, while critics believe it will increase discrimination against minorities.

- ***June 4:*** The Justice Department announces it will soon propose new regulations to require visa holders from countries posing the highest risk to national security to register with the government and be fingerprinted. Most of those subject to the requirement come from Saudi Arabia, Pakistan, and other Muslim nations. The government defends the plan as a necessary component of antiterrorism efforts, but critics call it blatant racial and ethnic profiling.
- ***September 11:*** The Rights Commissioner of the United Nations, Mary Robinson, criticizes the efforts of the United States to combat terrorism. She accuses the government of violating the civil rights of immigrants and profiling Arab Americans. A U.S. spokesman at the United Nations denies the accusations.

2003

- ***January 9:*** The state of New Jersey agrees to pay $575,000 in damages to 12 motorists who alleged they were victims of racial profiling by state troopers. The accusations of two of the plaintiffs had earlier led the state to change its policy in responding to complaints about officer misconduct.
- ***January 25:*** A former police officer, E. Anthony Bradley, was convicted for violating the civil rights of drivers stopped on Interstate 40 in Arkansas by confiscating cash seized from drug suspects. Accusations that officers were profiling Hispanic drivers led the FBI to investigate, and two other officers await trial on similar charges.
- ***January 27:*** In response to a decision of the FBI to fight terrorism in the United States by counting the number of mosques and Muslims in a neighborhood, Arab American leaders denounce the practice as a form of racial profiling. The FBI denies the information would be used to investigate Arab Americans but would simply provide a yardstick to guide the expected number of investigations for an area. However, critics argue that it treats all Muslims as potential terrorists and demand that the directive be withdrawn.
- ***February 27:*** In settling a racial profiling class-action lawsuit brought by the American Civil Liberties Union (ACLU) on behalf of African-American and Latino motorists stopped by highway officers, the California

Highway Patrol agrees to stop using minor traffic violations as a pretext to search cars for drugs. The agency also agrees not to ask permission to search the car unless there is probable cause. Opponents of racial profiling believe that changes in the procedure will reduce the opportunity for officers to use racial profiling.

- ***March 14:*** New Jersey governor James E. McGreevey signs legislation to make it a crime for New Jersey officers to engage in racial profiling. Punishment for the crime includes a fine up to $15,000 and up to five years in prison. While both police and civil organizations believe the legislation is a step in the right direction, they see it as largely symbolic. Police representatives argue that use of racial profiling is rare and civil rights representatives worry that prosecutors will not vigorously enforce the law.
- ***May 9:*** Two New Jersey state troopers accused of racial profiling, Kevin Goldberg and Howard Parker, resign after being rebuked by the acting superintendent of the New Jersey State Police. Tapes made during a stop in 1991 and given to state officials by the former wife of Officer Goldberg show the troopers using racial epithets and grabbing drugs that should have been sent to evidence. A lawyer for the troopers said that the presence of drugs contradicted the claim that the officers singled out blacks for arrest, but the troopers resigned because they did not believe they could obtain a fair hearing.
- ***May 21:*** A class-action civil-rights lawsuit against Macy's department store is filed in federal district court in Manhattan on behalf of blacks and other minorities who alleged that they were detained by the store on suspicion of shoplifting more often than whites. A victim of the alleged racial profiling, Sharon Simmons-Thomas, says she was handcuffed, detained, and pressured to make a false confession. Macy's releases a statement denying that it profiles, targets, or discriminates against any minority group or individual.
- ***May 25:*** After a judge dismisses charges in April against 13 Asian Indian teenagers arrested for criminal trespassing in a school playground on Long Island (New York), the district attorney resubmits the case to a grand jury. Members of the large Indian community in the area and the American Civil Liberties Union (ACLU) have accused authorities of racial profiling in the arrests. The issue extends controversy over racial profiling against African Americans and Latinos to Asian ethnic and national origin groups.
- ***June 2:*** A report from the U.S. government criticizes the treatment of 762 detainees jailed to prevent more terrorist attacks as unduly long and harsh. Despite being in the United States illegally, many detainees have no connection to terrorism. Arab groups accuse the Justice Department of singling out Arabs in the United States, as if coming from an Arab

country indicated terrorist connections. The Justice Department responds that its actions are legal and appropriate.

- ***June 8:*** Colonel Joseph R. Fuentes is sworn in as the new superintendent of the New Jersey State Police, the fifth one in the last 19 months. In the wake of controversies over the use of racial profiling that harmed the agency's image and led to instability in leadership, Colonel Fuentes promises to reduce crime through community policing. In New Jersey Senate hearings, he affirmed his intention to eliminate use of racial profiling.
- ***June 17:*** President George W. Bush announces guidelines barring agents in 70 federal law enforcement agencies from using race or ethnicity in routine investigations. However, they allow use of race and ethnicity in some circumstances to identify potential terrorists and protect national borders (but only to the extent permitted by the Constitution and laws). Critics of racial profiling argue that the guidelines do little to stop the practice and may even contribute to profiling of Middle Eastern men.
- ***June 17:*** Two nights of riots, arson, and violence begin in Benton Harbor, Michigan, after a black motorcyclist crashed and was killed while being chased by a white police officer. Rioters allege a long history of police abuse and racial profiling of blacks in the town.
- ***September 19:*** In settling a class-action lawsuit brought by black and Hispanic men who accused the New York City Police Department of racial profiling, the city agrees to report every instance of police stops and searches to an independent agency.
- ***October 7:*** Along with recalling Governor Gray Davis and electing Arnold Schwarzenegger, the voters in California rejected a ballot initiative to prohibit the sorting of people into racial categories by the state. Had it passed, the initiative would have exempted statistics on criminal suspects but would have limited the ability of police agencies to report figures on racial profiling.
- ***December 9:*** In response to a request from the principal of Stratford High School, outside Charleston, South Carolina, police raided the school in a search for drugs. Although no drugs were found, a disproportionate number of black students were caught up in the raid, which led to accusations of racial profiling and a class-action suit on behalf of the students, some of whom were confronted by police with guns drawn and were handcuffed. A spokesperson for the school denied singling out black students in the search for illegal substances.

2004

- ***January 7:*** The city of New York agreed to pay the parents of Amadou Diallo, who was shot while unarmed by four police offers on February 4,

1999, $3 million to settle a wrongful death suit. The killing of Diallo was viewed as an instance of racial profiling by critics of the police and as a tragic mistake by the police. After an acquittal of the police officers in a murder trial, the parents sued the officers and the city. In the settlement, the mayor, police department, and city did not admit wrongdoing but apologized to the family of Diallo.

- ***January 22:*** Joining many other cities that have taken similar actions, the Los Angeles City Council voted to oppose the USA PATRIOT Act, claiming that it encourages racial profiling. The vote does not affect the validity or enforcement of the law, but critics of the act and racial profiling see the formal opposition as an important step in the campaign to change the law.
- ***February 4:*** A study of data on contacts between drivers and police in 413 law-enforcement agencies in Texas finds African-American and Latino drivers are more likely to be pulled over and searched than whites. Law-enforcement representatives deny the differences stem from bias, but minority leaders see the results as part of a pattern of racial profiling that justifies further investigation and legal reform.
- ***April 17:*** Reports describe a pilot program under way at Boston's Logan International Airport to identify terrorists. Rather than rely on racial or ethnic appearance, the program uses a checklist of behaviors, such as wearing heavy clothes on a hot day, loitering without luggage, and observing security methods, to select certain travelers for further questioning. However, critics suggest that the methods could still become a means to allow racial profiling.

CHAPTER 4

BIOGRAPHICAL LISTING

This chapter contains brief biographical sketches of important participants in the events and controversies involving racial profiling in the United States. They include scholars and advocates in favor of and in opposition to racial profiling, police accused of racial profiling, minorities victimized by racial profiling, and judges and politicians setting policy on racial profiling.

Spencer Abraham, former U.S. senator from Michigan and current (as of 2004) head of the Department of Energy. In 2001, he sent a memorandum containing a statement of policy against racial profiling to department employees, many of whom play an important role in protecting national security. He specified that any practice of racial profiling be eliminated and prevented. Abraham is the grandson of Arab immigrants.

John Ashcroft, former Republican senator from Missouri and current (as of 2004) U.S. attorney general. As a senator, he chaired hearings on racial profiling in March 2000 and has publicly stated his opposition to the practice. As attorney general in the George W. Bush administration, however, his efforts to prevent terrorism have led critics to accuse the Department of Justice of violating the civil rights of immigrants and relying on practices that encourage profiling of Arab Americans. Officials at the Department of Justice deny these accusations and argue that policies follow the law, protect constitutional rights, and serve to prevent terrorism.

Tony Barksdale, African-American lieutenant in the Baltimore Police Department. In discussing the issue of racial profiling with Heather Mac Donald, the officer argues that police do not focus solely on race but concentrate on crime, which is often highest in minority neighborhoods. Barksdale worries that accusations of racial profiling may inhibit officers from stopping criminals.

William Bennett, head from 1989 to 1990 of the newly established Office of National Drug Control Policy. Informally known as the "drug czar," Bennett used an approach he called denormalization to make drug use socially unacceptable and supported drug treatment to help addicts end their habit. Along with aiming to reduce demand for drugs, he advocated vigorous law enforcement and drug interdiction to slow the supply of drugs.

Mary Francis Berry, since 1993 the chair of the U.S. Civil Rights Commission. She supported a controversial 2000 report criticizing New York City mayor Rudolph Giuliani for use of racial profiling and human rights abuses by city police. The report recommended the appointment of an independent prosecutor to investigate misconduct, but some members of the commission disagreed with the ruling, claiming that the evidence did not support the allegations. Others believed that the report was politically motivated to embarrass the popular and conservative mayor.

Len Bias, basketball star at the University of Maryland who had been drafted to play with the Boston Celtics of the National Basketball Association (NBA). His well-publicized death from a cocaine overdose in 1986, combined with the growing use of crack cocaine, contributed to increasing public concern about the drug problem in the United States. The public concern led to intensified efforts against drugs, which in turn encouraged the use of racial profiling in drug interdiction efforts.

Michael R. Bloomberg, current (as of 2004) mayor of New York City. The successor to Rudolph Giuliani, he pledged to continue the quality-of-life policing implemented by his predecessor. Publicizing the continued drop in the crime rate during 2002, he attributed the success in making the city safer to these anticrime initiatives of the police. Also responding to allegations that the police procedures led to harassment of minorities, he and New York City police superintendent William Kelly have prohibited use of racial profiling by police.

Brian Boykin, a law enforcement officer and representative of National Organization of Black Law Enforcement Executives. During congressional testimony in 2001, he stated the strong opposition of his organization to racial profiling and described the organization's training efforts to prevent use of the practice. Although police organizations generally oppose government efforts to ban racial profiling, Boykin's organization takes the opposite position.

William J. Bratton, chief of the New York City Police Department from 1994 to 1996 and, since October 2002, chief of the Los Angeles Police Department. While chief in New York City, he instituted decentralized policing procedures and focused on reducing quality-of-life crimes, both of which appear to have contributed to a steep drop in the crime rate in the city. Along with Mayor Rudolph Giuliani, he received much acclaim for the drop in the crime rate and much criticism for allegations that police used racial profiling in their procedures.

Dan Burton, Republican member of the House of Representatives from Indiana. As chairman of the House Committee on Government Reform, he explored in hearings in 2001 the potential to use audiovisual technology in addressing problems of racial profiling.

George H. W. Bush, Republican vice president of the United States under President Ronald Reagan and president of the United States from 1989 to 1993. As vice president, he led a 1982 task force to control drug trafficking in South Florida. As president, he established the Office of National Drug Control Policy and added substantially to the budget for agencies fighting the war on drugs. According to some, these antidrug efforts led to the use of racial profiling.

George W. Bush, Republican president of the United States. In 2001, he said of racial profiling, "It's wrong, and we will end it in America." However, concern over terrorism and homeland security has overshadowed any legislative effort to deal with racial profiling. After the September 11 terrorist attacks, Bush signed legislation that advocates say will enhance homeland security but critics say will lead to racial profiling and violate the civil rights of minorities.

Peso Chavez, a Hispanic private investigator from Santa Fe, New Mexico. To obtain proof that Illinois state troopers used racial profiling in searching for drugs, he was hired to drive along Interstate 80 in Illinois. Chavez was stopped for an illegal lane change and had his car searched without his consent or a search warrant. The American Civil Liberties Union (ACLU) used the incident to file a 1997 lawsuit on behalf of black and Hispanic drivers stopped by Illinois state troopers searching for drugs.

Arshad Chowdhury, a U.S. citizen working toward a master's degree at Carnegie-Mellon University and the child of parents who had emigrated from Bangladesh. Soon after the September 11 terrorist attacks, he was prevented from boarding a flight because his name sounded like that of a suspected terrorist. After security agents investigated and cleared him, he was allowed to board a later flight but filed suit over the incident, claiming airport personnel used racial profiling based on his Middle Eastern appearance. Several other similar cases occurred shortly after September 11.

Hillary Rodham Clinton, Democratic U.S. senator from New York. She cosponsored the End of Racial Profiling Act in the Senate and criticized the use of racial profiling by police. Early in her 2000 Senate campaign, she criticized New York City police for their treatment of minorities, leading New York City mayor Rudolph Giuliani to defend the department.

William J. Clinton, Democratic president of the United States from 1993 to 2001. In 1999, he called racial profiling a "morally indefensible, deeply corrosive practice" and "the opposite of good police work, where actions are based on hard facts, not stereotypes. It is wrong, it is destructive, and it must stop." He then directed the attorney general to begin collecting and reporting data on the race, ethnicity, and gender of people stopped at the nation's borders and airports.

Johnnie L. Cochran, Jr., well-known African-American attorney involved in the O. J. Simpson defense. Besides being the alleged victim of racial profiling, he represented four young black men shot by New Jersey troopers in 1998 after a highway stop. In a suit, the young men claimed they were stopped on the basis of racial profiling. The state of New Jersey settled the case by paying damages.

John Cohen, director of the Community Crime Fighting Project at the Progressive Policy Institute. He has developed proposals to end racial profiling along with modernizing police departments. By emphasizing the use of technology, a focus on high-risk offenders, better police training and accountability, and attacks on "hot spots," the modernized police procedures will, according to the proposals, make racial profiling unnecessary.

David Cole, professor at Georgetown University Law Center in Washington, D.C. Concerned about the double standard of justice for blacks and whites in the United States, he has written and spoken publicly against the practice of racial profiling. He sees racial profiling as part of a larger criminal justice system that treats minority and disadvantaged groups unfairly.

John Conyers, Jr., Democratic congressman from Detroit, Michigan, since 1968. A founder of the Congressional Black Caucus, he has been an outspoken advocate of the rights of African Americans and other minorities. In recent years, he has sponsored several pieces of legislation on racial profiling in the House of Representatives: The Traffic Stops Statistics Act was introduced in 1999 and 2000, and the End of Racial Profiling Act was introduced in 2001.

Katie Corrigan, legislative counsel on privacy at the American Civil Liberties Union (ACLU). In congressional hearings in 2002, she and her organization have opposed any proposal to use national origin in airport screening. Along with opposition to racial profiling in airports, she expressed concern that screening would violate privacy rights of travelers. The ACLU has led the fight against racial profiling.

Christopher Darden, former attorney in the Los Angeles District Attorney's office and current legal commentator and author. He became famous while prosecuting O. J. Simpson for the murder of Nicole Simpson and Ron Goldman but, despite his celebrity, believes he was stopped by police because he is black. He has spoken about the emotional toll racial profiling takes on minorities.

John Derbyshire, a critic, commentator, novelist, and writer on public issues. The author of columns in the print and online versions of *National Review*, he has written an article entitled "In Defense of Racial Profiling" and several follow-up articles that make the case for the practice.

Amadou Diallo, a black resident of New York City born in Guinea. He was shot 19 times (41 bullets fired) after a routine stop in 1999 by undercover police officers, who mistook Diallo's efforts to pull out his wallet to show identification as going for a gun. Police claimed it was a tragic accident, but critics viewed the killing as the result of police policies and racial profiling.

Viet Dinh, assistant attorney general, Office of Legal Policy, U.S. Department of Justice. He testified before Congress in 2001 about efforts of the Department of Justice to implement anti–racial profiling policies and provided information to Congress about the potential for using audiovisual technology to address concerns over racial profiling.

Dinesh D'Souza, fellow at the Hoover Institution (a Stanford-based think tank), a conservative commentator, writer, activist, and former policy analyst in the Reagan administration. He has written about racial profiling as a form of "rational discrimination." In his view, the need for police to respond to high rates of crime in minority neighborhoods and protect lawful citizens in those neighborhoods from criminals leads to racial profiling, not irrational prejudice.

Russell Feingold, Democratic senator from Wisconsin. He has strongly supported anti–racial profiling legislation in the U.S. Senate, sponsored the End of Racial Profiling Act of 2001, and participated in Senate hearings on racial profiling issues. His efforts have not yet had success, as none of the legislation on racial profiling has passed.

Ed Flynn, police chief in Arlington, Virginia. In response to requests for more aggressive policing against drug users from residents in minority neighborhoods, he implemented a strategy to battle drug dealers and users. The police began to stop cars with cracked windshields, darkened windows, expired tags, and excessive speed as part of the strategy. The police also cracked down on quality-of-life crimes such as public urination. The effort successfully eliminated drug hot spots in the neighborhoods, for which he received thanks from minority residents.

F. E. Francis, New Jersey judge. In a 1996 decision, *New Jersey v. Pedro Soto et al.*, he ruled on the basis of statistical evidence presented during the course of the trial that officers of the New Jersey State Police had used racial profiling. The decision led to the dismissal of charges against defendants stopped and searched as a result of racial profiling.

Joseph R. Fuentes (Rick Fuentes), superintendent since June 2003 of the New Jersey State Police. In the wake of controversies over the use of racial profiling that tarnished the agency's image and created instability in leadership, Colonel Fuentes promised to reduce crime through community policing. In New Jersey Senate hearings in 2003, he also affirmed his intention to eliminate use of racial profiling after critics accused him of supporting the practice.

Daniel E. Georges-Abeyie, professor of Administration of Justice at Arizona State University. He introduced the term "petite apartheid" in 1990 to describe the informal and subtle instances of discrimination against minorities that occur in the criminal justice system. This form of discrimination differs from formal segregation laws such as existed in the American South and South Africa but nonetheless has similarly harmful consequences. Racial profiling is one component of petite apartheid.

Rossano Gerald, an African-American member of the armed forces. In 1998, he was detained by Oklahoma state troopers who forced him and his 12-year-old son out of their car while they unsuccessfully searched it for drugs. The troopers detained Gerald for two hours, opened all the suitcases in the trunk, and removed the floorboards from the car. Arguing that the police had no grounds for the search other than his race, he sued the state over his mistreatment.

Mohammad Ghonoudian, an Iranian-born American citizen. After being ordered off an airplane and questioned for three hours in 1991, he filed a discrimination suit against Pan American Airlines. He claimed that he was singled out for this treatment on the basis of his national origin. Airlines had been in a state of high alert after the start of the Persian Gulf War against Iraq, but Pan Am said the suit was without merit. His case would foretell similar incidents after the September 11 terrorist attacks.

Rudolph W. Giuliani, mayor of New York City from 1994 to 2002. A former U.S. Attorney, he campaigned for mayor in 1993 by focusing on quality-of-life and crime issues. While mayor, he supported new approaches to policing that concentrated on apprehending those committing minor offenses in order to maintain order and reduce crime. Crime rates fell dramatically during his time as mayor and he gained popularity with voters. Critics, however, claimed that the policing policies led to racial profiling, harassment of minorities, and police brutality.

Danny Glover, African-American actor. He has complained publicly in 1999 about the difficulty of black men in obtaining a taxi in New York City, saying that drivers use racial profiling in deciding whom they will pick up.

Saul Green, the U.S. attorney for eastern Michigan, an African American, and a top federal law enforcement official. In a 1998 meeting with Attorney General Janet Reno and other law enforcement officials, academics, and representatives of advocacy groups to discuss racial profiling, he told a story about warning his 16-year-old son, who had just received his driver's license, that he would likely be stopped because he was black. Other African-American and Hispanic parents tell similar stories about having to warn their children of the mistreatment they will likely face.

David Harris, Balk Professor of Law and Values at the University of Toledo (Ohio) College of Law. A strong opponent of racial profiling, he authored a 1999 report published by the American Civil Liberties Union (ACLU) on the use of racial profiling. The report and Professor Harris's other writings and court testimony have done much to publicize and generate opposition to the practice. He has also testified before Congress in support of antiprofiling legislation and, most recently, has opposed proposals to select Arabs for special airport screening.

Johnny L. Hughes, a retired member of the Maryland State Police and representative of the National Troopers Association. In congressional testimony in 2000, he opposed legislation to end racial profiling as unnecessary and prone to interfere in proper police procedures. He argued that critics misunderstand and intentionally distort the value of using race, ethnicity, and national origin in a limited sense as part of a larger criminal profile, and he suggested that profiling based solely on race, ethnicity, or national origin does not occur.

Jesse Jackson, African-American religious leader, former candidate for the Democratic presidential nomination, and president, founder, and chief executive officer of the Rainbow/PUSH Coalition. Perhaps the best-known civil rights leader in the nation, Reverend Jackson has protested the use of racial profiling, the arrest and conviction of minorities in the drug war, and discrimination against minorities in the criminal justice system. He has also talked frankly about crime problems in the black community, unintentionally lending support to advocates of racial profiling.

George L. Kelling, professor at Rutgers University, research fellow at Harvard University, and adjunct fellow at the Manhattan Institute. With James Q. Wilson, he coauthored an influential article in 1982 that encouraged the use of quality-of-life policing to maintain order as well as to reduce serious crimes. Although the theory is viewed as contributing to the use of racial profiling by police, Kelling has defended quality-of-life policing in New York City as fair, effective, and popular.

Raymond W. Kelly, former commissioner of the U.S. Customs Service and New York City Police Department commissioner from 1992 to 1994 and again since 2002. In both positions, Kelly strongly opposed the use of racial profiling. At the Customs Service, he changed procedures starting in 1999 to insure fair treatment of minorities in searches at airports and at borders. As police commissioner, he announced guidelines to prevent police from using racial profiling.

Randall Kennedy, professor at the Harvard Law School and a leading critic of racial profiling. His work on race and the law critically addresses the role of racial prejudice in the criminal justice system and makes the case for the moral injustice of racial profiling.

Rachel King, legislative counsel of the American Civil Liberties Union (ACLU) in Washington, D.C. She has taken a lead in testifying and lobbying in support of congressional legislation to collect data on traffic stops and to end racial profiling, and in opposition to the use of national origin in airport screenings.

John Lamberth, emeritus professor of psychology at Temple University. He began studying racial profiling issues in 1993 and led the traffic surveys used in *New Jersey v. Soto.* The New Jersey judge in that case concluded from the results of the surveys that the New Jersey State Police had used racial profiling. Lamberth's research has also been used in other court cases and he has served as an expert witness. He recently founded Lamberth Consulting to provide services in measuring and deterring racial profiling practices.

Wen Ho Lee, former nuclear weapons scientist at the Los Alamos National Laboratory. Arrested in March 1999 on suspicion of spying for China and held in custody without bail, he denied all accusations. Asian groups accused the government of relying on racial profiling in their actions against Lee. A weak case against the scientist and a plea bargain that dismissed all but a single, minor charge gave credence to the claims. He was freed from jail after 279 days in solitary confinement.

Heather Mac Donald, fellow at the Manhattan Institute in New York City and contributing editor of *City Journal.* Her writings defend the actions of police in the face of persistent accusations of racial profiling and discrimination. She argues that police do not use race in a biased manner but do so when it is warranted by racial differences in the commission of crime. She has also been willing to publicly present and debate her views about what she sees as the myth of racial profiling.

Fedwa Malti-Douglas, an American citizen and professor of humanities and law at Indiana University. Because she was born in Lebanon, travels often in the Middle East, and has an Arabic sounding name, she has been detained at airports on the basis of ethnic profiling. Nonetheless, she wrote an op-ed piece for the *New York Times* in 2002 defending the practice. She says such profiling is a defensible tactic for picking out potential problem passengers.

James E. McGreevey, New Jersey governor. He signed legislation in 2003 to make it a crime for New Jersey police officers to engage in racial profiling. Punishment for the crime includes a fine up to $15,000 and prison time for up to five years.

Kenneth Meeks, a journalist and managing editor of *Black Enterprise* magazine in New York City. He has described the various forms racial profiling may take (on roads and sidewalks, in railroad stations, airports, and shopping malls). His writings also do more than most to describe the actions individuals should take during a stop based on racial profiling and after the incident to correct the mistreatment.

John L. Mica, Republican U.S. representative from Florida. As chairman of the Subcommittee on Aviation, he held hearings in 2002 on the use of racial profiling in airport security and expressed concern that "political correctness" in opposing profiling might threaten the public safety. He also authored legislation to create the new Transportation Security Administration, charged with responsibility for protecting aviation and other modes of transportation from future terrorist attacks.

Norman Mineta, head of the Department of Transportation since 2001. A victim when 11 years old of the internment of Japanese Americans during World War II, Mineta has opposed profiling in airports that selects Arabs and Muslims (on the basis of national origin or religion alone) for special screening. Acting on several incidents after the September 11 terrorist acts that removed Arab-appearing men from planes, the Transportation Department issued guidelines to airlines reminding them that use of race and ethnicity in such incidents is inappropriate.

Joe Morgan, former baseball player elected to the Hall of Fame and current sports announcer on ESPN. A 1988 incident, in which airport detectives questioned Morgan about carrying drugs and detained him for a search, reveals the potential for even African-American celebrities to be subject to racial profiling.

Eleanor Holmes Norton, Democratic representative from the District of Columbia. In 2002 congressional hearings and legislation, she took an active role in opposing racial profiling. Critical of President George W. Bush's guidelines announced in 2003 to eliminate use of racial profiling by federal law enforcement agencies as insufficient, she supports legislation that, rather than relying on guidelines alone, would include mechanisms for enforcement and implementation of the prohibition.

Ronald Reagan, Republican president of the United States from 1981 to 1989. While president, he created a cabinet-level task force to mobilize government resources against drug trafficking in South Florida and signed the Anti–Drug Abuse Act of 1986, which specified minimum sentences for drug crimes. These efforts led, according to critics, to the use of racial profiling in drug interdiction and neighborhood policing.

Richard Reid, a British citizen currently serving a life sentence in prison. On an American Airlines flight from Paris to Miami in 2001, he tried to ignite explosives hidden in his shoes but was subdued and arrested before he could do so. Some suggest that Reid's British citizenship and Caucasian appearance make profiling on the basis of national origin ineffective. Others suggest that the experience with Reid demonstrates the need for more detailed background checks of airline passengers.

Janet Reno, attorney general in the Clinton administration from 1993 to 2001. As attorney general, she implemented President Bill Clinton's directives to collect and report data on racial profiling and provide guidance to state and local law enforcement agencies to do the same. She also led efforts to evaluate the ability of passenger screening systems to avoid racial, ethnic, and national-origin discrimination.

Curtis V. Rodriguez, a Latino lawyer in San Jose, California. While driving with a colleague on a California highway in 1998, he observed police stopping cars with dark-skinned Latino drivers and suspected that the police were using racial profiling. Rodriguez was soon stopped himself, and the troopers accused his passenger of acting suspiciously and used the suspicion to justify a search but found nothing in the car. Rodriguez successfully sued the state of California over the incident.

Rafi Ron, former chief of security at the Israeli Airport Authority and currently chief executive officer of an airport security firm. He has criticized manual searches of air travelers and argued that, to uncover possible terrorists, security agents need to ask questions about travel plans and background. He further believes that procedures can be developed to obtain profiles relevant to terrorism that do not involve racial discrimination.

John Royster, Jr., New York City resident. He was found, after being apprehended and fingerprinted for fare-beating on the New York City subway, to be involved in a murder and four other unsolved crimes. His apprehension illustrated the effectiveness of quality-of-life policing that enforces violation of minor offenses to help reduce more serious offenses.

Katheryn K. Russell, professor in the Department of Criminology and Criminal Justice at the University of Maryland. She has written extensively on how use of racial profiling contributes, along with other practices, to the oppression of blacks and other minorities.

David Sampson, New Jersey state attorney general. After a study of racial profiling sponsored by the attorney general's office found that blacks were more likely than whites to speed, he opposed release of the report. He later released the report in 2002 but claimed that it did not undermine other evidence of the existence of racial profiling.

Al Sharpton, African-American religious leader, civil rights advocate, and Democratic candidate for the 2004 presidential nomination. He has been active in controversial New York City protests against alleged police brutality, in one case supporting accusations of racism and brutality that proved false. More recently, he helped lead protests against the 1999 killing of Amadou Diallo and use of racial profiling by police.

Larry Sykes, an African-American bank vice-president and local school board head in Toledo, Ohio. Stopped on the highway although he was not speeding, he was forced from his car and searched on the roadside. He believes the fruitless stop—the police found no evidence of drugs—was a result of racial profiling.

Jonathan Turley, law professor at George Washington University. In testimony before the House Subcommittee on Aviation in 2002, he argued that use of race, ethnicity, or national origin in airport screening could, if properly limited, meet constitutional standards. He urged Congress to consider legislation to this effect, as it would balance the need for national security with the rights of individuals for protection from unreasonable search and seizure.

C. Vang, a 14-year-old Laotian refugee living in Madison, Wisconsin. When riding in a car one night in 1992, he and his friends were stopped by police and forced at gunpoint to lie on the ground while police searched the car for weapons. That the police found no weapons suggests the stop was based on an ethnic profile that treated Asian youth as gang members.

Peter G. Verniero, New Jersey attorney general from 1996 to 1999 and New Jersey Supreme Court justice since 1999. As attorney general, he appointed a task force to investigate accusations of racial profiling and in 1999 concluded on the basis of the investigation that the New Jersey State Police officers had indeed used the practice. When Verniero was nominated for the New Jersey Supreme Court, critics accused him of having supported racial profiling.

John Welter, acting chief of the San Diego Police Department. He testified in Senate hearings in 2000 against racial profiling and about the efforts of the San Diego Police Department to address this area of concern through the collection of data. The experience of the department suggests that community policing can produce a drop in crime without resorting to use of race, ethnic, or national-origin profiles.

Christie Todd Whitman, governor of New Jersey from 1993 to 2001. In 1999 she fired Carl A. Williams, head of the New Jersey State Police, for remarks she believed were insensitive and harmed the credibility of the organization, which had for some time been fighting accusations of racial profiling. Much of the controversy over activities of the New Jersey State Police occurred during her time as governor.

Robert L. Wilkins, an African-American public defense lawyer in Washington, D.C. While Wilkins was driving through Maryland at night in 1992, his car was stopped by state police. He objected to a search of the car on the grounds there was no reason for such a search, but police proceeded anyway. Discovering later that the police were responding to a drug courier profile that directed officers to stop young African-American men driving rental cars with Virginia license plates, Wilkins sued the state of Maryland. In 1995, he settled the suit for $96,000 in damages and changes in police procedures to eliminate profiling.

Carl A. Williams, former head of the New Jersey State Police. He was fired in 1999 by New Jersey Governor Christie Todd Whitman after making comments about racial profiling that civil rights leaders found offensive. In noting the involvement of African Americans and Hispanics in drug trafficking, he stated that federal officials fighting the drug problem traveled to Mexico rather than to Ireland.

James Q. Wilson, former professor at Harvard University and UCLA and now Ronald Reagan Professor of Public Policy at Pepperdine University. The author of many books on public policy and crime, Wilson coauthored with George L. Kelling an influential article in 1982 that presented the "broken windows" theory of crime. The article and the theory it expressed became influential, encouraging the use of quality-of-life policing to maintain order as well as to make arrests for serious crimes. The theory is also viewed by some as indirectly contributing to the use of racial profiling by police.

Steve Young, national vice president of the Fraternal Order of Police, the nation's largest law enforcement labor organization. In Senate testimony in 2001, he stressed the organization's strong opposition to legislation to end racial profiling. He argued that the bill falsely accuses police of racism, confuses racial profiling with criminal profiling, makes police subject to second-guessing by outsiders, and has the potential to allow data to be misused.

James Zogby, the founder and president of the Arab American Institute in Washington, D.C. The institute serves the political and policy interests of the Arab-American community. He has been active in opposing discrimination and use of racial profiling against Arab Americans in the wake of the September 11 terrorist attacks.

CHAPTER 5

GLOSSARY

affirm To conclude that the decision of a lower court was correct and will stand.

aggressive policing Term used by critics to refer to quality-of-life policing and to emphasize the potential for misuse of the procedure by police.

anecdotal evidence Information that is based on unscientific reports, observations, or stories but is easily understood, persuasive, and emotionally powerful.

arrest data Figures on race differences in crime obtained from police agencies on the basis of arrests made. Some believe that arrest data are biased by police discrimination and exaggerate minority involvement in crime.

attrition rate Percentage reduction of numbers in an organization such as a police force due to resignation, retirement, or death.

audiovisual technology In this context, video cameras and microphones placed permanently in or on police vehicles to record illegal activity and contact between police and the public.

benchmark Point of reference in making measurements. Racial differences in criminal involvement would, for example, serve as a benchmark in examining racial differences in police stops. Benchmark data on racial profiling has proved difficult to obtain.

black codes Set up in the American South immediately after the Civil War, it made innocent actions of blacks subject to special laws and punishments.

"broken windows" theory Suggests that if a window in a building or home is broken and left unrepaired, the rest of the windows on the block will soon be broken. As an unrepaired window signals that no one cares and that breaking more windows costs offenders nothing, disorderly activity in a neighborhood signals lack of control and opportunity for crime.

certiorari Order from a higher court informing a lower court that it will reexamine a decision and require the record of the case.

civil rights Protections guaranteed to U.S. citizens by the Constitution and its Amendments, including protection from unreasonable search and seizure and selective enforcement of the law.

community policing Practices that aim to prevent crime and improve community relations by integrating police officers into the local community and having them work closely with neighborhood residents.

COMPSTAT (Computerized Statistics) Computerized crime data system used by New York City police to identify problem areas and direct police resources to these areas. Used along with quality-of-life policing, it helped reduce the crime rate in New York City.

concurring opinion Opinion of the Supreme Court that reaches the same conclusion or decision as the majority opinion but for different reasons.

consent decree Judgment accepted by all parties that requires the defendant to discontinue illegal activity but without having to admit guilt. The U.S. Department of Justice and several state and local police departments have signed consent decrees to end racial profiling.

consent search Search of personal belongings, property, or cars based on consent or permission of an individual rather than on a warrant or probable cause that evidence of a crime will be found.

conservative Person with political views that emphasize the importance of economic freedom and protecting the public from crime. Conservatives generally belong to the Republican Party and tend to support police actions more than do liberals or libertarians.

contraband Illegal or prohibited goods often transported across or within borders.

court of appeals State or federal court that reviews the legal soundness of verdicts and decisions of lower courts.

crack Powerful form of cocaine that users smoke rather than sniff through the nose. When inhaled as smoke, the drug reaches the brain quickly—in just a few minutes—and a higher proportion of the narcotic chemicals enter the bloodstream. The potent nature of the drug makes it relatively inexpensive, usable in small doses, and powerfully addictive.

criminal profiling Identification of a set of traits and behaviors of persons likely to be involved in crime. To be effective, the profile characteristics need to have a proven or well-known relationship with offending. It differs in principle from racial profiling but the two may overlap in practice.

cultural sensitivity training (multicultural training) Designed to improve the understanding and appreciation of cultural differences across groups defined by race, ethnicity, national origin, gender, class, and other characteristics.

discovery Process by which lawyers learn about their opponent's case in preparing for the trial. It includes, for example, obtaining depositions and requesting documents.

discretion Power or freedom of individuals to make choices or judgments within certain legal bounds. The more discretion police have, the greater the potential for the use of racial profiling.

discrimination Actions based on prejudice and dislike of minorities and serving to maintain inequality between majority and minority groups.

disparate impact Refers to the outcomes of practices that may not directly involve discrimination but have more harmful consequences for some groups (usually racial or ethnic minorities) than others. Some view disparate impact as the equivalent of discrimination.

disproportionate Being too large or too small, such as the number of stops of minority drivers relative to their representation in the population.

dissent Opinion in the Supreme Court that disagrees with the majority opinion. It does not have any legal effect but may influence later decisions.

double standard System of applying rules, laws, and expectations in different ways for different groups, such as stopping minorities for minor traffic violations more often than others.

driving while black (or brown) An informal name for racial profiling deriving from "driving while intoxicated." It implies that police treat being black (African American) or brown (Hispanic) and driving as a reason to stop a vehicle. The wide use of the phrase has led to similar ones such as "shopping while black" or "flying while Arab."

drug interdiction Effort to impede, hinder, or intercept the movement of drugs across and within national borders.

End of Racial Profiling Act of 2001 Legislation to ban racial profiling, allow the U.S. Department of Justice or individuals to file suit against those practicing racial profiling, and provide funds for state and local agencies in developing effective complaint, disciplinary, and data collection procedures. This bill has not passed either the Senate or House, in large part because the events of September 11, 2001, have come to dominate the attention of legislators.

Enhanced Border Security and Visa Reform Act Law passed in 2002 that bans the entrance to the United States of travelers from countries deemed sponsors of terrorism and sets up procedures to track the entry and exit of all foreign visitors to the United States. Advocates believe the law will help protect homeland security, while critics believe it will increase discrimination against minorities.

equal protection Right guaranteed by the Fourteenth Amendment that all persons be treated equally by the law and be free of selective enforcement of the law.

ethnicity Characteristic of a human group based on customs, nationality, language, background, and history.

federal court Part of the nationwide system that includes district (trial) courts, circuit courts of appeals, and the U.S. Supreme Court.

Fourteenth Amendment Addition to the Constitution in 1868 that guarantees equal protection of the law to all persons and prohibits racial discrimination in the enforcement of the law.

Fourth Amendment Addition to the Constitution as part of the Bill of Rights in 1791 that states, "The right of the people to be secure in their persons, houses, papers, and effects, against unreasonable searches, and seizures, shall not be violated."

hard profiling Use of race, ethnicity, or national origin alone to initiate a police action; it violates constitutional guarantees for equal protection and runs counter to good police procedures.

Hispanic A person of Latin American descent.

hit rate Percentage of searches in which drugs, weapons, or other contraband are found. Hit rates are similar across race and ethnic groups, but dispute remains over whether this similarity shows no race differences in illegal behavior or effective police efforts in selecting cars or persons to stop.

hot spot Small geographic area in a neighborhood where a large amount of crime tends to occur.

immigration Movement of individuals or groups from one nation across the border of another, usually for permanent or long-term residence.

institutional racism Day-to-day practices of an organization that have harmful effects on minorities. Unlike individual racism, institutional racism is built into the system.

internment Detainment and confinement within a country or restricted area, often used for aliens in a time of war (such as Japanese Americans during World War II).

Latino A person of Latin American descent.

liberal Person with political views emphasizing the importance of constitutional rights and support for disadvantaged, less powerful groups that need protection from the government. Liberals generally belong to the Democratic Party and tend to oppose racial profiling more than do conservatives.

libertarian Person with political views emphasizing the importance of social and economic freedom and the potential for government tyranny. Although critical of both major political parties, they tend to support Republicans on many issues but, like liberals and Democrats, generally oppose racial profiling.

loitering Remaining in an area for no obvious reason. Although a minor offense subject to police interpretation, laws against loitering can be enforced to help maintain order and reduce more serious crime. However, the Supreme Court has ruled that many loitering laws are unconstitutionally vague.

majority opinion Opinion of the Supreme Court that more than half of the nine justices support. It is generally authored by one justice to represent the views of the other supporting justices.

multicultural training (cultural sensitivity training) Designed to improve the understanding and appreciation of cultural differences across groups defined by race, ethnicity, national origin, gender, class, and other characteristics.

Operation Pipeline Nationwide highway interdiction program that trains law enforcement officers across the United States in the law, drug trafficking trends, and key characteristics shared by drug couriers. Critics have accused the program of promoting racial profiling.

"out of place" Reason used by police to stop minority motorists or pedestrians in a white neighborhood or whites in a minority neighborhood. Being "out of place" suggests criminal involvement according to some and may promote racial profiling according to others.

police brutality Illegal use of excessive force by police against suspects and citizens. Although often used against minority groups and an aspect of discrimination, it differs from racial profiling.

post-traumatic stress syndrome Mental disorder often diagnosed in Vietnam War veterans, victims of rape, and survivors of a natural disaster such as a flood. Some suggest that racial discrimination, including incidents of racial profiling, can cause the disorder.

pretext stop Stop based on a pretext, or false motive put forth to cover the real reason. It usually involves stopping vehicles for minor violations with the real purpose of looking for more serious crimes—even if the police do not have probable cause to search for evidence of a more serious crime.

probabilistic Based on likelihood rather than certainty, as in profiles which use traits that are often but not always associated with crime.

probable cause Reasonable belief that a crime is being or has been committed by a specific person. By requiring an officer to have a clearly expressed, objective, and factual basis for the belief, it limits police discretion and protects citizens from unreasonable search and seizure.

quality-of-life policing Focuses on stopping minor offending and disorderly behavior that worsen the quality of life in a neighborhood (for instance, the actions of panhandlers, drunks, addicts, rowdy teens, prostitutes, loiterers, gangs, drug sellers, and drug purchasers) and contribute to more serious crime.

race Human group set off from other groups by biological differences and physical appearance.

racial profiling Any police-initiated action that relies on race, ethnicity, or national origin rather than on the behavior of an individual or on information that leads police to a particular individual who has been identified as being or having been engaged in criminal activity.

racism Attitudes that specify the superiority of some races over others and lead to behaviors that discriminate, persecute, and dominate a racial group.

reasonable suspicion Lesser standard than probable cause that gives officers discretion in making stops and can more easily allow for the use of race, ethnicity, or national origin in police decision making.

remand Act of an appeals court in sending a case back to a lower court for further proceedings.

Section 14141 of Title 42, U.S. Code (42 USC § 14141) States that it is unlawful to deprive persons of civil rights and that individuals can bring civil action against agencies when this happens. The statute makes no reference to racial profiling, but the Department of Justice has, under the section, interpreted racial profiling as a form of police misconduct that violates civil rights.

segregation Separation of race, class, or ethnic groups in residence and social interaction.

self-fulfilling prophecy Assumption or prediction that in itself causes the expected outcome to occur and seemingly confirms the prophecy. For example, the belief that African Americans commit more crime leads police to target, investigate, and discover more crime among African Americans.

self-report data Figures based on the response of individuals to questions about their criminal activities. Such data show similar drug use by whites and blacks, but critics suggest that such measures do not accurately reflect involvement in serious offending.

soft profiling Use of race, ethnicity, and national origin as one of several characteristics in a profile. It appears legal in certain circumstances and is viewed by some as a part of good police work.

statistical evidence Evidence that is based on quantitative analysis of data collected from samples and populations and that, ideally, adheres to scientific standards of data quality. The technical nature of such evidence can, however, limit its persuasiveness.

stereotype Generalization to all members of a group based on the behavior or traits of a few members. Most people view a stereotype as fundamentally unfair and inaccurate, but some suggest that stereotypes often accurately reflect group differences.

terrorism Systematic use of terror or violence against civilians to attain political objectives.

Traffic Stops Statistics Study Act of 2000 Proposed legislation that would require the attorney general to collect data on racial profiling from police departments that voluntarily agree to participate. Although the bill passed in the House of Representatives, it did not pass in the Senate.

USA PATRIOT Act (Uniting and Strengthening America by Providing Appropriate Tools Required to Intercept and Obstruct Terrorism Act of 2001) Law signed in 2001 soon after the September 11 terrorist attacks that permits the U.S. attorney general to detain aliens certified as threats to national security for up to seven days without bringing charges. It also increases the government's ability to use wiretaps and share secret information across agencies. Some contend that, along with violating the civil rights of immigrants, the act will promote racial profiling of Muslims and Arabs.

vagrancy Having no established place of residence or means of support. Although a minor offense subject to police interpretation, laws against vagrancy can be enforced to help maintain order and reduce more serious crime. However, the Supreme Court has ruled that some vagrancy laws are unconstitutional.

victimization data Figures on race differences in crime obtained from surveys of victims on the basis of their observations. Unlike arrest rates, they do not reflect possible police bias but are limited to crimes such as rape and assault in which victims see offenders. Drug crimes are excluded.

zero-tolerance policing Term used sometimes to refer critically to quality-of-life policing.

PART II

GUIDE TO FURTHER RESEARCH

CHAPTER 6

HOW TO RESEARCH RACIAL PROFILING

The term *racial profiling*—and its equivalent, "driving while black or brown"—has come into widespread use only since the 1990s. Discrimination by law enforcement officials in the United States has certainly existed in a variety of forms for a much longer period. Conflict between minority groups and the police has been shown historically in mistreatment of Native Americans by settlers, the existence of slavery until 1865, oppression of blacks after slavery, abuse of Asian immigrants, internment of Japanese Americans during World War II, rioting and protests by African Americans during the 1960s, and efforts to stop Latino immigration.

Those interested in doing research on the more recent debates and controversies over racial profiling will confront a number of challenges. First, writings on the topic span a variety of fields of study. Racial profiling relates to general issues of race, ethnicity, discrimination, and inequality as well as to specific issues of police behavior. It links legal debates about the meaning of the Constitution for search, seizure, and enforcement of the law to the daily behavior and actions of law enforcement officers along highways, at national borders, on the streets, and in airports. It reflects underlying political beliefs about the importance of civil rights compared to the importance of maintaining order. It encompasses issues of the causes of crime and the nature of punishment in the United States. And it requires attention to issues of statistical methodology in evaluating studies. Sociology, law, criminology, political science, psychology, race and ethnic studies, and statistics all relate in various ways to the topic of racial profiling.

The diversity of material can be overwhelming. For instance, entering of the term "racial profiling" on the Google search engine results in 128,000 hits. The sheer number of web pages containing information on the topic is impressive but also daunting. One can find useful facts and perspectives on nearly any aspect of racial profiling—if only by working through the vast amount of information.

Second, the literature on the topic reflects strong political views and opinions. These views come into play when considering the question of how much emphasis society should give to the sometimes conflicting goals of protecting the civil rights of citizens and protecting citizens from crime. Disagreements stem in part from underlying political beliefs. Liberals, who are generally concerned with protecting the interests of disadvantaged groups and the civil rights of the public, tend to oppose racial profiling. Libertarians, who are generally concerned about the importance of personal choice, individual freedom, and the protection of citizens from the potential for government tyranny, also tend to oppose racial profiling (but differ from liberals on many issues). Conservatives, who are generally concerned with promoting business interests, maintaining order, and protecting citizens from crime, tend to support racial profiling. Other sources of political ideology make the sides in the debate more complex but nonetheless highlight the moral basis of the controversy. In any case, the disagreements over racial profiling make it hard to separate facts from beliefs.

The underlying political sources of these divergent viewpoints on racial profiling help shape public policy efforts. Although both Republican and Democratic politicians oppose racial profiling in its strongest form, Congress has been unable to pass legislation outlawing the practice. Democrats strongly favor such legislation, but some Republicans worry that proposed legislation will unnecessarily hamper the police and promote frivolous lawsuits. Presidents Bill Clinton and George W. Bush have implemented policies to help end racial profiling in executive-branch agencies, but these efforts do not have the force of law elsewhere.

Third, research on racial profiling often covers some technically difficult material. The problem has to do with determining acceptable differences by race, ethnicity, and national origin in stopping drivers, pedestrians, and airplane passengers. Some simply suggest that if the representation of a race or ethnic group in police stops exceeds their representation in the population, it reflects racial profiling. Others rightly note that the representation must be compared to some measure of involvement in behaviors that would lead to a police stop. Determining the benchmark measurement of criminal involvement raises a number of difficult problems. Measures of actual involvement in crime are hard to obtain since offenders do what they can to hide their actions. Although studies of the extent of racial profiling properly debate the strength and weaknesses of methods, those less familiar with these issues can find the scientific details confusing.

The methodological issues are, however, tied closely to beliefs in support or opposition to racial profiling. Advocates of racial profiling use the terms *junk science* and *worthless* to describe the evidence used to show minorities are wrongly stopped. In their view, stories and misleading statistics have much emotional impact but little scientific validity. They believe that "political correctness" trumps science and leads politicians to suppress studies that contradict their viewpoints and publicize studies that support their viewpoints. Opponents of racial profiling, on the other hand, believe that the misuse of racial profiling is so obvious that methodological criticisms are trivial and petty. Talk of benchmarks and comparison groups mistakenly shifts the focus away from the key issue of discrimination in modern society. Researchers need to be aware not only of the scientific issues debated in studies of racial profiling but also the political disagreements that often underlie the scientific debates.

TIPS FOR RESEARCHING RACIAL PROFILING

How can researchers overcome these challenges? Here are some general suggestions, followed by more specific advice about where to find material.

- Define the topic carefully. Racial profiling occurs on highways, city streets, in airports, at national borders, shopping malls, schools, and under a variety of circumstances. In some ways, it seems as if people sometimes use racial profiling even more broadly to mean racial discrimination. To narrow down the research, it helps to treat racial profiling more precisely as one type of discrimination. Further, it will help to focus on one of the realms in which racial profiling appears most common: Stopping minorities for traffic violations as a means to search for drug transportation; stopping minorities on city streets as part of quality-of-life policing; stopping minorities on roads near national borders to check for immigration papers; stopping minorities in airports for extra scrutiny to avert terrorism; or stopping minorities in a variety of other circumstances, such as shopping malls or stores, school hallways, and public places, to check for problem behavior. With so many choices, making the research manageable requires care and precision in the identification of the issue to study. Restricting the focus can help the researcher avoid feeling overwhelmed by the material.
- Consider the underlying viewpoints. The political beliefs of liberals and conservatives, Democrats and Republicans, and disadvantaged and advantaged groups affect opinions on racial profiling. Being familiar with the debates and how various studies fit in the spectrum of beliefs can help researchers put information into perspective and make sense of more specific arguments. Understanding the political foundation for the racial profiling debate can also help one to avoid relying on a single article or

book, particularly if it represents only one side of the debate. The annotated literature review in the next chapter includes a wide selection of readings that support and that oppose police use of race or ethnicity in their investigations.

- Link the issue to larger social disputes. The controversy over racial profiling reflects more than concern about a single issue but relates to basic conflict over inequality and government policy. Disagreements over the role of government versus the economic market, the value of equality versus personal accomplishment, and the importance of safety versus civil rights inform debates over racial profiling. Understanding these larger disagreements and their implications for racial profiling can help researchers organize the diverse literature.
- Do not accept statistics at face value. Newspaper, magazine, television, and radio reports do not always take the time and effort to present the complexities in measuring the extent of racial profiling. Instead, media sources may rely on stories and personal experiences to attract the interest of readers. While interesting and emotionally powerful, these stories lack scientific validity and need to be supplemented by statistical studies. When the popular media do report the results of studies, they may be misinterpreted. For example, presenting simple figures on the percentage of stops that involve minorities without providing benchmark statistics on the reasons for the stops can be misleading. Similarly, figures on hit rates or successful searches may reflect police efficiency rather than police bias. Researchers need to consider these complexities.
- Take care with Internet sources. Given the vast amount of information it contains about racial profiling, the Internet presents a quick and easy way to obtain sources for research. A simple word search turns up an astounding number and diversity of web pages, which makes it easy to jump right into the research. At the same time, however, the reliability of the information can be suspect. Personal opinions, misleading facts, and highly charged language can misinform rather than help. A review of the most important books and magazine articles on the topic offers more reliable information. With the knowledge gained from the books and magazines, one can most effectively evaluate and exploit the information on the Internet.

GETTING STARTED: HOW TO FIND HELPFUL SOURCES

Books

A few recent books provide good starting points for research on racial profiling. Kenneth Meeks, in *Highways, Shopping Malls, Taxicabs, Sidewalks:*

What to Do If You Are a Victim of Racial Profiling (New York: Broadway Books, 2000), presents a readable overview of the issue and sides clearly with those opposed to racial profiling. He views profiling as an inescapable component of daily life for African Americans and advocates private and public efforts to end the practice. David A. Harris, in *Profiles in Injustice: Why Racial Profiling Cannot Work* (New York: The New Press, 2002), provides the most comprehensive criticism of racial profiling. He offers an excellent resource for understanding the arguments and evidence against racial profiling. On the other side of the issue, Heather Mac Donald, in *Are Cops Racist?* (Chicago: Ivan R. Dee, 2003), vigorously defends police against charges of racial profiling (see, in particular, the first chapter, "The Myth of Racial Profiling"). Arguing that police use race, ethnicity, and national origin only to the extent that it helps in good police work, she believes that criticism of police for racial profiling can threaten public safety (if it has not already).

Most books fail to provide an evenhanded overview of both sides of the debate (and tend to oversimplify and exaggerate the views of the other side). To see both sides of the issues and compare competing arguments, it helps to consult records of congressional hearings. Four major hearings on racial profiling have been held:

1. U.S. Senate, *Racial Profiling within Law Enforcement Agencies*, March 30, 2000
2. U.S. House of Representatives. *The Benefits of Audio-Visual Technology in Addressing Racial Profiling*, July 19, 2001
3. U.S. Senate, *S. 989: The End of Racial Profiling Act of 2001*, August 1, 2001
4. U.S. House of Representatives. *Profiling for Public Safety: Rational or Racist*, February 27, 2002

These hearings not only record the statements and opinions of senators and representatives but include questions for experts giving testimony and discuss competing viewpoints. Moreover, publications of the hearings add useful background documents and testimony of those opposed and in favor of anti–racial profiling legislation. Most of these hearings can be obtained on the Internet.

For treatment of the legal issues, two books present different viewpoints. David Cole, in *No Equal Justice: Race and Class in the American Criminal Justice System* (New York: The New Press, 1999), presents a highly critical review of court cases that, he argues, contribute to racial profiling and discrimination of police against minorities. Stop-and-frisk procedures, consent searches, and pretext stops are discussed and criticized as violating the rights of citizens. James T. O'Reilly's *Police Traffic Stops and Racial Profiling:*

Resolving Management, Labor and Civil Rights Conflicts (Springfield, Ill.: Charles C. Thomas, 2002) also opposes racial profiling in its extreme form but has more sympathy for the difficulties faced by police in dealing with crime and outside criticism. O'Reilly reviews legal issues involving police traffic stops and administrative issues in dealing with allegations of racial profiling.

Two short volumes published by the U.S. government introduce readers to data collection matters. In *A Resource Guide on Racial Profiling Data Collection Systems: Promising Practices and Lessons Learned* (Washington, D.C.: U.S. Department of Justice, 2000), the authors describe in clear language how police agencies can gather and use data on traffic stops. The volume also considers the benchmark comparison problems faced in accurately interpreting results obtained from the data. In *How to Correctly Collect and Analyze Racial Profiling Data: Your Reputation Depends On It* (Washington, D.C.: U.S. Department of Justice, Office of Community Oriented Policing Services, 2002), the authors report on their literature review and evaluation of possible data collection and analysis techniques. The report criticizes overly simple methodologies and makes several recommendations for police agencies to follow. For a more advanced treatment of methodological issues, see *Racial Profiling: Limited Data Available on Motorist Stops: Report to the Honorable James E. Clyburn, Chairman Congressional Black Caucus* (Washington, D.C.: U.S. General Accounting Office, 2000).

Suggestions for additional books to consult follow in the annotated bibliography. Otherwise, researchers can search for books in library catalogues, bookstore lists, and databases. Most library catalogues will return a manageable list of books with a keyword search for "racial profiling." A similar search of electronic bookstores such as Amazon.com (http://www.amazon.com) and Barnes and Noble (http://www.barnesandnoble.com) may provide additional citations. The electronic bookstore listings sometimes helpfully include summaries and reviews of the books, as well as the comments of individual readers. Besides using a local public or university library, researchers can find references using the comprehensive listings of the Library of Congress (http://lcweb.loc.gov). Although the database includes subject headings on racial profiling, it is most efficient to use the term for a keyword search. More than 30 books will be listed.

ARTICLES

Three types of articles may be useful for those doing research on racial profiling: articles published in scientific journals that include original research, articles published in magazines that typically represent particular views, and articles in newspapers that report events and facts. The first type addresses specialists, while the last two target general audiences.

First, for access to scientific articles, one might begin with a search of two databases. Social Science Abstracts contains citations from journals in a variety of fields, such as economics, anthropology, political science, and sociology. A keyword search for "racial profiling" provides about 30 articles that, along with their abstracts, allow researchers to identify those of most interest. Criminal Justice Abstracts includes journal articles of special interest to those working in the criminal justice field. These databases are available as part of OCLC First Search, which users must access through subscribing libraries. Consult a librarian on whether the library owns such databases and how to use them.

In examining academic articles obtained from these sources, it helps to focus on conclusions and limitations. Few researchers, even if they are able, will want to wade through the complex details of the theory, methodology, and statistical procedures in research articles. Most published articles will have met a minimum standard for scientific quality—otherwise they would be weeded out in the scientific review process and not published. Readers can therefore most efficiently concentrate on the conclusions. Articles contain a one- or two-sentence summary of the conclusion in the abstract (a one-paragraph overview that precedes the article). The abstract contains crucial information in a compact form that can prove quite helpful. In addition, most articles include a few paragraphs at the end on the limitations of the study and qualifications of the conclusions. These paragraphs can be important as well: No study is perfect, and knowing the weaknesses can help one in understanding its importance.

For a summary of empirical studies of racial profiling through 2001, see Robin Shepard Engel, Jennifer M. Calnon, and Thomas J. Bernard, "Theory and Racial Profiling: Shortcomings and Future Directions in Research," *Justice Quarterly*, vol. 19, June 2002, pp. 249–273. The article lists 13 studies along with summaries of their data collection efforts, research design, and findings and conclusions. The authors criticize the studies for their inability to measure the expected stops of minority drivers in the absence of racial discrimination and suggest some alternative approaches. However, most readers will find the last part of the article, which discusses theoretical approaches, less useful.

Second, for access to less technical articles targeted at a general audience, researchers can use several databases. OCLC First Search contains an electronic version of Reader's Guide Abstracts that lists articles in a large number of magazines. Again, however, users generally need access to a subscribing library for this database. InfoTrac also compiles articles for general interest audiences and sometimes includes an abstract with the citation, or an abstract and a full-text article. It, too, requires library privileges. Ingenta Library Gateway (http://www.ingenta.com) includes

11 million citations from more than 20,000 journals and allows searches within specific subject areas, such as medicine and social science. Searching Ingenta is free but delivery of an article requires a fee.

More so than scholarly pieces, magazine articles usually take one side or the other on debates over racial profiling. *The National Review* and *The Weekly Standard*, conservative opinion magazines, have published several articles on racial profiling that counter criticisms of the practice and defend the police. On the left, magazines such as *The Nation* and *The New Republic* oppose racial profiling. Still, in making their cases for or against profiling, most articles offer facts that, if interpreted carefully, can be informative. *Time*, *Newsweek*, and *U.S. News and World Report* also contain opinion pieces on the topic as well as straight news stories.

Among articles on racial profiling, several summarize basic arguments for and against the practice. Randall Kennedy ("Suspect Policy," *The New Republic*, vol. 221, September 13–20, 1999, pp. 30–35) argues that, despite court rulings to the contrary, racial profiling is morally wrong, has severe costs in terms of the trust minorities have of the police, and represents a form of discrimination. In contrast, John Derbyshire ("In Defense of Racial Profiling," *National Review*, vol. 53, February 19, 2001, pp. 38–40) makes a case for the common sense of racial profiling. It is unapologetic in its tone and critical of the unwillingness of most people to discuss the issue frankly. Jeffrey Goldberg ("The Color of Suspicion: Racial Profiling," *New York Times Magazine*, June 20, 1999, pp. 50–57) considers the perspectives of both police and their critics.

Third, newspaper articles can usefully supplement other sources. If less valuable for obtaining research findings or in-depth analyses, newspapers may accurately report on events involving police action, litigation, government policies, and public opinion. Most stories explain complex legal issues in clear terms, highlight the importance of the topic to the general public, and get information to readers quickly. For example, three newspaper articles (available on the Internet) present valuable overviews of debates on the possible uses of racial profiling to prevent terrorist attacks: Henry Weinstein, Michael Finnegan, and Teresa Watanabe, "Racial Profiling Gains Support as Search Tactic. Law Enforcement: As Former Critics Temper Opposition, Some Feel Unfairly Targeted," *Los Angeles Times*, September 24, 2001; Derrick DePledge, "Federal Action on Profiling Held Up. Bill in Congress Slowed by Sept. 11," *The Cincinnati Enquirer*, April 22, 2002; and Leela Jacinto, "Flying While Arab: Profiling May Be a Dirty Word, But Some Say Targeting Certain Ethnic Groups Is a Good Thing," ABCNews.com, August 14, 2002.

The *New York Times*, *Washington Post*, and *Los Angeles Times* are particularly useful sources for stories. The *New York Times* has published many articles on racial profiling involving the New Jersey State Police and New

York City police officers. The *Washington Post* has covered stories involving the Maryland State Police and federal policy making. The *Los Angeles Times* has focused on issues relating to profiling of Latinos and suspected illegal immigrants. Libraries usually subscribe to databases that include these newspapers. For example, users can have access to abstracts and full articles through First Search (use LexisNexis Academic or ProQuest). Again, consult a librarian on how to use these databases.

RESEARCH ON THE INTERNET

Given the ease of obtaining information, the Internet may seem to be a good place to begin research on racial profiling. Simply typing "racial profiling" in a search engine will return a vast number of web pages. Finding one suitable web page among those listed often suggests links to other web pages, which in turn lead in new directions. Innovative ideas and fresh information emerge in this process.

The Internet also has a negative side, however. Although the Internet represents an extraordinary resource in terms of the wealth of information available to researchers, combing through all the web sites listed by searches can consume much time. Users need patience and persistence in dealing with the vast amount of information they obtain. Yet, patience and persistence can translate into wasted effort. Moreover, the information obtained does not always meet standards of reliability and balance. Most sites on racial profiling present strongly opinionated viewpoints that have not been reviewed or verified by others. Researchers must take care in using information obtained from these sites and inquire into the background of the site sponsors. Web pages also often include scientific facts and government reports that are useful and reliable, but all information cannot be accepted at face value. With these qualifications in mind, researchers can proceed in several ways.

Popular and general search engines such as Google (http://www.google.com), Yahoo! (http://www.yahoo.com), AltaVista (http://www.altavista.com), Excite (http://www.excite.com), Hotbot (http://www. hotbot.com), Lycos (http://www.lycos.com), and many others can identify web sites that contain information on racial profiling. Using these search engines effectively requires the thoughtful selection of narrow search terms—use of "racial profiling" as keywords will produce an enormous number of hits. On the other hand, taking the time to work through the web sites found by using the general terms can sometimes lead to an unexpected and intriguing discovery.

The search engines also include directories relevant to racial profiling. In Yahoo!, the directory under "Society and Culture > Cultures and Groups > People of Color > Racial Profiling" lists relevant web sites and information.

In Google, the directories do not contain categories specific to racial profiling, but those on law enforcement, criminal justice, and crime can be useful. Relevant directories include "Society > Issues > Race-Ethnic-Religious Relations > Race and Racism, > Racial Profiling" and "Society > Issues > Crime and Justice > Police Misconduct > Police Brutality."

It might also help to begin a search with particular sites. Perhaps most useful is the Racial Profiling Data Collection Resource Center at Northeastern University (http://www.racialprofilinganalysis.neu.edu). This web site provides information to guide the understanding and measurement of the extent of racial profiling. Specific pages cover the benefits and limitations of data collection, common challenges to data reporting and analysis, details on legislation, a glossary of terms, news items, reports, and articles. Avoiding the bias of most advocacy-group web sites, the data collection center contains many practical references and Internet links.

Another useful starting point comes from the U.S. Department of State's International Information Program. A page on racial profiling (http://usinfo.state.gov/usa/race/profile/official.htm#texts) allows access to key texts, documents, and legislation. Memos from the Clinton and Bush administrations, for example, describe policies on racial profiling, and legislative documents show how Congress has proposed to deal with the issue.

Other pages offer more in the way of advocacy positions. A strong opponent of racial profiling, the American Civil Liberties Union has a web page (http://www.aclu.org/RacialEquality/RacialEqualitylist.cfm?c=133) that includes press releases, legislative documents, legal documents, speeches, and fact sheets. The press releases reflect antiprofiling positions and catalog the varied activities of the organizations to help end the practice. Users can also find out about the organization's viewpoint on topics such as the Justice Department's battle against terrorism, the Maryland State Police, victims of profiling in New Jersey, mistreatment of airline passengers, airport screening practices, and federal and state legislative proposals. David A. Harris, author of *Profiles in Injustice* and a critic of racial profiling, maintains a web site (http://www.profilesininjustice.com) that contains information on research, news stories, laws, and policies relating to racial profiling. A web page sponsored by the Leadership Conference on Civil Rights (http://www.civilrights.org) contains stories, press releases, reports speeches, position papers, testimony, essays, and court decisions on racial profiling. This material appears in the directory under "Issues and Criminal Justice."

Advocates of racial profiling do not have a corresponding site, but a variety of articles and pages, although not contained by a central source, defend their viewpoints. For example, FrontPageMagazine.com (http://www.frontpagemag.com) contains several articles critical of the claims of racial profiling opponents. Adversity.Net (http://www.adversity.net) opposes reverse discrimination, racial preferences, and quotas—forms of prejudice and discrimination, in their view. It also includes a page in opposition to racial profiling with a number of case studies on the topic.

COURT CASES

Few court decisions address the issue of racial profiling directly (see the discussion in Chapter 2 for those that do). However, litigation involving accusations of racial profiling has grown since the 1990s. Settlements made by the Maryland State Police and New Jersey State Police have encouraged such action. Information on the suits, jury decisions, awards, appeals, and final judgments can be found through searches of newspapers *(New York Times)*, web sites (The Data Collection Resource Center at Northeastern University, the American Civil Liberties Union), and general search engines (Google, Yahoo!). To obtain the written decisions in racial profiling cases, electronic law libraries such as Westlaw and LexisNexis include court opinions. Opinions of the Supreme Court relevant to many issues can be obtained from the Legal Information Institute at Cornell Law School (http://www.law.cornell.edu). With knowledge of the specific case, a Web search that lists the names of the parties involved (in the form of the plaintiff v. the defendant, such as the *United States v. Brignoni-Ponce*) and the case number turn up the text of many rulings.

LEGISLATION

The most recent proposed but still unpassed federal legislation appears in Appendix D. For more information on legislation in specific states, the Center for Policy Alternatives offers a web page on recent developments (http://www.stateaction. org/issues/racialprofiling/index.cfm). The Data Collection Resource Center at Northeastern University (http://www. racialprofilinganalysis.neu.edu/legislation.php) shows a map of the U.S. states coded to indicate current legislative action in regard to racial profiling. Clicking on the state of interest describes its legislation. Otherwise, a Web search for "racial profiling" and the name of a state will provide some up-to-date information.

CHAPTER 7

ANNOTATED BIBLIOGRAPHY

The following annotated bibliography contains nine sections that cover the literature on racial profiling:

- Opposition
- Support
- Highway Stops and Drug Enforcement
- City Policing
- Immigration and Border Control
- Terrorism
- Data and Analysis Issues
- Policy Issues
- Background Issues

The sections correspond roughly to those in Chapter 1 but begin with opponents and supporters of racial profiling before moving to references on types of racial profiling and special issues relating to racial profiling. Within each of these sections, the citations are divided into subsections on books, articles, and Web documents. The topics and citations include technical and nontechnical works, in-depth and short treatments, and research and opinion pieces (see Chapter 6 for an overview on how to most effectively use the diverse materials).

OPPOSITION

BOOKS

Asim, Jabari, ed. *Not Guilty: Twelve Black Men Speak Out on Law, Justice, and Life.* New York: HarperCollins, 2001. Speaking of their experiences with police, the contributors to the volume, mostly educated and professional African Americans, reveal their anger and resentment. However, they do so in a personal way that also reflects the diversity of their experiences and ideas. Some of the chapters address the long-standing distrust between police and African Americans and suggest some ways to improve the situation. Nearly all the chapters aim to counter images of black men as criminals and drug users.

Cole, David. *No Equal Justice: Race and Class in the American Criminal Justice System.* New York: New Press, 1999. The author, a law professor at Georgetown University, argues that the criminal justice system fails to live up to its promise of equality before the law. The inequality shows in the mistreatment of lower-income groups and racial and ethnic minorities. Chapter 1 focuses on the double standard used by police in treatment of minority and majority race and ethnic groups, while later chapters focus on the double standard in legal proceedings and punishment.

Harris, David A. *Profiles in Injustice: Why Racial Profiling Cannot Work.* New York: New Press, 2002. A thorough and detailed critique of racial profiling, this book covers a variety of topics, offers a wealth of detail, and reviews much literature. Harris, a vocal opponent of racial profiling, has written often on the topic and testified in court cases and in front of Congress about the need to eliminate its use by police. More than other treatments, this book does much to suggest ways to eliminate the practice. It also includes many stories of the instances of racial profiling along with a review of the statistics. It is an essential reference for those studying racial profiling. A companion web site to the book can be found at http://www.profilesininjustice.com.

Kennedy, Randall. *Race, Crime, and Law.* New York: Pantheon Books, 1997. Criticizing the treatment of African Americans by the criminal justice system, this Harvard Law School professor addresses a number of issues relating to race, including the high rates of crime among blacks, racial profiling, and other forms of discrimination against blacks by police and prosecutors. However, he is also critical of unsubstantiated charges of racism and fully represents the complexity of the issues he discusses in the book.

Meeks, Kenneth. *Driving While Black: Highways, Shopping Malls, Taxicabs, Sidewalks: What to Do If You Are a Victim of Racial Profiling.* New York: Broadway Books, 2000. A clearly written introduction to the topic, this book offers a less technical and more readable overview of the problem of racial profiling than most other books (which are oriented toward academics and policy makers). Meeks writes for ordinary citizens who may be victims of racial profiling, want to know more about the issue and problem, and desire to do something about it.

Murphy, Laura W. "Additional Statement," in *S. 989: The End of Racial Profiling Act of 2001, Hearing before the Subcommittee on the Constitution, Federalism, and Property Rights of the Committee on the Judiciary, United States Senate, One Hundred Seventh Congress, First Session.* Washington, D.C.: U.S. Government Printing Office, August 1, 2001, pp. 79–84. The director of the American Civil Liberties Union in Washington, D.C., criticizes the continued widespread use of racial profiling, particularly by the Drug Enforcement Administration. She and her organization advocate the use of data collection procedures, litigation, and federal legislation to stop racial profiling. In addition, she argues more generally for laws to ban pretext stops and consent searches.

National Council of La Raza, Washington, D.C. "Statement," in *S. 989: The End of Racial Profiling Act of 2001, Hearing before the Subcommittee on the Constitution, Federalism, and Property Rights of the Committee on the Judiciary, United States Senate, One Hundred Seventh Congress, First Session.* Washington, D.C.: U.S. Government Printing Office, August 1, 2001, pp. 112–119. This civil rights organization representing Latinos across the United States argues that, as a growing part of the U.S. population, Latinos have been adversely affected by racial profiling. Three organizations, the U.S. Immigration and Naturalization Service, the U.S. Border Patrol, and the U.S. Customs Service, have, according to La Raza, discriminated against Latinos. The organization urges Congress to pass the End of Racial Profiling Act, to allocate funds to the Department of Justice to sue state and local police agencies using racial profiling, and to require federal agencies concerned with immigration and smuggling to end racial profiling.

Russell, Katheryn K. *The Color of Crime: Racial Hoaxes, White Fear, Black Protectionism, Police Harassment, and Other Macroaggressions.* New York: New York University Press, 1998. Highly critical of the treatment of African Americans, the author disputes claims that racial discrimination in the criminal justice system is a myth. In one chapter, she attacks evidence that minorities offend more commonly than others and therefore rejects this justification for excess police stops of minorities. Of special interest are the examples of the use of racial profiling against celebrities and hoaxes involving the claim that blacks committed crimes actually done by whites.

ARTICLES

Antonia, Kathleen. "A Lesson before Living." *The Humanist,* vol. 61, March/April 2001, pp. 43–44. Argues that racial and ethnic stereotypes lead to racial profiling and, more seriously, to harsher penalties for minorities than for whites. As a result, more regulations will not end the problem—increasing awareness of individuals about their own misleading stereotypes is needed.

Cole, David. "The Color of Justice. Courts and Racial Profiling." *The Nation*, vol. 269, October 11, 1999, pp. 12–14. Although recognizing the role of police in racial profiling, the author also argues that the courts have, by approving consent searches and pretext stops, contributed to the use of the practice. He presents the legal case against racial profiling and the challenges critics face in campaigning to end the practice.

Forman, James. "Arrested Development: The Cases against Conservative Support for Racial Profiling." *The New Republic*, vol. 225, September 10, 2001, pp. 24–27. A critic of racial profiling argues that conservative principles about work and responsibility should lead to the view that innocent blacks should be treated identically to innocent whites. Yet, conservatives often deny that police use unfair tactics against minorities. The article calls for conservatives to reconsider their views on this issue. However, the article was published shortly before terrorist attacks in 2001, which changed the context of debates over racial profiling.

Goldberg, Jeffrey. "The Color of Suspicion: Racial Profiling." *New York Times Magazine*, June 20, 1999, pp. 50–57. This cover story reviews the allegations of racial harassment made against the police and considers the perspectives of police in defending their actions. The author finds that, although police officers say they do not let race influence their actions, observing them on the job often shows the opposite.

Harris, David A., and Heather Mac Donald. "Race Wars: Discussion of the War on Police by H. Mac Donald, with Reply." *Weekly Standard*, vol. 7, February 4, 2002, pp. 6–8. David Harris, a well-known critic of racial profiling, challenges the facts and arguments made in an earlier article by Heather Mac Donald, a defender of police action. The exchange allows comparison of diverse views on the evidence of racial profiling.

Kennedy, Randall. "Blind Spot." *Atlantic Monthly*, vol. 289, April 2002, p. 24. This opponent of racial profiling describes an intriguing similarity between racial profiling and affirmative action. Both involve special attention to minorities, one in relation to crime investigation, and one in relation to educational opportunity. Ironically, those favoring racial profiling often oppose affirmative action, while those opposed to racial profiling often favor affirmative action. The different views reflect the complexities of issues involving race in the United States.

———. "Suspect Policy." *The New Republic*, vol. 221, September 13–20, 1999, pp. 30–35. The author notes that courts have not prohibited the use of race as a consideration in making a stop as long as it is done for legitimate law enforcement purposes and is one of several factors taken into account. Still, he asserts that the practice is morally wrong, has severe costs in terms of the trust minorities have of the police, and represents a form of discrimination.

Leitzel, Jim. "Race and Policing." *Society*, vol. 38, March/April 2001, pp. 38–42. The author believes that recent success in reducing crime has been tarnished by the methods used to reach that goal—including racial profiling. In the long run, real reductions in crime will require better relationships between minorities and police, and a stringent ban on race-based policing is needed to reach this goal.

Loose, Cindy, and Chris L. Jenkins. "Rallying to 'Redeem the Dream'; Rights Leaders Target Racial Profiling." *Washington Post*, August 27, 2000, p. C1. In a protest held at the Lincoln Memorial in Washington D.C., civil rights leaders led by Martin Luther King III and Reverend Al Sharpton protested police brutality against minorities and the use of racial profiling. According to the story, the organizers hoped to push the Clinton administration to address these issues. (They were successful.)

Morin, Richard, and Michael H. Cottman. "Discrimination's Lingering Sting; Minorities Tell of Profiling, Other Bias." *Washington Post*, June 22, 2001, p. A1. This article contains stories from minorities about their mistreatment by police.

Nurse, Jemelleh. "What Racial Profiling Feels Like." *New York Times Upfront*, vol. 135, February 7, 2003, p. 5. A personal story of an African American woman who was subjected to racial profiling.

"Rash of Racial Profiling Forces Black Parents to Prepare Young Drivers for Police Stops." *Jet*, vol. 95, March 29, 1999, pp. 7–8. This story reports on how the actions of New Jersey state troopers have heightened the concerns of minority parents about racial profiling. It describes how many of these parents felt it necessary to explain to their children that they can expect to be unfairly stopped simply because of their skin color.

Taylor, Stuart, Jr. "Racial Profiling—The Liberals Are Right." *National Journal*, vol. 31, April 24, 1999, pp. 1084–1085. In reviewing the emerging evidence of the widespread use of racial profiling and citing examples from New York City and New Jersey, the author emphasizes the immorality of the practice and the terrible harm it brings to minorities. Some practices, such as quality-of-life policing, reflect good police work rather than racial profiling, but other practices discriminate against minorities. Taylor recommends a variety of efforts to deal with the problem.

Web Documents

American Civil Liberties Union. "Racial Equality: Racial Profiling." American Civil Liberties Union web site. Available online. URL: http://www.aclu.org/RacialEquality/RacialEqualitylist.cfm?c=133. Downloaded in

July 2003. Strongly opposed to racial profiling, this organization offers a web page that includes its press releases on the issue along with legislative documents, legal documents, speeches, and fact sheets. The press releases reflect the antiprofiling position and present a one-sided perspective on the issue but also provide a useful starting place to understand the reasons behind the position. In addition, the information on the web page gives an overview of the many issues that involve racial profiling. Users can read about the organization's viewpoints of topics such as the Justice Department's battle against terrorism, the Maryland State Police, victims of profiling in New Jersey, mistreatment of airline passengers, airport screening practices, and federal and state legislative proposals.

American Civil Liberties Union Freedom Network. "Arrest the Racism: Racial Profiling in America." ACLU Online Archives. Available online. URL: http://archive.aclu.org/profiling. Downloaded in July 2003. Besides information on how to join the ACLU and report on incidents of racial profiling, this web page describes racial profiling and summarizes news stories on the topic.

Breakthrough. "End Racial Profiling: Promote Racial Equality." Breakthrough: Building Human Rights Cultures. Available online. URL: http://www.breakthrough.tv/act/act_now_subarticle.cfm?id_Article=40&id_SubArticle=22. Downloaded in July 2003. Along with presenting arguments against racial profiling, this web page includes links for users to test their knowledge of racial profiling, participate in a poll, act against racial profiling, and discuss the issue with others.

Harris, David A. "Profiling—A Self-Fulfilling Racist Policy." Media Awareness Project. Available online. URL: http://www.mapinc.org/letters/1999/03/lte86.html. Posted on March 19, 1999. In response to claims that high rates of criminal activity among members of minority groups lead to racial profiling, David Harris argues the opposite. In fact, stereotypes of minority crime lead police to search more for minority crime and therefore find more minority crime. Racial profiling is thus more a cause of minority arrests than a response to minority crime.

———. "Profiles in Injustice. Why Racial Profiling Cannot Work." Available online. URL: http://www.profilesininjustice.com. Downloaded in July 2003. On this web page that promotes Harris's book of the same name, one can find reviews, news, reports, resources, laws, and policies that relate to racial profiling. Because Harris has been one of the most active critics of racial profiling and his book is one of the most thorough treatments of the topic, this web site is worth examining.

Leadership Conference on Civil Rights. "Racial Profiling." Civilrights.org. Available online. URL: http://www.civilrights.org/issues/cj/_profiling. Downloaded in July 2003. This web page features stories, press releases, speeches, position papers, testimony, essays, and court decisions related to racial profiling issues. Sponsored by a coalition of civil rights organizations, the web site presents information against racial profiling and represents a good starting place for information on this viewpoint.

Muharrar, Mikal. "Media Blackface: 'Racial Profiling' in News Reporting." FAIR: Fairness and Accuracy in Reporting. Available online. URL: http://www.fair.org/extra/9809/media-blackface.html. Posted in September/October 1998. Although the media treatment of racial profiling has generally been fair and accurate, the media has, according to the author, been unfair in another way. It consistently presents news stories that link African Americans with crime, drug use, and welfare receipt. The false images worsen the position of minorities in society.

Rice, George. "Racial Profiling: Prejudice or Protocol." Horizon: People and Possibilities. Available online. URL: http://www.horizonmag.com/6/racial-profiling.asp. Posted in December 1999. In describing situations where police have the discretion to use racial profiling, this article offers a quiz for readers to identify incidents of racial profiling and the supposed characteristics of drug couriers. It also offers tips to follow when approached or detained by police.

United Automobile, Aerospace, and Agricultural Implement Workers. "Racial Profiling." UAW Community Action Program. Available online. URL: http://www.uaw.org/cap/03/issues/issue20.cfm. Posted in February 2003. This labor union addresses the problem of racial profiling as part of its community action program. It opposes the practice and sets forth its support of legislation to prevent its use. Unions have generally not taken an active role in this issue but, as illustrated by this web page, have not ignored it altogether.

Williams, Scott W. "Racial Profiling Web Pages." The Circle Brotherhood Association. Available online. URL: http://www.math.buffalo.edu/~sww/circle/raceprofiling/links.racial.profiling.html. Posted on January 14, 2000. Includes links to pages containing stories about "driving while black," other racial profiling stories, racial profiling questions, recommendations for action after a racial profiling incident, racial profiling solutions, and numerous documents. Headed by a quotation from comedian Chris Rock, "In America, an African-American is born a suspect," the site takes a strongly negative view of racial profiling.

Zoufal, Donald R. "Developments in Racial Profiling Litigation: 'A Tale of Two Cities.'" Americans for Effective Law Enforcement Legal Center. Available online. URL: http://www.aele.org/zoufal.html. Posted on August 30, 2000. This story contrasts the experiences of two small, affluent Chicago suburbs sued for racial profiling. After settling its suit, Mt. Prospect, Illinois, initiated policy reforms, and Highland Park, Illinois, signed a consent decree requiring the city to change its policing procedures. The two cities illustrate the effectiveness of bringing about changes in policy through litigation.

SUPPORT

BOOKS

Frederickson, Darin D., and Raymond P. Siljander. *Racial Profiling: Eliminating the Confusion between Racial and Criminal Profiling and Clarifying What Constitutes Unfair Discrimination and Persecution.* Springfield, Ill.: Charles C. Thomas, 2002. This book rejects discriminatory forms of racial profiling but defends criminal profiling as a legitimate law enforcement practice. It gives examples of both and highlights the potential for racial profiling, but not criminal profiling, to lead to racial discrimination. Along with its discussion of racial profiling, it devotes attention to ways for police to avoid more general racial prejudice and discrimination.

Hughes, Johnny L. "Statement," in *Racial Profiling within Law Enforcement Agencies, Hearing before the Subcommittee on the Constitution, Federalism, and Property Rights of the Committee on the Judiciary, United States Senate, One Hundred Sixth Congress, Second Session.* Washington, D.C.: U.S. Government Printing Office, March 30, 2000, pp. 41–44. A retired member of the Maryland State Police and representative of the National Troopers Association, Hughes is one of the few at the hearing to oppose legislation to collect data on traffic stops. Reflecting the views of many police officers, he calls the legislation unnecessary and prone to interfere in police activity, which properly relies on the use of race, ethnicity, and national origin in a limited sense—as part of a larger criminal profile. He argues that critics misunderstand the use of criminal profiles and intend to hamper police efforts with legislation.

Lee, Yueh-Ting, Lee J. Jussim, and Clark R. McCauley, eds. *Stereotype Accuracy: Toward Appreciating Group Differences.* Washington D.C.: American Psychological Association, 1995. The chapters in this edited volume are based on scientific research and experiments but take an unusual perspective: They argue that stereotypes are, by and large, useful and accurate. Although most view stereotypes as illogical generalizations, some researchers note that the generalizations have a kernel of truth. Defenders of racial profiling use this research to support their view that the use of race, ethnicity, or national origin in criminal profiling has some validity.

Mac Donald, Heather. *Are Cops Racist?* Chicago: Ivan R. Dee, 2003. A good place to start for those interested in understanding the viewpoints of the defenders of racial profiling. Most of the nine chapters in the book come from articles that appeared earlier in *City Journal*, a magazine published by the conservative Manhattan Institute. The first chapter, "The Myth of Racial Profiling," argues that to the extent that police use race or ethnicity in investigations, they do so appropriately, given the racial makeup of crime. Other chapters defend police actions in Cincinnati, where accusations of police brutality have led to riots, and in New York City, where the shooting of Amadou Diallo led to protests about police treatment of minorities. Still other chapters discuss how opposition to racial profiling threatens the ability of security agents to keep the nation safe from terrorism.

Tucker, William. "The Tragedy of Racial Profiling: It's Unjust—and It Works," in *S. 989: The End of Racial Profiling Act of 2001, Hearing before the Subcommittee on the Constitution, Federalism, and Property Rights of the Committee on the Judiciary, United States Senate, One Hundred Seventh Congress, First Session.* Washington, D.C.: U.S. Government Printing Office, August 1, 2001, pp. 125–129. In making the case for racial profiling, the author contrasts the complaints about the practice in New York City with the horrible violence committed by criminals. For example, while celebrities protest racial profiling by cabdrivers, cabdrivers are murdered by passengers. While some complain about racial profiling in tickets for traffic violations, drug-related murders occur daily. Tucker believes the seriousness of the crime problem in the United States warrants more concern with stopping the victimization of law-abiding citizens by criminals than with use of race and ethnicity by cabbies and cops.

Wilbanks, William. *The Myth of a Racist Criminal Justice System.* Monterey, Calif.: Brooks/Cole Publishing, 1987. The book offers a detailed, although somewhat dated, review of the social science literature on racism in the criminal justice system. Based on the literature, Wilbanks concludes that, despite racist individuals, the criminal justice system is not characterized by racial prejudice or discrimination. In making the case for the myth of a racist criminal justice system, the chapters consider perceptions of blacks and whites, and the actions of police, prosecution, sentencing, and parole. The focus on scientific studies makes the material technical and difficult for general readers.

Articles

Corry, John. "The Sounds of Silence: *New York Times* Tends to Exaggerate Racial Differences." *The American Spectator*, vol. 33, September 2000, pp. 46–47. Referring to stories in the *New York Times* about Amadou Diallo and a series titled "How Race Is Lived in America," the author suggests that the newspaper exaggerates the seriousness of the racial incidents it reports. Writers for the paper tend to assume that race and ethnicity must always divide rather than unite people.

Derbyshire, John. "In Defense of Racial Profiling." *National Review*, vol. 53, February 19, 2001, pp. 38–40. This article makes the case for racial profiling more clearly and strongly than most others. It is unapologetic in its tone and critical of the unwillingness of most people to discuss the issue frankly. Derbyshire emphasizes the high rates of criminal offending of minority groups and the validity of some stereotypes that have developed about race differences in crime. He views racial profiling as a commonsense approach to policing that simply involves investigation of people in places where crime is most likely to occur.

D'Souza, Dinesh. "Sometimes Discrimination Can Make Sense." *USA Today*, June 2, 1995, p. 15A. Available online. URL: http://www.hoover.stanford.edu/publications/digest/994/dsouza.html. Posted on June 2, 1999. This short editorial argues that racial profiling cannot be attributed to irrational prejudice but to the pursuit by police of those groups most involved in crime. However, the author also argues that rational discrimination is less acceptable in the public sector than the private sector and by police than private individuals. He believes that the cost of racial profiling in terms of racial polarization is more important than the benefits in terms of police efficiency.

Golab, Jan. "Probable Cause: Racial Profiling and Los Angeles Police." *Los Angeles Magazine*, vol. 44, August 1999, pp. 28ff. As reported in the article, a Los Angeles police representative claims that racial profiling as practiced by police considers time, place, and activity of the suspect in addition to race and ethnicity. Such procedures are effective in preventing and stopping crime. Still, others say that the profiles result in unjustified stops of Hispanics and African Americans.

Johnson, Scott. "Better Unsafe Than (Occasionally) Sorry?" *The American Enterprise*, vol. 14, January/February 2003, pp. 28–30. The article disputes the arguments of major critics of racial profiling, David A. Harris and the American Civil Liberties Union, about the widespread use of racial profiling. Not only is racial profiling absent from the highways and streets, it is absent where it is greatly needed—in airports and airlines. The author believes the misguided crusade against racial profiling, which has gathered momentum in recent years, leaves the nation vulnerable to terrorist attacks.

Kersten, Katherine. "Race to Conclusions: What the Activists Don't Tell You About Racial Profiling." *Weekly Standard*, vol. 6, August 20–27, 2001, pp. 27–29. The author criticizes studies using data on the race of drivers stopped by police because they do not properly consider criminal activity. Looking only at the race of drivers and not the neighborhood of the stop, the suspicions that led to the stop, and the involvement of minority groups in crime makes the figures meaningless. The end result, according to the article, is to fuel criticism of the police and slow the progress they have made in many cities to lower homicide and crime.

Lundman, Richard J., and Robert L. Kaufman. "Race, Ethnicity, and Gender on Citizen Self-Reports of Traffic Stops and Police Actions." *Criminology*, vol. 41, February 2003, pp. 195–220. Relying on self-reported traffic-stop encounters with police, this study, not unexpectedly, finds higher rates of stopping of African Americans and males, but also that African-American and Hispanic drivers less often "report that police had a legitimate reason for the stop and are less likely to report that police acted properly." The study recognizes the limitations of self-report data and discusses ways to gather additional kinds of data to better understand racial profiling.

Malti-Douglas, Fedwa. "Let Them Profile Me." *New York Times*, February 6, 2002, p. A21. The author has often been detained at airports on the basis of ethnic profiling but nonetheless believes the tactic makes sense for preventing terrorism. She argues that the procedures, although they inconvenience members of some national groups, protect people from terrorist acts.

Pope, Carl E., and Howard N. Snyder, "Race as a Factor in Juvenile Arrests," *Juvenile Justice Bulletin.* Office of Juvenile Justice and Delinquency Prevention, April 2003, pp. 1–8. Using data gathered by the FBI, the study finds that, once accounting for the seriousness of the offense, police are no more likely to arrest nonwhite than white juvenile offenders. The results therefore provide little evidence of racial profiling in arrests of young people.

Satel, Sally. "I Am a Racially Profiling Doctor." *New York Times Magazine*, May 5, 2002, pp. 56–58. Satel uses racial profiling in a different way than most. She argues that genetic differences between races influence disease and the response to drug treatment. The use of race in this way aims to help minorities rather than investigate or arrest them, but racial profiling in both cases uses information on racial groups to make decisions about individual members of the groups.

Toby, Jackson. "'Racial Profiling' Doesn't Prove Cops Are Racist." *Wall Street Journal*, vol. 233, issue 48, p. A22. Available online. URL: http://www.frontpagemag.com/Articles/Printable.asp?ID=3526. Posted on March 11, 1999. A criminologist defends police actions in stopping vehicles on highways and pedestrians in New York City by arguing that police respond to investigative clues rather than act with racist motivations.

Will, George F. "Exposing the 'Myth' of Racial Profiling." *Washington Post*, April 19, 2001, p. A19. In discussing Heather Mac Donald's writing, this well-known conservative columnist and commentator criticizes the unwillingness of most elites to admit a simple fact: Felons are not evenly distributed across society's demographic groups. Because police focus their efforts in neighborhoods where crime is highest, which are often minority neighborhoods, it does not imply discrimination and racial profiling but efforts to protect the public safety.

WEB DOCUMENTS

Adversity.net. Home Page. Available online. URL: http://www.adversity.net. Downloaded in July 2003. This organization opposes "reverse discrimination," racial preferences, and quotas—forms of prejudice and discrimination, in their view. It also includes a page with case studies of the alleged abuse of police by anti–racial profiling efforts of politicians, civil rights advocates, and courts.

Dunphy, Jack. "Racial Profiling." National Review Online. Available online. URL: http://www.nationalreview.com/comment/comment101600b.shtml. Posted on October 16, 2000. The author is a Los Angeles police officer who uses a pseudonym for his articles. In writing about racial profiling, he argues that police focus on race only because of its connection to crime.

Levy, Robert A. "Ethnic Profiling: A Rational and Moral Framework." Cato Institute. Available online. URL: http://www.cato.org/current/terrorism/pubs/levy-011002.html. Posted on October 2, 2001. In trying to draw the line between the need to protect both civil rights and the population from terrorism, the author tries to find a middle ground. Rejecting a complete ban on the practice and rejecting its arbitrary use, he supports racial profiling when certain conditions can be met. These conditions put the onus on users of racial and ethnic profiling, such as in airport screening, to demonstrate that it is effective and applied fairly.

Mac Donald, Heather. "Racial Profiling Myth Debunked." *City Journal*, vol. 12, no. 3, Spring 2002. Available online. URL: http://www.city-journal.org/html/eon_3_27_02hm.html. Posted on March 27, 2002. An article in this conservative journal (also included in the author's book, *Are Cops Racist?*) reports on efforts to bury a government report on racial differences in speeding. As the report finds blacks speed more than whites, it contradicts claims that state troopers arbitrarily stop blacks and use racial profiling. The author argues on the basis of the report that there is no credible evidence that racial profiling exists.

Police Executive Research Forum. "Racially Biased Policing: A Principled Response." Police Executive Research Forum web site. Available online. URL: http://www.policeforum.org/racial/RBP_Refs.pdf. Posted on July 16, 2000. Enter into http://www.policeforum.org as a guest, click "Racially-Biased Policing," and follow instructions to download. The forum has opposed racial profiling legislation, and the web page contains chapters on other ways to deal with the problem: changing police and citizen perceptions, developing policies to address racially biased policing, and improving recruitment, hiring, education, training, and minority outreach.

Rhetts, Bill. "Racial Profiling." Domelights: The Voice of the Good Guy. Available online. URL: http://www.domelights.com/racprof2.htm. Posted in July 2001. A retired police officer offers his opinion that racial profiling in some cases is necessary and suggests that much of the negative media publicity about the practice has been exaggerated. He gives examples of circumstances where race or ethnicity became relevant factors in an investigation. The article is personal rather than general but provides the perspective of a police officer on the issue.

Think Tank. "Is Racial Profiling Real?" PBS Online. Available online. URL: http://www.pbs.org/thinktank/transcript967.html. Posted on July 19, 2001. The transcript of this PBS television show brings Heather Mac Donald, the author of an article "The Myth of Racial Profiling," together with two opponents of the practice, Paul Butler and David Cole. The exchange contrasts views about the existence of biased racial profiling and the justification of using race and ethnicity as part of profiles. The discussion jumps quickly from topic to topic but presents both sides of the issue.

Weinkopf, Chris. "Shifting Gears on Racial Profiling." FrontPageMagazine.com. Available online. URL: http://www.frontpagemag.com/articles/printable.asp?ID=806. Posted on April 3, 2002. The author criticizes the actions of the then New Jersey attorney general, David Samson, for trying to suppress a study that showed a higher percentage of black than white speeders. The study supported claims of the New Jersey State Police that they did not unfairly target minorities for traffic stops but followed the law. The unwillingness of state politicians to release the report until pressured by the media and the public reflects, according to the author, bias against the police. Politicians accept less scientific studies critical of the police but not a strong study that contradicts their political views.

HIGHWAY STOPS AND DRUG ENFORCEMENT

BOOKS

Covington, Jeanette. "Round up the Usual Suspects: Racial Profiling and the War on Drugs," in Dragan Milovanovic and Katheryn K. Russell, eds., *Petit Apartheid in the U.S. Criminal Justice System.* Durham N.C.: Carolina Academic Press, 2001, pp. 27–42. The author argues that much of the concern about drug use stems from "drug scares" that exaggerate the seriousness of the problem and paint an unfair connection between minorities and drug crimes. Given the drug scares, police gain justification, according to the argument, for use of race and ethnicity in fighting the drug war. As with the public more generally, police appear to accept false stereotypes about minority involvement in drug crime.

Farmer, John J., Jr., and Paul H. Zoubek. *Final Report of the State Police Review Team Regarding Allegations of Racial Profiling.* Trenton, N.J.: New Jersey Office of the Attorney General, 1999. In responding to allegations of racial profiling by state troopers, the attorney general initiated an investigation and published this report. It concludes that state police had used racial profiling and procedures need to be changed to end the practice. The report makes recommendations to deal with the problem.

O'Reilly, James T. *Police Traffic Stops and Racial Profiling: Resolving Management, Labor and Civil Rights Conflicts.* Springfield, Ill.: Charles C. Thomas, 2002. Written largely for police managers by a professor at the University of Cincinnati, this book presents unbiased coverage of the issue of racial profiling with regard to traffic stops. The first section describes the legal rulings controlling police actions in stopping cars, the second section considers racial profiling specifically, and the remaining sections cover the negative consequences of racial profiling for police departments and how to deal with them.

U.S. General Accounting Office. *Racial Profiling: Limited Data Available on Motorist Stops: Report to the Honorable James E. Clyburn, Chairman, Congressional Black Caucus.* Washington, D.C.: U.S. General Accounting Office, 2000. This volume criticizes existing efforts to measure racial profiling. It finds that, in one way or another, previous studies have been flawed in their ability to properly compare the racial breakdown in traffic stops with measures of racial background in offending. It also offers a helpful summary of the studies. It concludes "A key limitation of the available analyses is that they did not fully examine whether different groups may have been at different levels of risk for being stopped because they differed in their rates and/or severity of committing traffic violations."

Wilkins, Robert L. "Statement," in *Racial Profiling within Law Enforcement Agencies, Hearing before the Subcommittee on the Constitution, Federalism, and Property Rights of the Committee on the Judiciary, United States Senate, One Hundred Sixth Congress, Second Session.* Washington, D.C.: U.S. Government Printing Office, March 30, 2000, pp. 16–21. The experience of Wilkins, an African-American public defense lawyer in Washington, D.C., who was stopped by state police while driving through Maryland, was an early and highly-publicized instance of alleged racial profiling. Wilkins sued the state of Maryland and settled in 1995 for $96,000 in damages and changes in police procedures to eliminate profiling. His testimony in Congress describes the incident, the settlement with the state of Maryland, and his efforts to monitor the continued use of racial profiling by the state.

ARTICLES

Barovick, Harriet. "DWB: Driving While Black: Incidents in New Jersey and Maryland Heat Up the Issue of Racial Profiling by State Highway Patrols." *Time*, vol. 151, June 15, 1998, p. 35. The article describes the suit by the American Civil Liberties Union against the Maryland State Police for the continued use of racial profiling. The suit points to the agency's own records on the high rates of stops of African Americans on the highways, but police counter with more recent data to show higher rates of whites stopped.

Bureau of Justice Statistics. "Fact Sheet: Traffic Stop Data Collection Policies for State Police, 2001." Washington, D.C.: U.S. Department of Justice, Office of Justice Programs, 2001, pp. 1–4. This publication gives information on various state policies concerning traffic stop data. Some states collect data on all stops, some only on stops for traffic violations, some for stops involving the use of force, arrests, or searches, and some have no collection system in place. It also gives sources for examining specific anti–racial profiling laws in the few states that have them.

Callahan, Gene, and William Anderson. "The Roots of Racial Profiling." *Reason*, vol. 33, August/September 2001, pp. 36–43. Espousing ideals of individual freedom, the authors argue that the drug war has fueled the use of racial profiling. They reject the claim that racial profiling is part of good police work, arguing instead that it involves treating persons as suspects on the basis of skin color rather than criminal activity. In any case, the pressure for racial profiling comes from the demands of the government to stop drug use and the ability of police to confiscate the property of suspected drug dealers. The drug war has, according to the authors, eroded civil liberties in general and contributed to racial profiling in particular.

Cannon, Angie. "DWB: Driving While Black: Racial Profiling." *U.S. News and World Report*, vol. 126, March 15, 1999, p. 72. The firing of New Jersey State Police superintendent Carl Williams by New Jersey governor Christie Todd Whitman for insensitive remarks about the racial characteristics of drug traffickers has stimulated much criticism by minorities. This article discusses minorities' viewpoints about racial profiling and presents some statistics on the topic.

Cornwall, Warren. "Study Disputes Bias Claims in Stops by Troopers." *Seattle Times*, June 20, 2003, p. B1. Available online. URL: http://seattletimes.nwsource.com/html/localnews/135039859_statepatrol20e.html. Posted on June 20, 2003. On the basis of an analysis of data collection mandated by law, it appears that Washington State Police do not disproportionately target minorities in stops but may do so in searching those whom they have stopped.

Annotated Bibliography

Drummond, Tammerin. "It's Not Just New Jersey: Racial Profiling." *Time*, vol. 153, June 14, 1999, p. 61. Reporting on the finding of the New Jersey attorney general that state police had engaged in racial profiling, the author considers the extent of the practice elsewhere. In so doing, Drummond relies on findings from the American Civil Liberties Union.

Grant, Leroy Jermaine, and David Evanier. "Playing Through: Experience of L. J. Grant, Shot by New Jersey State Troopers in 1998." *New York Times Magazine*, May 19, 2002, p. 90. Grant recounts the racial profiling incident in which New Jersey state troopers opened fire on Grant and three other African Americans in a van. When the transmission was accidentally moved to reverse and the van backed up, the police thought they were under attack and shot three of the passengers. The state of New Jersey settled a suit brought against the troopers by the young men.

Hewitt, Bill. "An Echo of Gunfire: Shooting of Black Student P. Jones by Off-Duty Officer Prompts Accusations of Racial Profiling." *People Weekly*, vol. 55, May 14, 2001, pp. 211–214. This story describes the circumstances of the death of an African American attending Howard University who was shot in suburban Virginia by an undercover narcotics officer. The officer claims that he stopped the student as part of a search for a suspected drug dealer and opened fire only after the young man tried to ram him. When the state decided not to bring charges against the officer, friends and relatives accused the officer of racial profiling and filed a wrongful death suit.

Hosenball, Mark. "'It Is Not the Act of a Few Bad Apples': Racial Profiling by New Jersey State Troopers." *Newsweek*, vol. 133, May 17, 1999, pp. 34–35. Citing the suit filed by four African-American men fired on by New Jersey state troopers, this article discusses evidence released by the New Jersey attorney general on the extent of racial profiling on the state's highways.

Jerrigan, Adero S. "Driving While Black: Racial Profiling in America." *Law and Psychology Review*, vol. 24, 2000, pp. 127–138. The paper argues that the support of police pretext stops by the Supreme Court has given legitimacy to racial profiling and argues that police departments should develop their own policy to end such stops.

Kocieniewski, David, and Robert Hanley. "Racial Profiling Was Routine, New Jersey Finds." *New York Times*, November 28, 2000, p. A1. Reports on the conclusion of an investigation by the New Jersey state attorney general that troopers had used racial profiling in stopping minority drivers on interstate highways. The attorney general said that despite success of the troopers in crime fighting, the racial profiling methods "had been a social disaster, and had inflicted a terrible scourge on the state's minority residents, who were stopped and searched solely because of their skin color."

Leavy, Walter. "Keep Your Head to the Sky." *Ebony*, vol. 55, September 2000, p. 24. This article notes how the drug war has concentrated on minority communities but ignored drug use in affluent neighborhoods and workplaces.

Montgomery, Lori. "Racial Profiling in Maryland Defies Definition—or Solution." *Washington Times*, May 16, 2001, p. A1. The article compares the reaction to traffic stop statistics in Maryland of the representatives of the American Civil Liberties Union, who see evidence of racial profiling, and by state police officials, who do not. Despite a Maryland law to prohibit race-based vehicle stops, minorities are still disproportionately subject to police action. The difficulty comes in determining if race differences in stops reflect racial profiling or legitimate enforcement of the law by police.

Most, Doug. "Shot through the Heart: Four Basketball Players Shot by New Jersey State Troopers." *Sports Illustrated*, vol. 93, July 10, 2000, pp. 86–97. This story provides background information on the four young African-American men who, while driving home from a basketball camp in North Carolina through New Jersey, were stopped by police for no apparent reason and shot when the van began to move backward. As a result of the incident, the officers were indicted and the New Jersey State Police came under criticism for continued racial profiling.

Perry, Tony. "San Diego Traffic Stops Higher for Blacks, Latinos; Activists Say Problem Is Greater Than the Numbers Show: Police Chief Acknowledges Some Officers Are Not Filling Out Forms." *Los Angeles Times*, January 14, 2003, part 2, p. 7. The police chief in San Diego, a city that has done more than most to gather data on racial profiling, must face two questions on the basis of data: The higher percentages of blacks and Latinos stopped suggests the use of racial profiling, and the drop-off in the number of reports suggests officers are not accurately recording the information. The story reveals the difficulty in using traffic-stop data to determine the extent of racial profiling and police discrimination.

Peterson, Iver, and David M. Halfbinger. "New Jersey Agrees to Pay $13 Million in Profiling Suit." *New York Times*, February 3, 2001, p. A1. Describes the settlement reached by the New Jersey attorney general and four African-American men shot at by police during an incident of apparent racial profiling. The state does not admit guilt but provides a large award. The attorney general also says he will drop other cases in which defendants claim they were stopped through the use of racial profiling. A police organization criticizes the settlement, while civil rights groups approve of the action.

Putta, Kishan Kumar, Errin Haines, and Akilah Johnson. "Alleged Racial Profiling Victims Tell of Stops; Some Who Have Been Pulled Over Say

They Understand Why, But Most Deem It Unfair." *Los Angeles Times*, January 8, 2003, p. 1. In obtaining reactions to a Los Angeles Police Department report that finds blacks and Latinos are disproportionately stopped, this story describes the experience of blacks who believe they have been victims of racial profiling.

Roane, Kit R. A Risky Trip through 'White Man's Pass': Racial Profiling by State Troopers in New Jersey." *U.S. News and World Report*, vol. 130, April 16, 2001, p. 24. Reviews the continuing controversy over racial profiling in New Jersey. Despite efforts by the federal government to require the agency to end racial profiling, critics, including state attorney general John Farmer, note that stops still include a disproportionately high percentage of African Americans and Hispanics. Perhaps state troopers are resisting the reform or perhaps minorities are more likely to violate traffic laws. In any case, the controversy has not disappeared as many had hoped.

Toby, Jackson. "Are Police the Enemy? Racial Profiling in New Jersey." *Society*, vol. 37, May/June, 2000, pp. 38–42. In describing the firing of New Jersey State Police superintendent Carl Williams for stating that it is naive to think race is not an issue in drug trafficking, this article discusses the use and justification for racial profiling.

Webb, Gary. "DWB: Federally-Funded Operation Pipeline Stops High Proportion of Black and Hispanic Motorists Suspected of Drug Trafficking." *Esquire*, vol. 131, April 1999, pp. 118–127. Operation Pipeline has since the early 1990s attempted to arrest so-called mules—people who carry drugs and cash for dealers. The article reviews the record of race-based stops by Operation Pipeline and the complaints lodged against it by minority motorists.

Williams, Patricia. "Road Rage: Racial Profiling Practice by New Jersey State Troopers." *The Nation*, vol. 268, March 22, 1999, p. 10. Discusses the efforts of the Black Ministers Council of New Jersey to stop racial profiling by police.

WEB DOCUMENTS

Bickel, Bill. "Racial Profiling." About.com. Available online. URL: http://crime.about.com/library/blfiles/blprofiling.htm. Posted on January 30, 2002. Describes the shooting of three young black men on the New Jersey Turnpike during an alleged incident of racial profiling and the search of a woman at the Newark, New Jersey, airport because she fit a drug courier profile. The page also includes a poll on racial profiling and links to more detailed stories.

Cable News Network. "Law Enforcement Practice of Racial Profiling under Fire." CNN.com. Available online. URL: http://www.cnn.com/US/9906/

09/race.police.02. Posted on June 9, 1999. An early story about concerns over racial profiling on U.S. highways.

Common Sense for Drug Policy. "Racial Profiling." Common Sense for Drug Policy web site. Available online. URL: http://www.csdp.org/news/profiling.htm. Downloaded in July 2003. This page contains recent news stories relating to racial profiling and drug law enforcement. For example, one story reports on 12 defendants accused of drug crimes who claim the racism of a narcotics officer led to the arrests and charges. The article links use of racial profiling to the war on drugs.

Drug Policy Alliance. "Drugs, Police, and the Law: Challenges to Racial Profiling." Drug Policy Alliance web site. Available online. URL: http://www.drugpolicy.org/law/searchandsei/challengesto/index.cfm. Downloaded in July 2003. Based on its concern over police abuses in the war on drugs, this page describes several legal suits against police use of racial profiling. It also includes links to related pages on race, human rights, and the war on drugs.

Drug Reform Coordination Network. "New Jersey Racial Profiling Archive." Stop the Drug War.org. Available online. URL: http://www.stopthedrugwar.org/njprofiling/#njarchive. Posted on December 15, 2000. The archive available on this web page contains primary documents relating to racial profiling controversies in New Jersey and elsewhere. The documents come from the office of the New Jersey state attorney general, the internal affairs division, and the state patrol. It may be more useful for those doing detailed research than those wanting basic information.

Frontline: Drug Wars. "Thirty Years of America's Drug War: A Chronology." PBS Online. Available online. URL: http://www.pbs.org/wgbh/pages/frontline/shows/drugs/cron. Posted in October 2000. Based on a PBS television show, this web page provides a chronology of important events in the war on drugs. It gives special attention to events involving the efforts to stop the import of drugs from Colombia into the United States but also touches on issues of drug interdiction within the United States.

Harris, David A. "Driving While Black: Racial Profiling on Our Nation's Highways." American Civil Liberties Union Special Report. Available online. URL: http://archive.aclu.org/profiling/report. Posted in June 1999. This early report on racial profiling helped publicize the extent of the problem and the need for corrective action. Both Harris and the American Civil Liberties Union participated in early suits against state police departments for racial profiling.

Lamberth Consulting. "Training Courses." Lamberth Consulting web site. Available online. URL: http://www.lamberthconsulting.com/about_org.asp. Downloaded in July 2003. The web page lists courses on preventing racial profiling for officers, supervisors, executives, and community members. It also offers courses on collecting traffic stop data and obtaining benchmark measures to study racial profiling. The courses aim to help police departments address issues of racially biased policing.

Riley, K. Jack. "Racial Profiling: Lessons from the Drug War." RAND Corporation web site. Available online. URL: http://www.rand.org/publications/randreview/issues/rr.08.02/profiling.html. Posted on August 2002. The author argues that drug profiling did not work because couriers quickly learned to adjust their methods to avoid a profile and because it led to accusations of racial profiling. He also argues, however, that procedures could be developed to use profiling in dealing with terrorism. The key is to use profiling to let people with verified credentials avoid searches rather than to pick out people for special searches. Efforts must be taken as well to prove that the procedures do not result in racial profiling.

Substance Abuse Mental Health Services Administration (SAMHSA). "National Survey on Drug Use and Health." SAMHSA web site. Available online. URL: http://www.samhsa.gov/oas/nhsda.htm. Updated October 28, 2003. Reports the analysis of data from the 2002 national survey of drug use. The data set comes from the response of individuals to questions about their drug activities and may not accurately reflect involvement in serious offending. Still, the figures reveal only small differences across race and ethnic groups in drug use. Opponents of racial profiling conclude from this information that the drug use of minorities does not justify the attention police give to them for drug crimes.

U.S. Drug Enforcement Administration. "Operation Pipeline and Convoy." Available online. U.S. Department of Justice web site. URL: http://www.usdoj.gov/dea/programs/pipecon.htm. Downloaded in June 2003. The Drug Enforcement Administration (DEA) describes its controversial drug interdiction program. The official statement denies use of race or ethnicity in profiling but the program has nonetheless been accused in the past of violating this stricture. In any case, the web page offers a brief history of the program, its goal to stop drivers carrying smuggled drugs across interstate highways, and the training provided to state troopers as part of the program.

CITY POLICING

BOOKS

Bass, Sandra. "Out of Place: Petit Apartheid and the Police," in Dragan Milovanovic and Katheryn K. Russell, eds., *Petit Apartheid in the U.S. Criminal Justice System.* Durham N.C.: Carolina Academic Press, 2001, pp. 43–54. In discussing racial bias in policing, this chapter gives particular attention to quality-of-life policing. It criticizes claims made by advocates of the ability of this form of policing to reduce crime and describes the ways the procedures can lead to harassment of minorities and racial profiling. It also argues that efforts to battle gang activity in particular have led to mistreatment of minorities.

Cohen, John. "Statement," in *Racial Profiling within Law Enforcement Agencies, Hearing before the Subcommittee on the Constitution, Federalism, and Property Rights of the Committee on the Judiciary, United States Senate, One Hundred Sixth Congress, Second Session.* Washington, D.C.: U.S. Government Printing Office, March 30, 2000, pp. 70–76. This testimony of the director of the Community Crime Fighting Project discusses how modernizing police departments can reduce crime without resorting to racial profiling. The key is for police to emphasize the use of technology, focus on high-risk offenders, strengthen police training and accountability, and concentrate on hot spots. Attention to community policing methods will make racial profiling unnecessary. The testimony also supports legislation to collect traffic stop data and to end racial profiling.

Davis, Kelvin R. *Driving While Black: Coverup.* Cincinnati: Interstate International Publishing, 2001. Along with arguing that he was illegally arrested on the basis of racial profiling, the author offers background information and strong criticism of the practice.

FBI. *Crime in the United States 2000: Uniform Crime Reports.* Washington, D.C.: Federal Bureau of Investigation, 2000. Available online. URL: http://www.fbi.gov/ucr/cius_00/contents.pdf. 2002. Downloaded in July 2003. The figures collated by the FBI from local police agencies across the nation reveal high rates of arrest of minority group members. Some believe the high arrest rates are biased by police discrimination and exaggerate minority involvement in crime. Others believe they accurately reflect criminal activity and help justify racial profiling in crime prevention and investigation.

Human Rights Watch. *Shielded from Justice.* New York: Human Rights Watch, 1998. Available online. URL: http://www.hrw.org/reports98/police/uspo16.htm. Posted in June 1998. Critical of aggressive or quality-of-life policing and its tendency to promote racial profiling, this book includes a list of recommendations to deal with the problem and information on police practices in major cities in the United States.

Serrie, Jonathan. "Seattle Cops, Wary of Race-Profiling Accusations, Cutting Back on Minority Arrests," in *S. 989: The End of Racial Profiling Act of 2001, Hearing before the Subcommittee on the Constitution, Federalism, and Property Rights of the Committee on the Judiciary, United States Senate, One*

Hundred Seventh Congress, First Session. Washington, D.C.: U.S. Government Printing Office, August 1, 2001, p. 123. This story finds that Seattle police officers, who fear that their use of aggressive policing will lead to accusations of racial profiling, have cut back on the number of arrests they make. Such actions may indicate the adverse effect on police of criticisms about racial profiling.

Sharpton, Al. *Al on America.* New York: Kensington Publishing, 2002. This African-American political activist from New York City has taken some controversial stands on issues involving racism, discrimination, and the police. In this book, he defends his positions, lays out his views on the need for political change, and helps make the case for his candidacy in the 2004 Democratic presidential primary. Parts of the book touch on his activities to protest racial profiling and police brutality.

U.S. Commission on Civil Rights. *Police Practices and Civil Rights in New York City.* Washington, D.C.: U.S. Commission on Civil Rights, 2000. Based on 32,000 pages of evidence subpoenaed from the New York City Police Department (NYPD) and publicity about the shooting of Amadou Diallo, this report finds that the NYPD has used procedures that result in racial profiling. It recommends new written policies to prohibit such procedures.

U.S. Department of Justice, Office of Justice Programs, Bureau of Justice Statistics. *Criminal Victimization in the United States, 2001 Statistical Tables.* Washington D.C.: U.S. Department of Justice, 2001. Available online. URL: http://www.ojp.usdoj.gov/bjs/pub/pdf/cvus0102.pdf. Posted on January 1, 2003, p. 28. The data in these tables rely on the survey responses of victims about the offenders who attacked them. They have the advantage of avoiding possible police bias (such as with arrest rates) but have the limitation of relating only to crimes such as rape and assault where victims see offenders and excluding drug crimes. The reported data indicate offending is higher among African Americans than whites and indirectly helps justify police stops of African Americans.

Vaj, Kabzuag, "Statement," in *S. 989: The End of Racial Profiling Act of 2001, Hearing before the Subcommittee on the Constitution, Federalism, and Property Rights of the Committee on the Judiciary, United States Senate, One Hundred Seventh Congress, First Session.* Washington, D.C.: U.S. Government Printing Office, August 1, 2001, pp. 86–89. The cofounder of the Asian Emancipation Project in Madison, Wisconsin, discusses racial profiling of the Hmong (refugees from Southeast Asia). The stories of eight Asians mistreated by the Madison police illustrate how racial profiling can extend to minorities other than African Americans and Hispanics.

Watt, Rodney. "Statement," in *Racial Profiling within Law Enforcement Agencies, Hearing before the Subcommittee on the Constitution, Federalism, and Property Rights of the Committee on the Judiciary, United States Senate, One*

Hundred Sixth Congress, Second Session. Washington, D.C.: U.S. Government Printing Office, March 30, 2000, pp. 50–54. As a patrol officer in the affluent Chicago suburb of Highland Park, Watt observed numerous instances of racial profiling and discrimination. He describes the police department's efforts to keep minorities out of the city's central business district by stopping drivers for minor traffic violations. His experiences depict some particularly serious instances of discrimination by police and justify legislation to help end such practices.

Welter, John. "Statement," in *Racial Profiling within Law Enforcement Agencies, Hearing before the Subcommittee on the Constitution, Federalism, and Property Rights of the Committee on the Judiciary, United States Senate, One Hundred Sixth Congress, Second Session.* Washington, D.C.: U.S. Government Printing Office, March 30, 2000, pp. 44–50. This testimony, based on experiences of Welter, the acting chief of the San Diego Police Department, describes efforts to address racial profiling through data collection and the need for proposed legislation to require national data collection. The statement provides details of how, in San Diego, data collection procedures were implemented, complemented community policing efforts, and added to the budget. In the end, the experience of the San Diego Police Department suggests that community policing can produce a drop in crime without resorting to use of race, ethnic, or national origin profiles.

ARTICLES

Associated Press. "Cincinnati Police Want Community Pact Ended." *Washington Post,* April 30, 2003, p. A8. After interested parties reached an agreement in Cincinnati that, among other things, would end racial profiling, the police union has said it wants out of the agreement. Earlier, the Black United Front dropped out over the pace of reforms. The agreement was reached in response to days of rioting after the shooting of a black youth by a white police officer.

Becker, Gary. "Tough Justice Is Saving Our Inner Cities." *Business Week,* no. 3690, July 17, 2000, p. 26. The author argues that minorities have, despite some instances of police discrimination and violence, benefited greatly from more aggressive police efforts to prevent crime. While police discrimination is wrong, it does not appear widespread. Evidence of racial profiling should show in lower success in finding illegal substances (or hit rates) during stops of blacks than whites. In fact, police find similar percentages of incriminating evidence across both groups.

Butterfield, Fox. "City Police Work Losing Its Appeal and Its Veterans." *New York Times,* July 30, 2001, p. A1. Although it is not always well publicized, police are facing a personnel crisis. This article describes the attrition rate among police, fall in recruitment of new officers, increasing unwillingness of officers to accept senior positions, and difficulty in hiring police chiefs. The problem appears national rather than local but affects major cities more than suburbs and smaller towns. Although the article does not consider this issue, false accusations of racial profiling and the misuse of data to support these accusations would, according to some, contribute to this problem.

Cloud, John. "What's Race Got to Do with It? Shooting of T. Healy and Racial Profiling." *Time*, vol. 158, July 30, 2001, pp. 42–47. The shooting death of a young black man by a police officer in Cincinnati sparked riots and claims of racial profiling. This article describes the actions of the police in the city after the riots and the tensions between police and the African-American community.

Dolan, Maura, and John M. Glionna. "CHP Settles Lawsuit over Claims of Racial Profiling: The Agency Promises Reforms: Officers Will No Longer Pull Over Drivers Based Only on Hunches." *Los Angeles Times*, February 28, 2003, part 1, p. 1. In settling a class-action lawsuit over stopping minority motorists, the California Highway Patrol (CHP) agreed to end traffic stops based solely on hunches, end searches without probable cause, and monitor racial profiling.

Graves, Earl G. "Living While Black." *Black Enterprise*, vol. 29, May 1999, p. 15. This editorial calls for a campaign to stop police harassment of African Americans. Police discrimination shows not only in the well-publicized killing of Amadou Diallo by New York City police officers but is an everyday occurrence faced by black men that deserves the description "living while black."

Hemmens, Craig, and Daniel Levin. "Resistance Is Futile: The Right to Resist Unlawful Arrest in an Era of Aggressive Policing." *Crime and Delinquency*, vol. 46, no. 4, 2002, pp. 472–496. The authors argue that a need remains for the right to resist an unlawful arrest, particularly with the emergence of aggressive policing and racial profiling.

Herbert, Bob. "Hounding the Innocent: Racial Profiling by Police." *New York Times*, June 13, 1999, p. 17. In an editorial column, the author argues that the New York City police under Mayor Giuliani have targeted young black and Hispanic males, "usually without good reason." He cites a claim from the American Civil Liberties Union that almost everyone targeted by police stops is innocent and nonwhite.

Herbert, Bob, and Jeffrey Goldberg. "Police and Racial Profiling." *New York Times Upfront*, September 6, 1999, p. 36. The two writers take opposite sides in presenting the cases for and against police use of racial characteristics in investigations.

Hogan, Wesley. "Cincinnati: Race in the Closed City." *Social Policy*, vol. 32, Winter 2001, pp. 49–54. After riots in Cincinnati over alleged police brutality and racial profiling, the city received much attention about the conflict between police and the minority community. This article blames police and the city government for the problem. By making little effort to improve the conditions of the poor and supporting gentrification, city leaders have contributed to the problem. By increasing their use of violence in response to crime, police have also worsened racial relations. The article argues that activists must protest police treatment and demand economic inequality.

Kelling, George L. "A Policing Strategy New Yorkers Like." *The New York Times*, January 3, 2001, p. A23. Available online. URL: http://www.manhattan-institute.org/html/_nyt-a_policing.htm. Posted on January 3, 2002. One of the early advocates of quality-of-life policing, the author defends it against criticisms that it results in discrimination. He believes that it is popular with New Yorkers because of its effectiveness and fairness in reducing crime.

Noel, Peter. "When Clothes Make the Suspect: Portraits in Racial Profiling." *The Village Voice*, March 21, 2000, p. 46. Available online. URL: http://www.villagevoice.com/issues/0011/noel.php. Posted on March 15–21, 2000. Reports on claims that police use clothing styles, particularly for members of minority groups, as a basis for making stops. Such practices represent a form of racial profiling.

"NYPD Raps: NYPD Launches Hip-Hop Patrol." *New York*, vol. 34, April 30, 2001, p. 13. A new intelligence unit of the New York City Police Department has, according to the article, started to gather information on the cars owned by high-profile hip-hop musicians involved in past run-ins with police. The department denies the existence of such a database. If it exists, it would extend racial profiling to certain African-American lifestyles and cultures.

"'Offensive' Memo on Blacks by White Baltimore Cop Forces Him to Retire." *Jet*, vol. 101, March 25, 2002, p. 21. The story of Maj. Donald Healy, a white Baltimore ex-commander of the department's Northeast District, illustrates, in the words of one state senator, racial profiling at its worst. Healy was forced to retire after a memo he wrote told officers to question all black men at a bus stop where a rape occurred. Superiors in the police department called the memo offensive and illegal.

O'Sullivan, John. "Black and Blue: New York Erupts Over a Race-Tinged Killing—Again." *National Review*, vol. 51, April 19, 1999, pp. 33–34. The author presents a conservative viewpoint on the controversy over the killing of Amadou Diallo by New York City police. He defends the police against charges of racism, commends them for the difficult task of lowering crime rates in the city, and argues for the benefits of stop-and-frisk police procedures.

"Photo of New Jersey's White Governor Frisking Unarmed Black Man Draws Minorities' Criticism: She Won't Apologize: C. T. Whitman." *Jet*, vol. 98, July 31, 2000, pp. 36–37. Several years earlier, a publicity photo showed Christie Todd Whitman, the New Jersey governor, performing a search of an unarmed black suspect while accompanying a police patrol. Minorities criticized the governor for insensitivity, but she insisted the incident had nothing to do with racial profiling or discrimination and has refused to apologize. This story provides the background of the controversy over the photo.

"Photographer Howard Bingham Sues Police over Traffic Stop." *Jet*, vol. 98, July 24, 2000, p. 33. Driving through Manhattan Beach, California, after attending a fund-raising event for President Bill Clinton in Beverly Hills, Bingham was stopped by police. A famed photographer known for his pictures of the boxer Muhammad Ali, he alleges the stop was racially motivated. The police arrested, handcuffed, and jailed him for an expired license, which led Bingham to file a $3 million lawsuit for wrongful arrest.

Randall, Laura. "What Ever Happened To—An Uneasy Calm in a Troubled City: Aftermath of Riot in Cincinnati, Ohio, over Police Shooting." *Time*, vol. 158, December 31, 2001/January 7, 2002, p. 137. The article reviews the outcome after riots in Cincinnati over police brutality and the verdict of not guilty for the officer accused of shooting a young black man (the incident that sparked the riots). It also describes how the city has worked to negotiate a settlement of a racial profiling lawsuit over possible police misbehavior.

Rosen, Jeffrey. "Excessive Force: R. Giuliani's Zero Tolerance Policy." *The New Republic*, vol. 222, April 10, 2000, pp. 24–27. The article criticizes the New York City mayor for his support of zero-tolerance policing tactics. It argues that efforts to enforce laws against minor offenses in order to prevent major offenses have shifted to something more extreme and less effective: Widespread use of search-and-arrest tactics. The zero-tolerance policy has, according to the article, worsened relations with the minority community.

Tabak, Ronald, et al. "The Challenge of Urban Policing." *Fordham Urban Law Review*, vol. 28, 2000, pp. 363–617. This special issue includes articles on a variety of topics such as the broken windows theory, lawsuits, police action, and the causes of the crime drop. The issue also includes a roundtable discussion with William Bratton, former commissioner of the New York City Police Department, and defense attorney Johnnie L. Cochran, Jr.

Weiser, Benjamin. "U.S. Detects Bias in Police Searches." *New York Times*, October 5, 2000, p. A1. The article describes the decision of federal prosecutors to investigate the use of racial profiling by the New York City Police Street Crimes Unit, which was responsible for the death of Amadou Diallo. In reviewing records, prosecutors noted that blacks and Hispanics were disproportionately stopped and searched, and high crime rates in minority neighborhoods could not explain the excess stop-and-search rates.

Wilson, James Q., and George L. Kelling. "Broken Windows." *The Atlantic Monthly*, vol. 249, March 1992, pp. 29–38. Available online. URL: http://www.theatlantic.com/politics/crime/windows.htm. Downloaded in July 2003. This article presents a theory based on the claim that if a window in a building or home is broken and left unrepaired, the rest of the windows will soon be broken. An unrepaired window implies that no one cares and that breaking more windows costs offenders nothing. The argument helped justify quality-of-life policing, which aims to restore order and prevent serious crime by enforcing laws against minor offenses.

Winton, Richard. "Politicians Back Gang Loitering Law." *Los Angeles Times*, February 12, 2003, part 2, p. 12. Concerned about protecting citizens, leaders in Los Angeles have backed "a proposed ordinance that will allow police to arrest loitering street gang members who show an intent to intimidate." Critics worry that the ordinance will give police discretion to use racial profiling in their arrests.

Winton, Richard, and Andrew Blankstein. "Report Says LAPD May Miss Reforms Deadline." *Los Angeles Times*, May 16, 2003, part 2, p. 3. A federal monitor examining the movement of the Los Angeles Police Department toward compliance with a federal consent decree finds the department is making steady progress, but problems could prevent it from reaching its goals by the 2006 deadline. Among the problems, the department has failed to analyze racial profiling data from the last half of 2002 and has been slow to investigate citizen complaints.

WEB DOCUMENTS

Associated Press. "Cincy Profiling Deal OK'd." CBSNews.com. Available online. URL: http://www.cbsnews.com/stories/2002/04/09/national/main505736.shtml. Posted on April 9, 2002. This report describes a lawsuit accusing Cincinnati police of harassing black citizens and the agreement aiming to end racial profiling by the police. A spokesperson for the police states they do not use racial profiling but can accept the terms of the agreement.

Golub, Andrew, et al. "Quality-of-Life Policing, Net Widening, and Crime Specialization." National Criminal Justice Reference Service. Available online. URL: http://www.ncjrs.org/pdffiles1/nij/grants/196674.pdf. Posted on October 3, 2002. This research article considers the relationship between quality-of-life policing and racial profiling. Specifically, it examines how widening the scope of offenses affects the characteristics of persons arrested. Using data on a survey of those arrested in New York City in 1999, the authors find that those arrested for serious offenses do not differ in racial makeup from those arrested for less serious offenses. Since it did not increase minority arrests, the use of quality-of-life policing does not appear to encourage racial profiling.

Hohman, Kimberly. "NYPD Blues: Big Trouble in the Big Apple?" About.com. Available online. URL: http://racerelations.about.com/library/weekly/aa051300a.htm. Posted on May 13, 2000. Summarizes a controversial report of the U.S. Civil Rights Commission accusing the New York City Police Department of using racial profiling. It also lists links to stories about police brutality in the city and the response of Mayor Giuliani to these criticisms.

New York City Police Department. "COMPSTAT Process." NYPD web site. Available online. URL: http://www.nyc.gov/html/nypd/html/chfdept/compstat-process.html. Downloaded in June 2003. In providing background information on successful police efforts to reduce crime in New York City, this web page describes the COMPSTAT process. Along with computerized data on crime location and trends, the process involves weekly problem-solving meetings of commanders. The department views the process as a revolution in the way police agencies are managed and offers a model for other police departments throughout the nation.

IMMIGRATION AND BORDER CONTROL

BOOKS

Andreas, Peter. *Border Games: Policing the U.S.-Mexico Divide.* Ithaca, N.Y.: Cornell University Press, 2001. The book identifies a contradiction between the desire to prevent the smuggling of illegal immigrants, drugs, and goods across the Mexican border and a liberalized trade policy between the United States and Mexico that promotes the movement of goods and people across the border. It then examines the confrontation between border security and immigrants. Efforts at law enforcement—including forms of racial profiling—have had limited effect given the larger forces that promote the desire of Mexicans to come to the United States.

Lin, Ann Chih, and Nicole W. Green, eds. *Immigration.* Washington, D.C.: CQ Press, 2002. Along with a brief discussion of racial profiling on pages

75–76, this book provides an introductory overview of the issues and players involved in the movement of people across our borders.

Martinez, Ruben. *Crossing Over: A Mexican Family on the Migrant Trail.* New York: Metropolitan Books, 2001. This book presents the viewpoint of Mexican immigrants in the battle with border control agents and police to cross into the United States. The author describes the death of three brothers traveling in a truck that crashed when trying to outrace border patrol agents and then travels to their hometown to learn more about the motives of the immigrants. He follows other family members north and discovers how immigrants avoid apprehension and manage to find work and prosper. The book does not address racial profiling directly but depicts the dealings of immigrants with law enforcement agents in the United States.

Nevins, Joseph. *Operation Gatekeeper: The Rise of the 'Illegal Alien' and the Remaking of the U.S.-Mexican Border.* New York: Routledge, 2002. In 1994, the Clinton administration doubled the budget for fences and trained agents along the U.S.-Mexican border between San Diego and Tijuana. Called Operation Gatekeeper, this effort to prevent illegal border crossings faced problems from the start because economic opportunities in the United States for Mexicans were growing. The author argues that, although the program has done little to stem the flow, it may have moderated anti-immigrant feelings.

Tichenor, Daniel J. *Dividing Lines: The Politics of Immigration Control in the United States.* Princeton, N.J.: Princeton University Press, 2002. Focused on battles over immigration policies dating back to the founding of the United States, the book discusses the new forms of the battles in the 1990s. A key to this period is the surge in immigration that, despite new calls for restrictions, has mobilized the growing political power of immigrant groups and prevented strong enforcement of immigration laws. This book provides background information on debates over immigration and enforcement policies that can inform the understanding of controversies over use of racial profiling in immigration control.

Welch, Michael. *Detained: Immigration Laws and the Expanding I.N.S. Jail Complex.* Philadelphia: Temple University Press, 2002. Concerned about anti-immigration sentiments and the detention efforts of the Immigration and Naturalization Service (INS), this book also discusses issues of racial profiling. The larger benefit of the book, however, is its more general critique of efforts to apprehend illegal immigrants.

ARTICLES

Ching, Frank. "Wen Ho Lee: A Witchhunt?" *Far Eastern Economic Review,* vol. 163, January 20, 2000, p. 30. Although initially accused of passing nuclear weapons secrets to China, Wen Ho Lee has pleaded guilty to the minor charge of downloading sensitive materials to a nonsecure computer—an action that happens quite often. The case has received attention as an instance of racial profiling that targets Chinese Americans in investigations of spying. The article opposes such efforts, arguing that suspicion should not be based on ethnicity in investigating nuclear secrets any more than it should in making police stops on highways or streets.

Chua-Eoan, Howard. "Profiles in Outrage: Discrimination Against and Profiling of Asian Americans." *Time*, vol. 156, September 25, 2000, pp. 40–42. The story notes that Asian Americans are subject to racial profiling when treated according to stereotypes that assume disloyalty and lack of commitment to America. The article discusses the experiences with racism and discrimination of a number of high-profile Asian Americans.

Constable, Pamela. "INS Accused of Targeting Latinos in Recent Raids; Activists Speak Out in Wake of Arrests of Suspected Undocumented Workers at Bethesda Café." *Washington Post*, February 5, 1998, p. D3. After workers at a café were questioned, handcuffed, and taken away by Immigration and Naturalization Service (INS) agents, civil rights groups protested. They say agents single out Latinos, but representatives of the INS claim that they check all employees of a business.

Gray, Katti. "The Whistle-Blower: Customs Inspector C. Harris Challenges Agency for Racial Profiling of Black Women." *Essence*, vol. 31, February 2001, pp. 148–150. Based on the experiences of a customs inspector, this story describes the racial profiling of black women and the intrusive searches they had to endure. The accusations of Harris led to congressional investigations, a class-action suit, and reforms in the U.S. Customs Service.

Huie, Nancy. "Search and Seizure: Racial Profiling by U.S. Customs Service Agents." *Black Enterprise*, vol. 29, July 1999, p. 162. Reviews the accusations made against customs agents who search a disproportionate number of black women, and the response of politicians to the accusations. The accusations will lead to reform of the agency's practices.

Isikoff, Michael. "A Question of Profiling." *Newsweek*, vol. 136, September 18, 2000, p. 68. In describing the case of Edward T. Fei, who was investigated for spying, this article discusses charges of bias and racial profiling against Asian Americans.

Lichtblau, Eric. "U.S. Report Faults the Roundup of Illegal Immigrants after 9/11." *New York Times*, June 3, 2002, p. A1. This story summarizes the criticisms made of the Justice Department in a government report about the detainment of illegal aliens and the effort to protect homeland security.

McCollum, Sean. "Bias of War." *New York Times Upfront*, vol. 134, November 12, 2001, p. 14. The article reviews the movement of Japanese

Americans to relocation centers with barbed-wire fences and the negative reactions to the internment decades later. It cites the opinion of Paul Osaki of the Japanese American Cultural and Community Center in San Francisco that Japanese Americans, given their past treatment, must work to prevent the same treatment of Arab Americans.

Peretz, Martin. "Entry Level." *The New Republic*, vol. 225, October 15, 2001, pp. 20–24. In speculating about the future, the writer notes that concerns about terrorism will lead to racial profiling and examines the way immigration procedures will be tightened as a result of the terrorist attacks. Conflict between natives and immigrants could become more important than conflict between blacks and whites.

Scheer, Robert. "The Spy Who Wasn't: W. H. Lee." *The Nation*, vol. 271, October 2, 2000, pp. 4–5. This liberal columnist argues that the prosecution of Dr. Lee for giving nuclear weapons secrets to the Chinese had no basis in fact but resulted from political disputes over ties of members of the Clinton administration to China. Lee's treatment resulted more from racial profiling than evidence of treason.

Streisand, Betsy. "L.A. Chooses Sides: Cops Vs. Aliens: Illegal Mexicans Beaten by Deputies." *U.S. News and World Report*, vol. 120, April 15, 1996, pp. 10–11. An incident involving the beating of two illegal aliens by Riverside County sheriff's deputies raises issues about the relations between police and illegal immigrants. The incident intensifies conflict between those concerned about immigration in California and those concerned about police brutality.

Tharp, Mike, and David Whitman. "Hispanics' Tale of Two Cities." *U.S. News and World Report*, vol. 112, May 25, 1992, pp. 40–41. The article contrasts the experience of Mexican immigrants in East Los Angeles with that of immigrants from Guatemala, Salvador, and other Central American nations in south central Los Angeles. It suggests that the Mexican-American community gets along better with police than the other Latino communities and participated less in recent riots.

Verea, Monica. "Closing the Borders: U.S.-Mexico Migration Debate." *World Press Review*, vol. 49, April 2002, pp. 10–11. Concerned about anti-immigrant backlash brought on by the terrorist attacks, the article contends that the government and immigration critics need to recognize that work-seeking immigrants have little similarity to terrorists.

Young, Cathy. "Guilty by Association." *Reason*, vol. 34, March 2003, pp. 18–19. The article criticizes the tendency, especially among those with anti-immigration views, to confuse immigrants with terrorists. Policy making should keep the two issues separate, avoid profiles of terrorists that include immigration status, and offer opportunities to those who come to this country for freedom and a better life.

WEB DOCUMENTS

Bustos, Sergio. "New Law Will Mean Closer Monitoring of Foreign Visitors." Gannett News Service. Available online. URL: http://www.gannettonline.com/gns/911/feature1.htm. Downloaded in June 2003. Draws out the implications of laws passed after terrorist attacks and considers the potential of the new laws to produce racial profiling.

Nixon Center. "Profiling: Does It Make Good Immigration Policy?" Nixon Center web page. Available online. URL: http://www.nixoncenter.org/publications/Program%20Briefs/PBrief%202003/030503profiling.htm. Posted on March 5, 2003. This brief report summarizes a longer discussion of the pros and cons of using profiling to deal with the problem of illegal immigration.

Weinstein, Harvey, Michael Finnegan, and Teresa Watanabe, "Racial Profiling Gains Support as Search Tactic," *Los Angeles Times*, September 2, 2001. Available online. URL: http://www.latimes.com/news/nationworld/nation/la-092401racial.story. Posted on September 21, 2001. In considering racial profiling issues in regard to immigration from Mexico and more recently with regard to the entrance of terrorists into the nation, this article examines changes in opinions and policies. It provides a helpful overview of contemporary debates and legal opinions.

TERRORISM

BOOKS

Brill, Steven. *After: How America Confronted the September 12 Era.* New York: Simon and Schuster, 2003. This book offers a day-by-day chronicle of the U.S. response to the events of September 11, 2001. It considers the actions not only of political leaders and interest groups but also of individuals victimized by the attacks and involved in border patrol and customs. Issues of balancing civil rights protection—including freedom from racial profiling—versus national security appear throughout the narrative.

Cole, Richard, and James X. Dempsey. *Terrorism and the Constitution: Sacrificing Civil Liberties in the Name of National Security.* New York: New Press, 2002. The authors criticize the efforts of the government to fight terrorism in ways that limit the civil rights of the population. The book reviews the history of such efforts dating back to the 1950s, but the Anti-Terrorism Act of 1996 and the USA PATRIOT Act in 2001 come in for particular criticism, as does the use of racial profiling methods in investigating possible terrorists. The authors make recommendations about how the United States should deal with terrorist threats without giving the federal government unchecked powers.

Corrigan, Katie. "Profiling Systems Violate Individuals' Privacy Rights," in *Profiling for Public Safety: Rational or Racist, Hearing Before the Subcommittee on Aviation of the Committee on Transportation and Infrastructure House of Representatives, One Hundred Seventh Congress, Second Session.* Washington, D.C.: U.S. Government Printing Office, February 27, 2002, pp. 38–48. In supporting the author's testimony before Congress, this document lays out the case against use of national origin in airport screening. A legal counsel for the American Civil Liberties Union, which has been active in its opposition to racial profiling, the author extends the case to current debates over stopping terrorist activities. She argues that such practices in the airport would be both ineffective and immoral.

Gertz, Bill. *Breakdown: How America's Intelligence Failures Led to September 11.* Washington, D.C.: Regnery, 2002. This book describes the mistakes and blunders in "the most damaging intelligence failure since Pearl Harbor." The author criticizes intelligence agencies such as the CIA and FBI for focusing on budget increases and bureaucratic power rather than effectiveness and cooperation. Reflecting the problems described in the book, the FBI failed to react to reports of Arab men, some with terrorist ties, enrolling in flight schools. This failure resulted in part because of concerns about ethnic profiling.

Malkin, Michelle. *Invasion: How America Still Welcomes Terrorists, Criminals, and Other Foreign Menaces to Our Shores.* Washington, D.C.: Regnery, 2002. Blaming the September 11 terrorist attacks in part on lax immigration control, the author harshly criticizes the failure of border control agencies and politicians to enforce immigration laws. She believes proper screening in airports is essential and should not be misdirected by concerns about racial profiling. In fact, she argues that immigrant profiling is a simple and necessary component of any rational security system.

Ron, Rafi. "Remarks," in *Profiling for Public Safety: Rational or Racist, Hearing before the Subcommittee on Aviation of the Committee on Transportation and Infrastructure House of Representatives, One Hundred Seventh Congress, Second Session.* Washington, D.C.: U.S. Government Printing Office, February 27, 2002, pp. 62–64. The remarks of Ron, former chief of security for the Israeli Airport Authority, provide a perspective on airport screening from outside the United States. He argues that screening must involve more than X-rays for luggage and metal detectors for passengers. It should also include interviews of some passengers about their travel plans, travel history, and recent residences. He further suggests that procedures can be developed to obtain profiles relevant to terrorism that do not involve racial discrimination.

Turley, Jonathan. "Aviation Security and Passenger Profiling at United States Airports," in *Profiling for Public Safety: Rational or Racist, Hearing before the Subcommittee on Aviation of the Committee on Transportation and Infrastructure House of Representatives, One Hundred Seventh Congress, Second Session.* Washington, D.C.: U.S. Government Printing Office, February 27, 2002, pp. 65–79. In testimony before Congress, the George Washington University law professor reviews legal precedents that—if properly specified to meet constitutional standards—would allow the use of race, ethnicity, or national origin in airport screening. The author urges Congress to consider airport screening legislation that would balance the need for national security with the rights of individuals to be free from unreasonable search and seizure.

ARTICLES

Ahmad, Muneer. "Homeland Insecurities: Racial Violence the Day after September 11." *Social Text,* vol. 20, Fall 2002, pp. 101–115. This article views violence against Arabs, Muslims, and South Asians after September 11 as a continuation of oppression of minorities in the United States. It illustrates the argument by describing similarities in treatment of Arab Americans to that of African Americans and Hispanics.

Braber, Liam. "Korematsu's Ghost: A Post–September 11th Analysis of Race and National Security." *Villanova Law Review,* vol. 47, June 2002, pp. 451–490. This article considers constitutional issues related to profiling by country of origin during times of national emergency. In so doing, it examines a case relating to the internment of Japanese during World War II.

Cole, David. "Blind Sweeps Return." *The Nation,* vol. 276, January 13–20, 2003, p. 5. The author accuses U.S. Attorney General John Ashcroft of using the war against terrorism to round up Arab and Muslim men. He terms the program of detaining these men under immigration charges as ethnic profiling because it targets those innocent of involvement with terrorism. Such efforts actually harm the fight against terrorism by alienating citizens who could help.

Derbyshire, John. "Racial Profiling, Burning Hotter." *National Review,* vol. 52, October 15, 2001, pp. 43–44. Building on his earlier article, "In Defense of Racial Profiling," Derbyshire considers debates over racial profiling in regard to screening of Arab and Arab-American passengers in airports. He believes that, given group differences in behavior, profiling is a useful (although not perfect) tool. "So long as the authorities treat everyone with courtesy and apologize to the inconvenienced innocent, racial profiling is a practical and perfectly sensible tool for preventing crime and terrorism. To those who claim ethnic profiling is based on false stereotypes, the author replies that the photograph of the leader of the September 11 attacks, Mohamed Atta, looked exactly like his mental conception of an Arab terrorist."

Dreyfus, Robert. "Spying on Ourselves: Danger of Homeland-Security Team of J. Ashcroft and T. Ridge Building a Surveillance State." *Rolling Stone*, no. 892, March 28, 2002, pp. 31–33. The author sees efforts to protect the United States from a terrorist threat as directed against political opponents and dependent on racial profiling. He strongly criticizes legislation that gives the federal government such powers and the Bush administration for use of the powers.

Hope, Lori. "Did I Save Lives or Engage in Profiling? Alerting Flight Attendants to a Suspicious-Looking Passenger." *Newsweek*, vol. 139, April 1, 2002, p. 12. The writer alerted flight attendants on an airplane about a "suspicious-looking" passenger but has doubts about whether she in fact based her concerns on stereotypes and racial profiling. The title reflects the dilemma police and security agents face: How should they balance the need to protect the public with the need to protect the rights of members of certain race, ethnic, and national-origin groups?

Krauthammer, Charles. "The Case for Profiling: The Expansion of Profiling since September 11." *Newsweek*, vol. 159, March 18, 2002, p. 104. Calling random searches of airline passengers "an unnecessary farce," the author notes that such searches make a clearly false assumption: Suicidal terrorism comes equally from all gender, ethnicity, age, and religious groups. He advocates airport checks based at least partly on demographic characteristics.

Lewin, Tamar. "Cleared after Terror Sweep, Trying to Get His Life Back." *New York Times*, December 28, 2001, p. A1. This article tells the story of Nacer Fathi Mustafa, who was held in jail for 67 days for allegedly altering his passport. The arrest occurred on September 15, 2001, just a few days after the terrorist attacks on the United States. Mustafa was eventually found not to have altered his passport (the lamination had simply come loose). The story describes his efforts to recover legal costs for his case and restore relations with his neighbors.

Lowry, Richard. "Profiles in Cowardice." *National Review*, vol. 54, January 28, 2002, pp. 32–36. *Cowardice* in the title refers to the unwillingness of politicians to risk criticism for recognizing a clear fact: Modern terrorism requires profiling of travelers from Arab countries. The author argues that the background of terrorists makes such profiling a matter of common sense.

Polakow-Suransky, Sasha. "Flying While Brown: Must Arab Men Be Racially Profiled?" *American Prospect*, vol. 12, November 19, 2001, pp. 14–16. The answer to the title's question is, in short, no. By the author's count, 12 brown-skinned men have been removed from U.S. flights since the September 11 terrorist attacks simply because they were thought to be from the Middle East. To avoid these mistakes and the use of racial profiling in general, Americans need more education about Islamic and South Asian cultures.

Quindlen, Anna. "Armed with Only a Neutral Lipstick: State of Airport Security Measures to Prevent Terrorist Acts." *Newsweek*, vol. 139, May 18, 2002, p. 72. The writer sees flaws in randomly searching airline passengers, including those who are not the faintest risk to security, but also believes that inconveniencing and even humiliating innocent Arabs is wrong and ineffective. She calls for a middle ground between random screening and screening based only on ethnicity and race.

"Racism Allegations with Airport Profiling Prompt Justice Department to Examine Computerized Profiling System." *Jet*, vol. 92, October 13, 1997, p. 15. Increasing complaints about intensive screening of minorities at airports led the Justice Department to examine the computerized profiling system. The results of the study will show no evidence of race, ethnic, or national-origin discrimination in the system.

Risen, James. "FBI Told of Worry over Flight Lessons before Sept. 11." *New York Times*, May 4, 2002, p. A10. This story examines the failure of the FBI to follow up on leads that Arab terrorists were preparing an action involving airplanes. It mentions, as one source of the failure, the concerns of the agency that investigating the Arab men might lead to criticisms for ethnic profiling.

Satchell, Michael. "Everyone Empty Your Pockets? State of Airport Security Measures to Prevent Terrorist Acts." *U.S. News and World Report*, vol. 132, April 1, 2002, pp. 18–21. In discussing debates over profiling at airports, the article describes the procedures used effectively for several decades in Israel. Israel's system identifies high-threat travelers on the basis of watch lists as well as ethnic background. The United States, however, may be less willing to adopt these procedures given opposition to other forms of racial profiling. Also, some believe that terrorists identify the profiles and avert them.

Smith, Angie. "Measure Challenges Racial Profiling at Airports." *Houston Chronicle*, March 7, 2003, p. 35. Available online. URL: http://www.chron.com/cs/CDA/ssistory.mpl/special/03/legislature/1808085. Posted on March 7, 2003. This news story describes legislation proposed in Texas to impose criminal penalties on airport security screeners who use racial profiling. The article discusses the applicability of state law to federal airport screeners but otherwise emphasizes that the proposed legislation reflects opposition to racial profiling in all forms, including airport screening. The backers of the bill claim that African Americans, like Arab Americans, are subject to extra screening at airports.

Steinberg, Jacques. "U.S. Has Covered 200 Campuses to Check Up on Mideast Students." *New York Times,* November 12, 2001, p. A1. The article describes efforts of federal investigators to obtain information on college students. Law enforcement officials' attention to campuses in their antiterrorism actions pits goals of security with campus freedom from racial profiling.

Taylor, Stuart, Jr. "The Case for Using Racial Profiling at Airports." *National Journal,* vol. 33, September 22, 2001, p. 2877. Available online. URL: http://www.theatlantic.com/politics/nj/taylor2001-09-25.htm. Posted on September 25, 2001. The author has written in opposition to use of racial profiling on the nation's highways but in this article presents arguments in favor of the practice at airports. He believes that the older forms of racial profiling too often end up as police harassment of minorities. Use of profiles involving ethnicity and national origin at airports not only aims to stop more serious criminal actions but correctly recognizes the link between radical Islam and terrorism. Airport profiling should be done respectfully and politely, and should be combined with the search for other indicators of suspicious activity, but it still needs to be done in a way that protects passengers from terrorist violence.

Telhami, Shibley. "Arab and Muslim America." *Brookings Review,* vol. 20, Winter 2002, pp. 14–15. In describing the composition of the Arab-American community at a time of concern about terrorism and profiling, this article argues that the community differs in many ways from common assumptions. Most Arab Americans are not Muslim and most Muslim Americans come from Africa or South Asia rather than the Middle East. It also appears that government support for Arab-American communities has defused hostility of mainstream America toward the group.

Verhovek, Sam Howe. "Americans Give in to Racial Profiling." *New York Times,* September 23, 2001, p. A1. Americans, who generally believe that racial profiling of black drivers by police is wrong, now must reconsider their opinions in light of terrorist activities of Middle Eastern men. The article describes the ambivalent attitudes of Americans about the issue after the events of September 11.

Vibig, Peter. "Guilty of Looking Arab." *New York Times Upfront,* vol. 134, November 12, 2001, p. 13. In addressing debates over screening of Arabs in airports, the author reviews the history of racial profiling in the United States and considers differing opinions on the value of the practice.

Ward, Janet. "Police Departments Balk at Ashcroft's Request." *American City and County,* vol. 117, January 2002, p. 4. This brief article focuses on the reaction of police officers in Portland, Oregon, to a request by U.S.

Attorney General John Ashcroft for aid in homeland security efforts. The request involves interviewing persons that the federal government has reason to believe could be involved in terrorist activities. The local police officers worry that the interviews involve racial profiling and ask intrusive questions of a personal nature. Other city governments and police departments have opposed the request from the federal government.

"Where Gumshoes Fear to Tread." *The Economist*, vol. 363, June 1, 2002, p. 34. This brief article from a magazine published in Britain describes the dilemma Americans face in dealing with the terrorist events of September 11. On one hand, Americans deeply dislike the idea of the government spying on them and discriminating against minority groups. On the other hand, the failure of the FBI to investigate the terrorist pilots before the attacks because of concerns about racial profiling leads them to wonder if changes in security and attitudes toward racial profiling are needed. This dilemma appears in controversies over new homeland security laws and their administration by the U.S. Department of Justice.

Williams, Patricia J. "Better Safe? The Expression of Profiling since September 11." *The Nation*, vol. 274, March 11, 2002, p. 9. This article expresses concern about the possible emergence of a new international, militarized police force after the September 11 attacks. This police force will have increased power to use profiling, a practice that, given its potential for abuse, should concern travelers.

Web Documents

Al-Arian, Abdullah. "Summer Storm—Experiencing Racial Profiling." U-Wire. Available online. URL: http://www.uwire.com/content/topops092701003.html. Posted on September 27, 2001. While working as an intern, this young Arab American was part of a group invited to the White House for a meeting on President George W. Bush's policy initiatives. Once there, however, he was told by a Secret Service agent that he had to leave. The author tells about his reactions and those of the media to being racially profiled.

American Civil Liberties Union. "Keep America Safe and Free." Available online. URL: http://www.aclu.org/SafeandFree.cfm?11765&c=206. Downloaded in June 2003. The American Civil Liberties Union (ACLU) has opposed most of the actions of the Bush administration and the Department of Justice under Attorney General John Ashcroft that aim to apprehend and detain potential terrorists. The result of administration policies has, according to the ACLU, violated the civil liberties of citizens and immigrants, undermined enforcement of civil rights laws, and encouraged use of racial profiling. This page offers a strongly negative response to homeland security efforts.

Bloom, Richard. "Racial Profiling: Should It Be Used for Aviation Security?" Embry-Riddle Aeronautical University. Available online. URL: http://comm.db.erau.edu/leader/fall99/perspec.html. Posted on December 23, 1999. An overview of research in psychology points out that profiles can be inaccurate and even under the best of circumstances need to be continually revised.

Cable News Network. "Airlines, Passengers Confront Racial Profiling." CNN.com. Available online. URL: http://www.cnn.com/2001/ TRAVEL/ NEWS/10/03/rec.airlines.profiling/index.html. Posted on October 3, 2001. This news story summarizes the reactions of Arab Americans and Arab-American civil rights groups to incidents of racial profiling on airlines. It notes that the airlines have denounced racial profiling, but stories about several Arab-American travelers removed from their planes contradict the airline claims.

Colb, Sherry F. "The New Face of Racial Profiling: How Terrorism Affects the Debate." FindLaw's Writ—Legal Commentary. Available online. URL: http://writ.news.findlaw.com/colb/20011010.html. Posted on October 10, 2001. Worried that terrorist concerns might lead police to rely more on racial profiling, the author defines and criticizes the practice. She also describes some court cases relevant to the issue.

Harris, David A. "'Flying While Arab,' Immigration, Issues, and Lessons from the Racial Profiling Controversy." Profiles in Injustice: Why Racial Profiling Cannot Work. Available online. URL: http://www.profilesininjustice.com/images/02_flyingwhilearab.pdf. Posted on October 12, 2001. Critical of the use of racial profiling in other circumstances, the author of this brief testimony extends his concerns to the potential for renewed abuse of the practice in the aftermath of the terrorist attacks. He believes that, during times of national threat, the tendency to abuse civil rights becomes strongest and the stereotyping of a whole group on the basis of a few members becomes common. Yet, because group membership poorly predicts behavior, whether in regard to drug distribution or terrorism, the use of race, ethnicity, and national origin as a source of police investigation should be prevented.

"Harvard Study Examines Trade-Offs of Civil Liberties to Reduce Terrorism Risk." *Harvard University Gazette.* Available online. URL: http://www.news.harvard.edu/gazette/2003/03.20/10-racial.html. Posted on March 20, 2003. A survey examines support for selective racial profiling in airports relative to support for the slower waiting times needed to examine all persons. The survey makes explicit the costs in terms of safety and inconvenience that come from protecting civil rights and avoiding use of race, ethnicity, and national origin in any form during airport screening.

Jacinto, Leela. "Flying While Arab: Profiling May Be a Dirty Word, But Some Say Targeting Certain Ethnic Groups Is a Good Thing." ABCNEWS.com. Available online. URL: http://abcnews.go.com/sections/world/DailyNews/visa020814.html. Posted on August 14, 2002. Along with telling the stories of persons subject to airport profiling soon after the events of September 11, this article describes the benefits and costs of new efforts to prevent terrorist hijacking of airplanes.

Leadership Conference on Civil Rights. "Wrong Then, Wrong Now: Racial Profiling before and after September 11, 2001." Civilrights.org. Available online. URL: http://www.civilrights.org/publications/reports/racial_profiling. Posted on February 27, 2003. This report compares traditional street-level racial profiling with profiling of Arabs, Muslims, and South Asians after the September 11 terrorist attacks, arguing that both practices, despite their apparent differences, are wrong. It reviews the evidence that traditional profiling is both widespread and contrary to American values. Rather than disappearing, the practice may extend to new groups associated in the minds of many with terrorism. The report calls for a ban on racial and ethnic profiling of any type.

Lydersen, Kari. "War Brings Boom in Racial Profiling." AlterNet.org. Available online. URL: http://www.alternet.org/story.html?StoryID=15517. Posted on March 31, 2003. Just as the government has come to recognize that stopping minorities on the highway is wrong, new tendencies to use ethnic profiling in the fight against terrorism have emerged. This article describes incidents of both types of profiling and argues that profiling has many negative consequences.

Siggins, Peter. "Racial Profiling in an Age of Terrorism." Markkula Center for Applied Ethics, Santa Clara University, Available online. URL: http://www.scu.edu/ethics/publications/ethicalperspectives/profiling.html. Posted on March 12, 2002. As chief deputy attorney general for California, the author expresses concern that after the September 11 attacks, law enforcement agencies may feel pressure to cast their net too wide in looking for terrorists. Although it may appear that the world has changed because of the terrorist attacks, the need to protect civil liberties remains, according to Siggins. To avoid ethnic profiling, all citizens, rather than just those with Middle Eastern backgrounds, should prepare to face more government intrusion and intensive searches.

DATA AND ANALYSIS ISSUES

Books

Cleary, Jim. *Racial Profiling Studies in Law Enforcement: Issues and Methodology.* St. Paul, Minn.: Minnesota Research Department, House of Representatives, 2000. This report discusses definitions of racial profiling, justifications for racial profiling, data collection methodologies, potential uses of the data, and challenges facing law enforcement agencies in dealing with the problem. It gives special attention to issues facing lawmakers and policymakers.

Langan, Patrick A. *Contacts between Police and the Public: Findings from the 1999 National Survey.* Washington, D.C.: U.S. Department of Justice, Office of Justice Programs, 2001. This report summarizes survey results on the perceptions of individuals about their contacts with police. It provides much detail on the characteristics of each stop and the public's views on racial profiling, unjustified stops, and excessive force. The vast majority of persons (92 percent) experiencing threatened or actual use of force said the police acted improperly. The data show higher rates of police stops of blacks but cannot determine if police stops are warranted or not.

McMahon, Joyce, et al. *How to Correctly Collect and Analyze Racial Profiling Data: Your Reputation Depends on It.* Washington, D.C.: U.S. Department of Justice, Office of Community Oriented Policing Services, 2002. As part of giving technical assistance to four police agencies—those of Baltimore, Phoenix, Chattanooga, and St. Paul—on how to collect racial profiling data, the authors report on their literature review and evaluation of planned data methodologies. The report criticizes overly simple methodologies but finds little consensus among parties involved in the racial profiling controversy on how to proceed. Despite these problems, the report makes several recommendations for police agencies to follow.

Minnesota Department of Public Safety. *Recommendations on Racial Profiling Data Collection: Final Report of the Workgroup.* St. Paul, Minn.: Minnesota Department of Public Safety, 2000. Minnesota addressed concerns about the use of racial profiling with an effort to set up guidelines for data collection. The guidelines include contracting to set up, review, and analyze data.

Ramirez, Deborah, Jack McDevitt, and Amy Farrell. *A Resource Guide on Racial Profiling Data Collection Systems: Promising Practices and Lessons Learned.* Washington, D.C.: U.S. Department of Justice, 2000. Written as part of a project funded by the Department of Justice, this short monograph considers in some detail—but clear language—how to gather data on traffic stops. In so doing, it briefly reviews the debates over racial profiling, describes case study experiences in gathering and analyzing data, and makes recommendations for collecting additional traffic stop data. It does not, however, solve all the benchmark problems required for accurate interpretation of the results.

ARTICLES

Barlow, David E., and Melissa Hickman Barlow. "Racial Profiling: A Survey of African American Officers." *Police Quarterly*, vol. 5. no. 3, 2002, pp. 334–358. More than two-thirds of 167 African-American police officers in Milwaukee, Wisconsin, say in a survey that they have been the object of racial profiling sometime during their life. The authors argue that the views about racial profiling of these police officers, who are generally supportive of crime control and investigative procedures, cannot be easily dismissed and urge administrators to take action to end the practice.

Buerger, Michael E., and Amy Farrell. "The Evidence of Racial Profiling: Interpreting Documented and Unofficial Sources." *Police Quarterly*, vol. 5, no. 3, 2002, pp. 272–305. This essay reviews four major court cases that established racial profiling as an important public problem and the debate over use of the practices that has resulted from the cases. In discussing the issue, it makes a distinction between racial profiling due to the willful misconduct of individual police officers and unintentional racial profiling based on the existence of cultural stereotypes.

Eisenmen, Russell. "Demographic Profiling." *Policy Evaluation*, vol. 7, Summer 2001, pp. 4–11. This study of how African-American and white children are assigned for special academic help and health treatment extends the usual topic of racial profiling—police stops—to schools. The evidence presented shows that African-American children in grades one through four are seen as having serious academic and physical health problems more often than white children. The author concludes that this form of racial profiling occurs early in the lives of children and contributes to racial inequality later in life.

Engel, Robin Shepard, Jennifer M. Calnon, and Thomas J. Bernard. "Theory and Racial Profiling: Shortcomings and Future Directions in Research." *Justice Quarterly*, vol. 19, June 2002, pp. 249–273. This article reviews research on racial profiling and criticizes the methods and conclusions. It also offers a framework to understand the explanations of racial profiling. The details of the theoretical framework are necessarily abstract, but the review of previous studies usefully organizes the empirical research on racial profiling.

Feldstein, Dan. "City's Plan to Probe Racial Profiling Flawed. Some HPD Officers Ignore Form." *Houston Chronicle*, April 15, 2001, p. A21. Available online. URL: http://www.kpoa.org/news1.htm. Posted on April 15, 2001. Despite attempts in 1999 by Houston mayor Lee Brown to require Houston Police Department officers to document every traffic stop they make, the effort has, according to the article, faced problems and revealed the difficulties of implementing a policy to measure racial profiling. A high error rate in recording information and incomplete forms mar the process.

Fetto, John. "The Usual Suspects."*American Demographics*, vol. 24, June 2002, p. 14. This brief article describes the results of a survey of the

American public (done both over the phone and online) concerning racial profiling. In addition to asking general questions about support for racial profiling, the survey probes the respondents about use of the practice in more specific circumstances. The results present a more nuanced, and sometimes conflicting, picture of American attitudes. For example, a near majority opposes racial profiling in any circumstance, but a clear majority approve of the use of racial profiling to combat terrorism.

"Half of All Black Men Are Victims of Racial Profiling, Poll Finds." *Jet*, vol. 100, July 9, 2001, p. 4. Summarizes the results of a poll that indicates the wide extent of the problem of racial profiling as perceived by African Americans.

Heumann, Milton, and Lance Cassak. "Profiles in Justice? Police Discretion, Symbolic Assailants, and Stereotyping." *Rutgers Law Review*, vol. 53, no. 4, 2001, pp. 911–978. The author draws on research that police officers typically construct pictures of "symbolic assailants" for specific crimes that often include race along with other characteristics. Even if laws were to prohibit the use of race, images of symbolic assailants would keep it as a relevant factor in police action.

Knowles, John, Nicola Persico, and Petra Todd. "Racial Bias in Motor Vehicle Searches: Theory and Evidence." *Journal of Political Economy*, vol. 109, no. 11, 2001, pp. 203–229. This study of stops by Maryland state troopers finds that the "hit rates" differed little by suspects' race or ethnicity. Although blacks were stopped more than whites, about 34 percent of blacks and 32 percent of whites—statistically identical figures—were found to be carrying contraband. If police had discriminated against black drivers and had stopped more innocent black drivers, it would show in lower hit rates. That police were equally effective in finding contraband in vehicles with both black and white drivers shows they appropriately targeted drivers to maximize the potential for success in finding drugs. The study thus discounts claims that officers unfairly target minorities.

Kruger, Karen J. "Collecting Statistics in Response to Racial Profiling Allegations." *FBI Law Enforcement Bulletin*, vol. 71, May 2002, pp. 8–12. Collecting data seems an easy way to appease critics of racial profiling, but the data can, as discussed in this article, worsen rather than moderate concerns about the problem. The author summarizes the problem: "If agencies do not base their collection methodology on well-designed scientific models, then the resulting statistics can be easily manipulated to act as a weapon against them." Other solutions to the problem must be developed to deal with public concerns.

Malakoff, David. "The Reverend Bayes Goes to Court." *Science*, vol. 286, November 19, 1999, p. 1462. For the more scientifically and mathematically oriented, this article describes the use of Bayesian statistics to support allegations that New Jersey state troopers used racial profiling. It gives some background on the 18th-century clergyman, Reverend Thomas Bayes, who developed the statistical approach, and on the technique itself.

Meehan, Albert J., and Michael C. Ponder. "Race and Place: The Ecology of Racial Profiling African American Motorists." *Justice Quarterly*, vol. 19, no. 3, 2002, pp. 399–430. This study of police stops on a roadway separating a white suburban community from a predominantly African-American community finds clear evidence of racial profiling. The authors argue that community patterns of residential segregation contribute to biased policing.

Myers, Samuel L., Jr. "Presidential Address—Analysis of Race and Policy Analysis." *Journal of Policy Analysis and Management*, vol. 21, Spring 2002, pp. 169–190. The author highlights the conflict between the goal of police efficiency and the goal of social equality. Racial profiling involves efforts to most efficiently target those likely to be involved in crime, but in so doing, it leads to inequity in the detention of minority groups. This article addresses this conflict in general terms, considering issues involving race differences in access to loans, scholarships, and child protection services as well as police stops.

Persico, Nicola. "Racial Profiling, Fairness, and Effectiveness of Policing." *American Economic Review*, vol. 92, December 2002, pp. 1472–1497. This article uses economic models to identify the conditions under which forcing police to behave more fairly reduces the total amount of crime. The model begins with two groups that differ in their legal opportunities, engagement in crime, and likelihood of being stopped, and then draws out the implications of assumed differences between the groups. The material is highly technical but represents the kind of approach economists take in dealing with the issue of racial profiling.

Petrocelli, Matthew, Alex R. Piquero, and Michael R Smith. "Conflict Theory and Racial Profiling: An Empirical Analysis of Police Traffic Stop Data." *Journal of Criminal Justice*, vol. 31, January/February 2003, pp. 1–11. Based on data gathered in Richmond, Virginia, the study examines racial differences in police stops in black and white neighborhoods. In addition, the study considers the crime, poverty, and unemployment rates of the neighborhoods. The authors conclude from their analyses that racial profiling does not appear early in the crime detection process but may emerge after the initial stop, when police search vehicles.

Schott, Richard G. "The Role of Race in Law Enforcement." *FBI Law Enforcement Bulletin*, vol. 70, November 2001, pp. 24–32. Addressed to law enforcement officers, this article emphasizes the difference between legitimate and illegitimate use of race in law enforcement activities. The author believes police must act in ways that maintain credibility within the communities they serve and suggests ways to respond to accusations of racial profiling that enhance their credibility. The article also contains a brief history of constitutional challenges to racial profiling.

Sullivan, Philip R. "Profiling." *America*, vol. 186, March 18, 2002, pp. 12–14. A review of research suggests that the human brain has developed the ability to profile and this ability stems from the need of human ancestors to respond quickly to threats. Even if the profiles proved statistically incorrect, the ability to generalize about people on the basis of appearance may have contributed to the survival of ancient humans. The author also notes that higher-level thinking skills can prevent the use of profiling and lead people to recognize the mistakes their brain can make.

Taylor, Jared, and Glayde Whitney. "Crime and Racial Profiling by U.S. Police: Is There an Empirical Basis?" *The Journal of Social, Political, and Economic Studies*, vol. 24, Winter 1999, pp. 485–510. This review of race patterns of criminal offending suggests that public perceptions of racial profiling and racism have little validity. Although the empirical data show that police investigate a higher percentage of black and Hispanic suspects than white or Asian suspects, the data also show higher crime rates for the first two groups than the latter two groups. To illustrate their case, the authors examine instances of interrace violent crimes, noting that 90 percent are committed by blacks against whites and only 2 percent to 3 percent are committed by whites against blacks.

Thompson, Anthony C. "Stopping the Usual Suspects: Race and the Fourth Amendment." *New York University Law Review*, vol. 74, no. 4, pp. 956–1013. The article criticizes the Supreme Court's decisions on search and seizure for failing to recognize that apparent "racially neutral" actions actually reflect hidden perceptions, implicit judgments, and racial profiling. The author argues that the Fourth Amendment, as intended by the framers of the Constitution, aimed to protect disfavored minorities and should be used to disallow search-and-seizure practices that end up disproportionately affecting minorities.

Walker, Samuel. "Searching for the Denominator: Problems with Police Traffic Stop Data and an Early Warning System Solution." *Justice Research and Policy*, vol. 3, no. 1, 2001, pp. 63–95. Responding to the use of new forms of data collection to address allegations of racial profiling, the author points to some problems in baseline measurements. The use of resident population data or official arrest data has serious flaws. A better solution would compare officers working in the same area in order to identify those most likely to selectively stop minorities.

Weitzer, Ronald. "Racializing Policing: Residents' Perceptions in Three Neighborhoods." *Law and Society Review*, vol. 34, no. 1, 2000, pp. 129–155.

In-depth interviews of 169 Washington, D.C. residents reveal widespread belief that police treat blacks differently than whites. Those subjects residing in African-American communities are most likely to attribute the different treatment to racism.

Weitzer, Ronald, and Steven A. Tuch. "Perceptions of Racial Profiling: Race, Class, and Personal Experience." *Criminology*, vol. 40, May 2002, pp. 435–456. This study uses a national survey done by the Gallup organization to examine how people view racial profiling. According to the data, the vast majority of blacks and whites disapprove of racial profiling and believe it is widespread. About 40 percent of blacks and 5 percent of whites felt they were stopped because of their race or ethnicity, and about 39 percent of blacks and 13 percent of whites have an unfavorable opinion of local police. Besides these descriptive statistics, the paper presents some more complex analysis of how social class, age, gender, and other characteristics affect attitudes toward racial profiling.

Web Documents

Bureau of Justice Statistics. "Contact between Police and the Public: Findings from the 1999 National Survey." Bureau of Justice Statistics web site. Available online. URL: http://www.ojp.usdoj.gov/bjs/abstract/cpp99.htm. Downloaded in July 2003. Files available for downloading from this page include data on the nature and characteristics of police and citizen contacts based on a national survey of persons age 16 and over. The data allow for comparisons of contact rates by race as well as by many other social and demographic characteristics.

Gallup Organization. "Racial Profiling Is Seen as Widespread, Particularly among Young Black Men." Gallup Poll News Service. Available online. URL: http://www.gallup.com/subscription/?m=f&c_id=10343. Posted on December 9, 1999. Although access to the details of this report requires a subscription, the web page includes some basic statistics obtained before September 11, 2001. Most important, 81 percent of Americans disapprove of racial profiling, according to the poll.

O'Connor, Eileen. "Psychology Responds to Racial Profiling." Monitor on Psychology. Available online. URL: http://www.apa.org/monitor/may01/raceprofile.html. Posted in May 2001. This article describes a session on racial profiling at the 2001 American Psychological Association Annual Convention. Psychologists have begun to explore the psychological impact of racial profiling, gather data on the practice, and develop ways to increase respect for cultural differences. Their expertise on use of stereotypes can also help to understand perceptions of criminality among law enforcement officers.

Racial Profiling Data Collection Resource Center at Northeastern University. "Background and Current Data Collection Efforts." Resource Center web site. Available online. URL: http://www.racialprofilinganalysis.neu.edu. Downloaded in July 2003. The web site provides information useful to understanding and measuring racial profiling. Specific pages cover the benefits and limitations of data collection and common challenges to data reporting. Still others provide details on legislation, a glossary of terms, news items, reports, and articles. Avoiding the bias of most advocacy-based web sites, the data collection resource center provides much useful information for researchers on the topic. The site serves as a good starting place for those wanting to do in-depth research on racial profiling.

Rate It All. "Racial Profiling." Rate It All Opinion Network. Available online. URL: http://www.rateitall.com/item.asp?I=04D3AA7E-D7BB-4ECB-A037-39F3215FDBF8. Downloaded in July 2003. While most web pages include the writings of experts, this web page does more to reflect the views of the public. In particular, it includes comments and political views about racial profiling from individuals who differ strongly in their opinions.

Vera Institute of Justice. "Racial Profiling." Vera Institute of Justice web site. Available online. URL:http://www.vera.org/publications/publications_5.asp?publication_id=162. Posted in May 2002. Interested users can download a copy of a paper from the Police Assessment Resource Center on the impact of the criminal justice system on minorities and new ways to deal with the problem of racial inequality in crime and imprisonment.

Zingraff, Matthew, et al. "Evaluating North Carolina State Highway Patrol Data: Citations, Warnings, and Searches in 1998." Available online. URL: http://www.nccrimecontrol.org/shp/ncshpreport.htm. Posted on November 1, 2000. The study compares race data on traffic stops with race data on drivers in the state of North Carolina. It finds greater racial disparities in searches than stops but notes that the data do not allow an accurate determination of the extent of racial profiling.

POLICY ISSUES

BOOKS

Community Oriented Policing Services, U.S. Department of Justice. *Mutual Respect in Policing: Lesson Plan.* Washington, D.C.: Community Oriented Policing Services, U.S. Department of Justice, 2001. This lesson plan goes along with a video designed to increase mutual respect in policing and to explore the misleading assumptions officers may hold about the persons they stop. One lesson involves discussing the proper grounds for probable cause and reasonable suspicion. Another lesson addresses the components of good criminal investigation and the inappropriateness of using racial profiling in such investigation. This effort represents one of many by the federal government to help state and local police eliminate racial profiling.

Dinh, Viet. "Testimony," in *The Benefits of Audio-Visual Technology in Addressing Racial Profiling, Hearing before the Committee on Government Reform, House of Representatives, One Hundred Seventh Congress, First Session.* Washington, D.C.: U.S. Government Printing Office, July 19, 2001, pp. 25–49. The assistant attorney general, Office of Legal Policy, U.S. Department of Justice, Dinh testifies about efforts of the Department of Justice to implement anti–racial profiling polices and provides information to Congress about the potential for using audiovisual technology to address concerns over racial profiling. He supports the use of audiovisual technology and cites grants made by the Department of Justice to state and local police agencies for the purchase of equipment. However, he also recognizes the limitations of the technology, makes other recommendations to eliminate racial profiling, and cites grants made by the federal government to state and local agencies to support other procedures.

Dunbar, Charles, Jr. "Testimony," in *The Benefits of Audio-Visual Technology in Addressing Racial Profiling, Hearing before the Committee on Government Reform, House of Representatives, One Hundred Seventh Congress, First Session.* Washington, D.C.: U.S. Government Printing Office, 2001, p. 68–72. The then superintendent of the New Jersey State Police offers an example of the benefits of audiovisual technology. A driver stopped by New Jersey State Police filed a complaint alleging he was stopped for no apparent reason and treated rudely by the officer. In fact, the videotape taken by a camera on the officer's car demonstrated the driver had been speeding and the officer treated him with respect and courtesy. Based on the videotape, prosecutors filed charges against the driver for the false accusations.

Fridell, Lori. "Statement," in *S. 989: The End of Racial Profiling Act of 2001, Hearing before the Subcommittee on the Constitution, Federalism, and Property Rights of the Committee on the Judiciary, United States Senate, One Hundred Seventh Congress, First Session.* Washington, D.C.: U.S. Government Printing Office, August 1, 2001, pp. 49–58. As research director of the Police Executive Research Forum, Fridell reviews practices police can use to respond to accusations of racially based policing and perceptions of racial profiling. However, she also presents arguments in opposition to Senate legislation, particularly provisions that allow use of statistics on motor vehicle stops to be cited as evidence of racially biased policing. Given the weakness of such data in demonstrating racial profiling, their use in court would, she believes, wrongly implicate officers and agencies in racial profiling practices.

Kelly, Raymond W. "Testimony," in *The Benefits of Audio-Visual Technology in Addressing Racial Profiling, Hearing before the Committee on Government Reform, House of Representatives, One Hundred Seventh Congress, First Session.* Washington, D.C.: U.S. Government Printing Office, pp. 133–141. The former commissioner of the U.S. Customs Service describes the reforms he implemented to eliminate racial profiling. Responding to allegations of the use of race, ethnicity, and national origin in selecting persons for detailed searches, an outside commission was appointed to investigate the problem. On the basis of commission recommendations, Kelly changed supervision and management polices and appears to have largely ended complaints about profiling.

Maloney, Chris. "Testimony," in *Profiling for Public Safety: Rational or Racist, Hearing Before the Subcommittee on Aviation of the Committee on Transportation and Infrastructure House of Representatives, One Hundred Seventh Congress, Second Session.* Washington, D.C.: U.S. Government Printing Office, 2002, pp. 146–152. Maloney, the president of TriTech Software Systems, does not address issues of racial profiling in his testimony but does offer background technical information on the use of audiovisual technology. He describes how software his company has developed and sells can overcome problems of cost, data storage, and data retrieval, and how its use by police can benefit law enforcement agencies.

U.S. Department of Justice. "Report by the Department of Justice to the Department of Transportation on the Civil Rights Review of the Proposed Automated Passenger Screening System," in *Profiling for Public Safety: Rational or Racist, Hearing before the Subcommittee on Aviation of the Committee on Transportation and Infrastructure House of Representatives, One Hundred Seventh Congress, Second Session.* Washington, D.C.: U.S. Government Printing Office, 2002, pp. 87–97. Written in 1997 to review the proposed Computer Assisted Passenger Screening System but reprinted for this hearing, this report found that the system does not discriminate on the basis of race, color, national or ethnic origin, religion, or gender. It also made recommendations to further insure that the system is implemented in a nondiscriminatory fashion. Some wonder if, with all the care to make profiling evenhanded, the screening is likely to be ineffective in identifying potential terrorists. Still others worry that the screening criteria might be changed in the future to select members of particular national origin groups.

U.S. House of Representatives. *The Benefits of Audio-Visual Technology in Addressing Racial Profiling, Hearing before the Committee on Government Reform, House of Representatives, One Hundred Seventh Congress, First Session.*

Washington, D.C.: U.S. Government Printing Office, 2001. Dan Burton, a Republican representative from Indiana and the chair of the committee, discusses an alternative to proposed anti–racial profiling legislation—installing cameras and microphones in police vehicles to record traffic violations and interactions with occupants of stopped vehicles. Although concerned with the cost and practical problems of making, examining, and saving videotapes, those testifying at the hearing support the idea of using audiovisual technology. Critics of racial profiling believe the tapes will help protect innocent drivers, and police believe the tapes will protect them from unfounded accusations.

U.S. House of Representatives. "H.R. 2074," in *The Benefits of Audio-Visual Technology in Addressing Racial Profiling, Hearing before the Committee on Government Reform, House of Representatives, One Hundred Seventh Congress, First Session.* Washington, D.C.: U.S. Government Printing Office, 2001, pp. 161–177. House bill H.R. 2074—a proposal to gather data on traffic stops across the United States—has not passed, but those wanting a detailed description of the proposed legislation can find the full text in this volume.

U.S. House of Representatives. *Profiling for Public Safety: Rational or Racist, Hearing before the Subcommittee on Aviation of the Committee on Transportation and Infrastructure House of Representatives, One Hundred Seventh Congress, Second Session.* Washington, D.C.: U.S. Government Printing Office, 2002. Comments and questions in the hearing from congressional representatives reveal the disputes over the use of racial or ethnic profiling in airports as a means to protect national security and prevent terrorism. Some worry that concern about racial profiling reflects an unnecessary form of "political correctness" and leads to searches of wheelchair-bound women and decorated soldiers. Others oppose any form of screening in airports that relies on race, ethnicity, or national origin, much as they have opposed racial profiling of African Americans on highways.

U.S. Senate, *Racial Profiling within Law Enforcement Agencies, Hearing before the Subcommittee on the Constitution, Federalism, and Property Rights of the Committee on the Judiciary, United States Senate, One Hundred Sixth Congress, Second Session.* Washington, D.C.: U.S. Government Printing Office, 2000. The discussion in this hearing relates to the proposed Traffic Stops Statistics Study Act. The legislation would require the attorney general to collect data on racial profiling from police departments that voluntarily agree to participate. The senators present at the hearing largely support the legislation, although some suggest modest changes in the details. Of most interest are the stories presented by witnesses of their experiences in being stopped by police because, in their view, of their skin color or ethnicity.

U.S. Senate, *S. 989: The End of Racial Profiling Act of 2001, Hearing before the Subcommittee on the Constitution, Federalism, and Property Rights of the Committee on the Judiciary, United States Senate, One Hundred Seventh Congress, First Session.* Washington, D.C.: U.S. Government Printing Office, 2001. Members of the Senate, including Richard J. Durbin (D.-Ill.), John Edwards (D.-N.C.), Edward M. Kennedy (D.-Mass.), Hillary Rodham Clinton (D.-N.Y.), Orrin G. Hatch (R.-Utah), and Strom Thurmond (R.-S.C.) discuss proposed legislation intended to ban racial profiling, allow the U.S. Department of Justice or individuals to file suit against those practicing racial profiling, and provide funds for state and local agencies in developing effective complaint, disciplinary, and data collection procedures. Based on comments of the senators, support for the bill appears strong, but Republican senators express concerns about some of the provisions.

Young, Steve. "Statement," in *S. 989: The End of Racial Profiling Act of 2001, Hearing before the Subcommittee on the Constitution, Federalism, and Property Rights of the Committee on the Judiciary, United States Senate, One Hundred Seventh Congress, First Session.* 2001, pp. 32–38. This testimony of Young, the national vice president of the Fraternal Order of Police, the nation's largest law enforcement labor organization, opposes recent legislation to end racial profiling. He argues that the bill falsely accuses police of racism, confuses racial profiling with criminal profiling, makes police subject to second-guessing by outsiders, and has the potential to allow the collected data to be misused. To support his case, he presents maps of homicides for Washington, D.C., noting higher rates in minority neighborhoods than white neighborhoods.

ARTICLES

Alter, Jonathan. "Hillary Raises Her Profile. H. Clinton Proposes Legislation on Racial Profiling." *Newsweek*, vol. 137, June 25, 2001, p. 34. Arguing that no one can deny the prevalence of official and unofficial racial profiling, the author considers the advantages and disadvantages of legislation proposed by Senator Hillary Rodham Clinton to outlaw the practice.

Beinart, Peter. "Duty Free." *The New Republic*, vol. 225, December 17, 2001, p. 6. Criticizes President George W. Bush and Attorney General John Ashcroft for publicly opposing racial profiling but then supporting the roundup of Arabs in the United States because of their national origin. The author calls for continued criticism of the Bush administration for what he views as extreme antiterrorist actions.

Borger, Gloria. "Bush's 'Third Way.'" *U.S. News and World Report*, vol. 130, March 12, 2001, p. 40. Based on the president's 2001 State of the Union address, it appears he will use opposition to racial profiling as part of an effort to adopt some of the agenda of his opponents and reduce their grounds for criticizing the administration.

Buerger, Michael. "Supervisory Challenges Arising from Racial Profiling Legislation." *Police Quarterly*, vol. 5, no. 3, 2002, pp. 380–408. Recent legislation places special burdens on police supervisors to implement anti–racial profiling policies. Many officers view such policies as an insult to their professionalism and honesty, while many citizens do not trust police to fairly implement the policies. Police supervisors must therefore make officers aware of new expectations, deal with resistance, mediate disputes with citizens, exert discipline, and provide needed resources. This article gives suggestions for how to reach these goals.

Carrick, Grady. "Professional Police Traffic Stops: Strategies to Address Racial Profiling." *FBI Law Enforcement Bulletin*, vol. 69, November 2000, pp. 8–10. In promoting the use of professional standards for police traffic stops, the author views use of race and ethnicity in selecting criminal suspects as improper. Officers must have sound and defensible legal and moral grounds relating to the safety of citizens or police when they make a stop. To ensure professional police traffic stops and eliminate racial profiling, the author recommends that law enforcement agencies set up new organizational policies, training programs, and data collection procedures.

Cashmore, Ellis. "The Experiences of Ethnic Minority Police Officers in Britain: Under-Recruitment and Racial Profiling in a Performance Culture." *Ethnic and Racial Studies*, vol. 24, July 2001, pp. 642–659. Issues of police racism and racial profiling have emerged in Britain as well as the United States, with British residents of African-Caribbean (Jamaican, Bermudan) and South Asian (Indian, Pakistani, Bangladeshi) communities complaining about mistreatment by police. This article interviews minority police officers about such problems and their views on how to address them. The officers describe their experiences with discrimination in their departments and their difficulties in recruiting other minority officers.

Holmes, Steve. "Clinton Orders Investigation on Possible Racial Profiling." *New York Times*, June 10, 1999, p. A22. Describes the background and likely consequences of President Bill Clinton's order for federal law enforcement agencies to gather data on the race and ethnicity of persons stopped by police. The president hoped actions by the federal government would encourage state and local agencies to follow suit and to eliminate the "morally indefensible" practice of racial profiling.

"Martin Luther King III and Rev. Al Sharpton to Lead March on Washington. March on Washington Set for August 26, 2000." *Jet*, vol. 98, July 10, 2000, pp. 4–5. The march, meant to commemorate Martin Luther King, Jr.'s historic march in 1963, aims to put pressure on the White

House and Congress to require an end to racial profiling and punishment of those who use it.

Minter, Brendan. "Video Vindication." *The American Enterprise*, vol. 11, September 2000, p. 7. This review of the use of videotapes installed in New Jersey State Police vehicles suggests the equipment exonerates officers from accusations of racial profiling. By May 2000, 40 complaints about officer treatment during a traffic stop had been made when equipment was used to record the stop. In each case, the tapes revealed that the troopers acted properly. These results indicate, as many police have claimed, that accusations of racial profiling are seldom valid.

Roane, Kit R. "Strategic or Stupid? R. Giuliani and H. Clinton Attack Each Other on Opposing Views of P. Dorismund Shooting." *U.S. News and World Report*, vol. 128, April 3, 2000, pp. 16–18. Patrick Dorismond, a 26-year-old African-American security officer, was shot during a struggle when a Hispanic New York City police officer mistook him for a drug dealer. Senatorial candidate Hillary Rodham Clinton used the incident to criticize her possible opponent, New York City mayor Rudolph Giuliani, who in turn defended the police. The disagreement highlights the conflicting views over relations between police and minorities in the city.

Sterngold, James. "California Racial Profiling Bill Is Vetoed." *New York Times*, September 30, 1999, p. A20. Governor Gray Davis vetoed a bill strongly supported by civil rights leaders that would require collecting data on racial profiling. The governor worried about the cost of the measure but will require state police to collect the data and recommend to local police that they do the same.

Stewart-Brown, Rachael. "Community Mobilization: The Foundation for Community Policing: City Heights Neighborhood Alliance, San Diego" *FBI Law Enforcement Bulletin*, vol. 70, June 2001, pp. 9–17. Based on a case study of a San Diego neighborhood, this article describes how community members can participate with police in efforts to solve drug crimes and quality-of-life problems. The mobilization can lead community members to help solve problems once left for police to handle. Critics of quality-of-life policing in New York City (and the alleged racial profiling that is associated with such policing) point to the success of San Diego in reducing crime problems through community policing, without use of aggressive policing practices.

Trende, Sean P. "Why Modest Proposals Offer the Best Solution for Combating Racial Profiling." *Duke Law Review*, vol. 50, 2000, pp. 331–380. This article takes a middle ground between condemning and defending the racial profiling. It notes that efforts to stop profiling by bringing individual lawsuits will likely have little success because courts have allowed the use of race in some form by police and have erected high barriers for proof in such cases.

"U.S. Muslim Coalition Endorses Bush: American Muslim Political Coordination Council." *The Christian Century*, vol. 117, November 8, 2000, p. 1144. In the 2000 presidential election, the political action committee of a Muslim coalition supported George W. Bush because of his stated opposition to racial profiling and concerns about the rights of Arab Americans.

Ward, James D. "Race, Ethnicity, and Law Enforcement Profiling: Implications for Public Policy." *Public Administration Review*, vol. 62, November/December 2002, pp. 726–735. This article provides a review of congressional legislation—up to 2001—aimed at reducing racial profiling and the detention of minority motorists on the highway. The most recent proposal, the End of Racial Profiling Act of 2001, follows earlier unsuccessful legislative proposals (indeed, this proposal would not pass either). Despite the failure to pass new laws, the review of the goals and details of the proposals in the article describes public policy efforts to address this issue.

WEB DOCUMENTS

Americans for Effective Law Enforcement (AELE). "Hot Issues." AELE web site. Available online. URL: http://www.aele.org/hotissues.html. Downloaded in July 2003. The page includes a list of documents and papers on racial profiling, including proposed federal legislation, conference papers on current legal and police issues in racial profiling, and state court cases.

Buckman, W. H. "Materials on Racial Profiling Challenges." William H. Buckman Law Firm. Available online. URL: http://whbuckman.com/profiling/profiling.html. Downloaded in July 2003. The web page contains briefs on behalf of those challenging police racial profiling tactics in court. It also includes other racial profiling links and documents that demonstrate the use of racial profiling.

Bush, George W. "Text of Bush's Address to Congress." Washingtonpost.com on Politics. Available online. URL: http://www.washingtonpost.com/wp-srv/onpolitics/transcripts/bushtext022701.htm. Posted on February 27, 2001. The text of the 2001 State of the Union Address includes the president's George W. Bush's statement of opposition to racial profiling.

Cassel, Elaine. "Bush Plays the Racial Profiling Card." Counterpunch. Available online. URL: http://www.counterpunch.org/cassel06192003. html. Posted on June 19, 2003. In this highly critical piece, the author suggests that President George W. Bush's new guidelines to prohibit racial profiling by federal law enforcement agencies are actually a "nefarious smokescreen for race and ethnic-based roundups." Since the ban allows for exceptions related to national security, it can have only limited effectiveness. According to the author, the ban would not have prevented the detention of illegal immigrants suspected of terrorism and the major violations of their constitutional civil rights.

Cato Institute. "Racial Profiling: Good Police Tactic—Or Harassment?" Policy Forum. Available online. URL: http://www.cato.org/events/010515pf.html. Posted on May 15, 2001. This web page allows users to view or listen to this forum or read the transcript. It includes three speakers—a police chief, a law professor, and a policy expert—who discuss the possible justifications for profiling, the reasons to curb the practice, and other issues.

Community Oriented Policing Services (COPS). "Promoting Cooperative Strategies to Reduce Racial Profiling." COPS web site. Available online. URL: http://www.cops.usdoj.gov/Default.asp?Item=463. Downloaded in July 2003. On this web page, the Community Oriented Policing Services agency of the U.S. Department of Justice describes the grants that it has made to state and local agencies for the purpose of reducing racial profiling.

DePledge, Derrick. "Federal Action on Profiling Held Up: Bill in Congress Slowed by September 11." *The Cincinnati Enquirer.* Available online. URL: http://www.enquirer.com/editions/2002/04/22/loc_federal_action_on.html. Posted on April 22, 2002. The article describes in more detail than most newspaper stories the background of federal legislation to end racial profiling and then discusses how the debates have changed with more recent concerns about terrorism.

EthnicMajority.com. "Racial Profiling News." EthnicMajority.com web site. Available online. URL: http://www.ethnicmajority.com/racial_profiling_news.htm. Downloaded in July 2003. This organization notes that ethnic minorities have become a majority of the U.S. population and deserve power commensurate with their size. The web page contains stories on racial profiling from articles in major newspapers and links to numerous other news stories.

Florida Highway Patrol. "Racial Profiling." Florida Highway Patrol web site. Available online. URL: http://www.fhp.state.fl.us/html/census/profile.html. Downloaded in July 2003. The Florida Highway Patrol, an agency that in the 1980s appeared to use profiling to stop drug transport across the state, has since 1999 prohibited racial profiling. This page presents a memorandum to employees, the statement of prohibition on profiling, and an analysis of racial profiling data.

Florida Police Chiefs Association. "Racial Profiling." Florida Police Chiefs Association web site. Available online. URL: http://www.fpca.com/profiling.htm. Downloaded in July 2003. Concerned about perceptions that police use racial profiling and the need for trust between police and the community, this association has made recommendations for local agencies to deal with the problem. The recommendations include having a written policy to prohibit the practice, procedures to investigate complaints about use of the practice, community outreach programs, special training, and in-car video.

NewsTrove.com. "Racial Profiling: Latest News Stories." Racial Profiling. Available online. URL: http://racialprofiling.newstrove.com. Downloaded on July 11, 2003. This web page lists dozens of local stories on racial profiling and provides references that typically do not appear in most library databases. For example, stories in New Haven, Connecticut; Harrisburg, Pennsylvania; Fort Wayne, Indiana; and Newport, Rhode Island, extend the usual reports about large cities to smaller cities.

PoliticalCircus.com. "Racial Profiling." PoliticalCircus.com web site. Available online. URL: http://www.politicalcircus.com/archive/racialprofiling.shtml. Downloaded in July 2003. A source of information for the Asian and Pacific Islander–American community, this web site contains news and commentary on racial profiling as it relates in particular to the treatment of Asians in government labs.

Racial Profiling Data Collection Resource Center at Northeastern University. "Legislation and Litigation." Resource Center web site. Available online. URL: http://www.racialprofilinganalysis.neu.edu/legislation.php. Downloaded in July 2003. A map describes current racial profiling legislation for each of the states. Clicking a state on the map lists the current legislation there.

StateAction.com. "Racial Profiling." StateAction.com web site. Available online. URL: http://www.stateactionl.org/issues/racialprofiling/index.cfm. Downloaded in July 2003. The page summarizes state action against racial profiling and describes model legislation. It is designed to help make state policy and legislators aware of activities in other states.

U.S. Department of Justice. "Fact Sheet: Racial Profiling." Available online. URL: http://www.usdoj.gov/opa/pr/2003/June/racial_profiling_fact_ sheet.pdf. Posted on June 17, 2003. This sheet describes the opposition to racial profiling of the Department of Justice and reviews steps taken to prevent the practice. It also defends its efforts to protect national security, which some view as involving the use of racial profiling.

———. "Guidance Regarding the Use of Race by Federal Law Enforcement Agencies." Civil Rights Division. Available online. URL: http://www.usoj.gov/crt/split/documents/guidance_on_race.htm. Posted in June 2003. Claiming that racial profiling in law enforcement is not merely wrong but also ineffective, these guidelines prohibit federal law enforcement officers from using race or ethnicity in any form in routine or spontaneous decisions (except when looking for a specific suspect). In investigating threats to national security, federal law enforcement officers may not consider race or ethnicity except to the extent permitted by the Constitution and laws of the United States. The document (included in the appendices) provides details on carrying out these guidelines.

U.S. Department of State. "International Information Programs. Racial Profiling." Race and Ethnic Diversity. Available online. URL: http://usinfo.state.gov/usa/race/profile/official.htm. Posted on May 10, 2002. As part of the State Department's effort to provide information about the United States to those outside the country, this page contains statements from the president and attorney general, documents from government agencies, and proposed legislation.

BACKGROUND ISSUES

BOOKS

Ayers, William, Bernardine Dohrn, and Rick Ayers, eds. *Zero Tolerance: Resisting the Drive for Punishment in Our Schools.* New York: New Press, 2001. Beginning as a strictly enforced prohibition of guns, zero-tolerance policies in schools have, according to the authors, become excessive and rigid. Moreover, they appear to be used primarily against black and Latino children and thus contribute to a form of racial profiling. Articles in this edited volume illustrate the unfairness of the policies and the harm they do to individual students. Along with describing the problem, the book offers recommendations for removing racial bias in school discipline.

Bireda, Martha R. *Eliminating Racial Profiling in School Discipline: Cultures in Conflict.* Lanham, Md.: Scarecrow Press, 2002. Although focused on school discipline, the description of cultural norms for African Americans and the misunderstandings of these norms by other groups have implications for use of racial profiling by police. A basic idea is that innocent behaviors among African Americans may appear threatening or suspicious to others.

D'Souza, Dinesh. *The End of Racism.* New York: The Free Press, 1995. The author provides an analysis of race relations in the United States from a conservative political perspective. He argues that civil rights organizations promote black dependency with the policies they advocate and fail to understand the nature of racism and discrimination in the United States today. Chapter 7 ("Is America Racist?") argues that racial discrimination exists but is based on group conduct rather than irrational prejudice or a sense of racial superiority of whites. The arguments are consistent with those of the advocates of racial profiling and contrast with those who focus on the victimization of minorities by the criminal justice system.

Georges-Abeyie, Daniel E. "Petit Apartheid in Criminal Justice: The More 'Things' Change, the More 'Things' Remain the Same," in Dragan Milovanovic and Katheryn K. Russell, eds., *Petit Apartheid in the U.S. Criminal Justice System.* Durham, N.C.: Carolina Academic Press, 2001, pp. ix–xiv. In this foreword, the author discusses the term *petit apartheid,* which describes the informal and subtle instances of discrimination that occur in the criminal justice system in dealing with minorities. This form of discrimination differs from formal segregation laws such as existed in the American South and South Africa but nonetheless has similarly harmful consequences. Racial profiling is one component of petite apartheid.

Hacker, Andrew. *Two Nations: Black and White, Separate, Hostile, Unequal.* New York: Scribner, 2003. In a newly updated edition of a book first published in 1992, the author emphasizes the extent and strength of racial inequality in the United States. Chapter 11 discusses the role of race in crime and describes blacks' distrust of police—a distrust that persists in the face of high risks of threat from criminals in minority communities. The book also discusses race differences in arrest and punishment to illustrate the larger theme of persistent separation of whites and blacks.

Hawkins, Homer, and Richard Thomas. "White Policing of Black Populations: A History of Race and Social Control in America," in Ellis Cashmore and Eugene McLaughlin, eds., *Out of Order? Policing Black People.* London: Routledge, 1991, pp. 65–86. This book explores a variety of issues relating to the role of police in asserting the dominance of more powerful white groups over less powerful minority groups. This chapter focuses more specifically on the United States and the history of relations between police and African Americans. In strong, unqualified language, it argues that this history reveals police efforts to keep blacks in their place and the hate and distrust that emerged among blacks. It also considers how election of black mayors in some cities has improved traditionally hostile relations between police and blacks.

Lelyveld, Joseph, ed. *How Race Is Lived in America: Pulling Together, Pulling Apart.* New York: Times Books, 2001. As part of a special project on race relations in the United States, reporters for the *New York Times* followed subjects across the nation for more than a year. This book presents the stories written by the reporters, which give a personal and inside look at both the new connections and continuing divisions between whites and blacks. Chapter 13 ("Why Harlem Drug Cops Don't Discuss Race") considers issues of racial profiling as viewed by white and black New York City police officers.

McWhorter, John. *Authentically Black: Essays for the Black Silent Majority.* New York: Gotham Books, 2003. Generally critical of the adoption of victim status by minorities, this African-American professor examines racial profiling particularly in Chapter 2. He worries that racial profiling contributes to the largely mistaken perception that racism prevents black progress.

Milovanovic, Dragan, and Katheryn K. Russell, eds. *Petit Apartheid in the U.S. Criminal Justice System.* Durham, N.C.: Carolina Academic Press, 2001. *Petit apartheid* refers to the hidden, informal types of racial bias that contrast with the formal, legal racial bias in the past (such as apartheid in South Africa and segregation in the American South). This book examines how informal racial bias occurs in the criminal justice system. It offers a critical perspective on race relations and criminal justice, arguing that petit apartheid leads to continued mistreatment of minorities in the United States.

Rabinowitz, Howard N. "The Conflict between Blacks and the Police in the Urban South, 1865–1900," in Donald G. Nieman, ed., *Black Southerners and the Law, 1865–1900.* New York: Garland Publishing, 1994, pp. 284–299. This article describes the long history of violence between police and blacks. Viewed by blacks as responsible for enforcing racist laws, the police became the object of black resentment and anger. As a result, violence between blacks and police occurred often in the South during the last half of the 19th century. These riots protesting police treatment show some similarity to riots in more recent years.

Reed, Ishmael. *Another Day at the Front: Dispatches from the Race War.* New York: Basic Books, 2003. Reed, an African-American poet, novelist, and critic, argues in some of the essays in this book that white-on-black violence remains an essential component of black life in America today. From his view, blacks live in a police state where racial profiling is common of the experience blacks have with law enforcement agents.

Ruth, Henry, and Kevin R. Reitz. *The Challenge of Crime: Rethinking Our Response.* Cambridge, Mass.: Harvard University Press, 2003. Noting that expansion of the prison population has led to the most punitive decade in America's history, this book examines the recent changes in the response of the government to crime. It sees abuse of police discretion, such as in racial profiling, as part of this trend and argues for new approaches to the crime problem in the United States.

Walker, Samuel, Cassia Spohn, and Miriam DeLone. *The Color of Justice: Race, Ethnicity, and Crime in America.* 2d ed. Belmont, Calif.: Wadsworth, 2000. This clearly written textbook covers diverse topics on the intersection of criminal justice with race and ethnicity. The chapters cover issues of racial profiling and police treatment of minorities but also address topics of race differences in criminal offending and victimization by crime, and discrimination by prosecutors, judges, and prison officials.

ARTICLES

Alozie, Nicholas O. "Segregation and Black and Hispanic Group Outcomes: Policing in Large Cities." *American Politics Quarterly*, vol. 27, July

1999, pp. 354–375. This article addresses the question of how the residential segregation of a city affects relations between minorities and police. On one hand, segregation may encourage discrimination by police, but on the other hand, segregation may lead to more minority police personnel in minority neighborhoods. The study results find support for the thesis that segregation increases police discrimination against African Americans but not against Hispanics.

Bass, Sandra. "Policing Space, Policing Race: Social Control Imperatives and Police Discretionary Decisions." *Social Justice*, vol. 28, Spring 2001, pp. 156–176. This article views police discretion as reinforcing racial segregation and discrimination: "Since the demise of legal segregation and discrimination, discriminatory policies and practices have perpetuated a substantially authoritarian, regulatory, and punitive relationship between racial minorities and the police."

Brown, Judith. "Racial Profiling in School?" *Essence*, vol. 31, January 2001, p. 138. Extending controversy over police actions in regard to race, this article examines school discipline by race. Zero-tolerance policies are criticized as a means to exclude nonviolent black children from educational opportunities available to others.

Buntman, Fran Lisa. "Race, Reputation, and the Supreme Court: Valuing Blackness and Whiteness." *University of Miami Law Review*, vol. 56, October 2001, pp. 1–24. This article is critical of Supreme Court rulings dating from the 1850s to the present, and covering issues ranging from slavery to racial profiling. It argues that the Court, like most Americans, tends to accept the superior reputation of whites relative to blacks.

Butterfield, Fox. "Racial Disparities Seen as Pervasive in Juvenile Justice." *New York Times*, April 26, 2000, p. A1. The article summarizes a report that finds minority juvenile offenders are treated differently than their white counterparts. Although the article does not offer explanations of the reasons for the disparities in treatment, the higher rates of arrest, detention, and conviction, and the longer sentences for African Americans and Hispanics suggest discrimination in the criminal justice system.

Cureton, Steven R. "Justifiable Arrests or Discretionary Justice: Predictors of Racial Arrest Differentials." *Journal of Black Studies*, vol. 30, May 2000, pp. 703–719. The study examines the use of police power to discriminate against minorities in law enforcement. Its findings reveal that the difference in arrest rates between blacks and whites relates to economic inequality across races in U.S. cities and suggest that racial discrimination in policing exists.

Eisenman, Russell. "Is There a Bias in U.S. Law Enforcement?" *Journal of Social, Political, and Economic Studies*, vol. 20, Summer 1995, pp. 229–240. Based on analysis of data from the FBI, this study concludes that high rates of criminal offending among African Americans rather than racial discrimination in law enforcement account for differences in arrest rates.

Lee, Charles S., and Lester Sloan. "'It's Our Turn Now': Hispanics and Blacks in Compton, California." *Newsweek*, vol. 124, November 21, 1994, p. 57. In an interesting sidelight on police relations in minority communities, this article describes the circumstances of a disadvantaged Los Angeles suburb. There, African Americans dominate the government and police force, but Latinos represent the majority of the city's population. Latinos complain about their treatment by police, indicating conflict between race and ethnic groups outside the majority white community.

Lopez, Steve. "Death on the Beat: M. Davila Investigates When Phoenix Police Officer M. Atkinson Is Shot by a Mexican Alien." *Time*, vol. 153, June 28, 1999, pp. 56–61. In reporting on a shooting in Phoenix, the article describes the more general conflict between mostly white police forces and the minorities they police. It also discusses actions by city leaders to ease tension over the shooting and to improve relations between the Hispanic community and police officers.

Phillips, Julie A. "White, Black, and Latino Homicide Rates: Why the Difference." *Social Problems*, vol. 49, August 2002, pp. 349–373. Based on data for 129 American cities in 1990, the study finds that equalizing certain social conditions across race and ethnic groups could substantially reduce the black-white gap in homicide and reduce the entire white-Hispanic gap. As background to the topic of police relations with non-Latino whites, Latinos, and African Americans, the article describes race and ethnic patterns of murder in the United States today.

Roberts, Dorothy E. "Forward: Race, Vagueness, and the Social Meaning of Order-Maintenance Policing. Chicago Anti-Gang Loitering Law." *The Journal of Criminal Law and Criminology*, vol. 89, Spring 1999, pp. 775–836. The Supreme Court has ruled that a Chicago antiloitering ordinance was unconstitutionally vague and gave police excessive powers in dispersing individuals suspected of belonging to a gang. While some see the law as leading to harassment of minorities, others see it as a way to protect minority communities. This article examines the Supreme Court decision as part of a special issue on the work of the Supreme Court.

Rose, William. "Crimes of Color: Risk, Profiling, and the Contemporary Racialization of Social Control." *International Journal of Politics, Culture and Society*, vol. 16, Winter 2002, pp. 179–205. Argues that the actions of police in racial profiling reflect larger efforts of racial social control rather than individual racism. Accordingly, simple efforts to measure and expose the practice will not result in much change unless larger issues of inequality are addressed.

Sigelman, Lee, Susan Welch, and Timothy Bledsoe. "Police Brutality and Public Perceptions of Racial Discrimination: A Tale of Two Beatings: Malice Green and Rodney King." *Political Research Quarterly*, vol. 50, December 1997, pp. 777–791. This study examines the effects of well-publicized police beatings on perceptions of racial discrimination in public opinion surveys. The incidents appear to have influenced the views about how local police deal with blacks but not the views on the extent of racial discrimination generally.

Sorensen, Jon, and Don Stetman. "The Effect of State Sentencing Policies on Incarceration Rates." *Crime and Delinquency*, vol. 48, July 2002, pp. 456–475. Sentencing policies in states appear to have less effect on incarceration rates than do factors such as the crime rate and, interestingly, the percentage of the population that is black.

Steele, Shelby. "Hailing While Black." *Time*, vol. 158, July 30, 2001, p. 48. The author argues that views on racial profiling reflect underlying beliefs about the extent of racism in the United States. Opponents to racial profiling see racism as a major problem, while advocates view the problem today as much less serious than in the past. He suggests that the real debate concerns the distribution of power by race rather than stops and searches on the highway.

WEB DOCUMENTS

Hohman, Kimberly."About Race Relations." About.com. Available online. URL: http://www.racerelations.about.com. Downloaded in July 2003. This site includes links to pages on a variety of topics relating to race relations. The links to racial profiling are few, but other topics on stereotypes, discrimination, hate crimes, race and justice, civil rights, and racism may be useful.

Expose Racism and Advance School Excellence. "Report Charges Racial Profiling in U.S. Public Schools." Applied Research Center. Available online. URL: http://www.arc.org/erase/profiling_nr.html. Posted on October 30, 2001. This report argues that high-stakes testing and excessive security measures in schools have particularly harmed minority students and represent a form of racial profiling. The web page summarizes the report but also allows interested parties to download the full report.

McGoey, Chris E. "Shoplifting: Racial Profiling." Crime Doctor. Available online. URL: http://www.crimedoctor.com/shoplifting5.htm. Downloaded in July 2003. The author argues that most stores use profiling to prevent shoplifting and that profiles are necessary to limit inventory loss. However, he also argues that use of racial or ethnic profiling in places of business is wrong and recommends training and supervising employees to avoid the practice.

Online NewsHour. "Profile of a Terrorist." PBS Online. Available online. URL: http://www.pbs.org/newshour/bb/terrorism/july-dec01/racial_profile.html. Posted on September 26, 2001. This transcript from a PBS television show includes a roundtable discussion of the acceptability and benefits of racial profiling to prevent terrorism.

Sentencing Project. "Report Summary: Young Black Americans and the Criminal Justice System: Five Years Later." Sentencing Project web site. Available online. URL: http://www.sentencingproject.org/pubs_08.cfm. Posted in 1995. This study finds that 32 percent of black men ages 20–29 (compared to about 7 percent of white men in the same age group) fall under court supervision in prison, on probation, or on parole. The Sentencing Project and critics of the criminal justice system believe this disparity results from discrimination in laws and by police.

WordSpy. "Racial Profiling." WordSpy web site. Available online. URL: http://www.wordspy.com/words/racialprofiling.asp. Posted on May 4, 1999. This web page defines *racial profiling* as the inclusion of race in a profile of traits that allegedly identify the most likely perpetrators of a crime. It also presents part of a 1994 story in the *Philadelphia Daily News* that used the term and may be the earliest such use. The WordSpy site includes many other unusual and interesting words that relate to policing and discrimination.

CHAPTER 8

ORGANIZATIONS AND AGENCIES

The organizations and agencies listed in this chapter fall into three categories:

- federal government agencies
- state and local law enforcement agencies
- advocacy organizations

The categories overlap because, for example, federal, state, and local agencies often take advocacy positions. Still, most organizations fit better in one category than the other, and the classification helps organize an otherwise diverse domain. For each organization, the listings include the web site and e-mail addresses when available (if no e-mail address is listed, it is sometimes possible to send comments to the organization through the web site). The listings then include phone numbers (when available), postal addresses, and brief descriptions.

FEDERAL GOVERNMENT AGENCIES

Bureau of Citizenship and Immigration Services (BCIS)
URL: http://www.bcis.gov
Phone: (800) 375-5283
425 I Street, NW
Washington, DC 20536
Formerly the Immigration and Naturalization Service (INS), this agency has resided since March 1, 2003, in the U.S. Department of Homeland Security. It is responsible for immigration and naturalization administration rather than enforcement.

Bureau of Justice Statistics (BJS)
URL: http://www.ojp.usdoj.gov/bjs
E-mail: askbjs@ojp.usdoj.gov
Phone: (202) 307-0765
810 Seventh Street, NW
Washington, DC 20001

As part of the federal government's effort to fight racial profiling, the bureau has sponsored surveys, recommended traffic stop data collection procedures, published papers, and funded studies of traffic stops. It also provides statistics on crime, victimization, law enforcement, courts, sentencing, and corrections.

Community Oriented Policing Services (COPS)
URL: http://www.cops.usdoj.gov
E-mail: tellcops@usdoj.gov
Phone: (800) 421-6770
1100 Vermont Avenue, NW
Washington, DC 20530
Part of the Department of Justice, this agency promotes the use of community policing strategies to reduce crime and improve confidence in the police. In this role, it advocates procedures to eliminate the use of racial profiling and lessen conflict between minority groups and police. It also provides funding for community policing programs.

Customs and Border Protection
URL: http://www.customs.ustreas.gov
Phone: (202) 354-1000
1300 Pennsylvania Avenue, NW
Washington, DC 20229
Formerly part of the Treasury Department, the agency has been merged into the Department of Homeland Security as part of the Border and Transportation Security directorate. Once accused of racial profiling, it has instituted procedures to prevent discrimination in making customs and border searchers.

Federal Bureau of Investigation (FBI)
URL: http://www.fbi.gov
Phone: (202) 324-3000
J. Edgar Hoover Building
935 Pennsylvania Avenue, NW
Washington, DC 20535
This well-known agency has for some time had a policy to avoid the use of racial, ethnic, or national origin information in selecting individuals for investigation. However, concerns about use of ethnic profiling may have led to the failure to follow up on warnings before September 11, 2001, of Arabs attending U.S. flight schools.

Los Alamos National Laboratory (LANL)
URL: http://www.lanl.gov
E-mail: lanl-web@lanl.gov
Phone: (505) 667-7000
P.O. Box 1663
Los Alamos, NM 87545
Focused historically on nuclear weapons research, development, and safety, the lab experienced negative publicity over accusations of ethnic profiling in relation to an Asian scientist, Wen Ho Lee, who was accused, falsely it appears, of spying for China.

National Criminal Justice Reference Center (NCJRC)
URL: http://www.ncjrs.org
E-mail: tellncjrs@ncjrs.org
Phone: (800) 851-3420
P.O. Box 6000
Rockville, MD 20849-6000
A federally funded resource sponsored by the U.S. Department of

Justice and the Executive Office of the President that offers information on justice issues and aid to those wanting to use the information. Its web site includes information and publications on racial profiling.

National Institute of Justice (NIJ)
URL: http://www.ojp.usdoj.gov/nij
E-mail: askncjrs@ncjrs.org
Phone: (202) 307-2942
810 Seventh Street, NW
Washington, DC 20531
The research, development, and evaluation agency of the U.S. Department of Justice, this institute funds research on criminal justice programs and provides knowledge to state and local agencies to help them meet their law enforcement goals.

Office of National Drug Control Policy (ONDCP)
URL: http://www.whitehousedrugpolicy.gov
E-mail: ondcp@ncjrs.org
Phone: (800) 666-3332
P.O. Box 6000
Rockville, MD 20849-6000
Part of the White House Office, it establishes policies, priorities, and objectives for the nation's drug control efforts and offers guidelines for cooperation among federal, state, and local entities.

Substance Abuse and Mental Health Services Administration (SAMHSA)
URL: http://www.samhsa.gov
E-mail: info@samhsa.gov
Phone: (301) 443-8956
5600 Fishers Lane
Rockville, MD 20857
A resource center for data, the agency provides access to the results of national surveys of drug use that allow comparisons across races. The response of individuals to questions about drug-related behavior offers information that does not depend on police reports.

Transportation Security Administration (TSA)
Office of Civil Rights
Mail Stop TSA-6
400 Seventh Street, SW
Washington, DC 20590
URL: http://www.tsa.gov
Created by the Transportation Security Act signed into law on November 19, 2001, this organization took over airport screening and other tasks involved in protecting the nation's transportation system. It has recently become part of the U.S. Department of Homeland Security.

U.S. Commission on Civil Rights (USCCR)
URL: http://www.usccr.gov
E-mail: wwwadmin@usccr.gov
Phone: (202) 376-8312
624 Ninth Street, NW
Washington, DC 20425
This agency of the federal government has the mission to investigate complaints alleging that citizens are being deprived of their rights because of race, color, religion, sex, age, disability, or national origin. Under this mandate it has investigated policing practices in New

York City and accused the New York City Police Department of racial profiling.

U.S. Department of Homeland Security (DHS)
URL: http://www.dhs.gov/dhspublic
Washington, DC 20528
This newly created department, which does not provide a phone but allows interested parties to send an e-mail via its web page, supervises various agencies concerned with border protection and airport security.

U.S. Department of Energy (DOE)
URL: http://www.energy.gov
E-mail: secretary@hq.doe.gov
Phone: (800) 342-5363
1000 Independence Avenue, SW
Washington, DC 20585
Under Secretary Spencer Abraham, the DOE set guidelines to oppose racial profiling, which became particularly important in regard to protection of the U.S. domestic energy supply from terrorist activities.

U.S. Department of Justice (DOJ)
URL: http://www.usdoj.gov
E-mail: askdoj@usdoj.gov
Phone: (202) 353-1555
950 Pennsylvania Avenue, NW
Washington, DC 20530-0001
As the major legal and justice agency of the federal government, the Justice Department oversees law enforcement, immigration, security, and drug interdiction—all issues related to controversies over racial profiling.

U.S. Department of Transportation (DOT)
URL: http://www.dot.gov
E-mail: dot.comments@ost.dot.gov
400 Seventh Street, SW
Washington, DC 20590
Transportation Secretary Norman Mineta acted to end incidents of alleged racial profiling on airplanes in the aftermath of the September 11, 2001, terrorist attacks.

U.S. Drug Enforcement Administration (DEA)
URL: http://www.dea.gov
Phone: (202) 307-1000
2401 Jefferson Davis Highway
Alexandria, VA 22301
The DEA is a major federal agency for the enforcement of controlled-substance laws. Critics have alleged that some of its programs to train state law enforcement agents in drug interdiction techniques serve to promote racial profiling.

U.S. General Accounting Office (GAO)
URL: http://www.gao.gov
E-mail: webmaster@gao.gov
Phone: (212) 512-3000
441 G Street
Washington, DC 20598
As the agency that audits, evaluates, and investigates government programs, the GAO works to improve the performance and accountability

of government. In a report to the Congressional Black Caucus, it developed guidelines for measuring and collecting data on racial profiling.

U.S. House Committee on Government Reform
URL: http://reform.house.gov
Phone: (202) 225-5074
2157 Rayburn House Office Building
Washington, DC 20515
This committee has held hearings on the use of audiovisual technology to obtain evidence on racial profiling and help eliminate the practice.

U.S. House Committee on Transportation and Infrastructure
URL: http://www.house.gov/transportation
Phone: (202) 225-9446
2165 Rayburn House Office Building
Washington, DC 20515
The Subcommittee on Aviation of this committee has sponsored hearings on use of racial profiling methods to detect and prevent terrorist activities on airplanes.

U.S. Senate Committee on the Judiciary
URL: http://judiciary.senate.gov
Phone: (202) 224-5225
224 Dirksen Senate Office Building
Washington, DC 20510
The Subcommittee on the Constitution, Federalism, and Property Rights of this committee has sponsored hearings on the extent of racial profiling and legislation to end the practice.

U.S. Sentencing Commission (USSC)
URL: http://www.ussc.gov
E-mail: pubaffairs@ussc.gov
Phone: (202) 502-4500
One Columbus Circle, NE
Washington, DC 20002-8002
As the agency of the judicial branch of the federal government that establishes guidelines for sentencing, the USSC recommended changes in the punishment for possession of crack cocaine, but Congress overturned the recommendations.

White House
URL: http://www.whitehouse.gov
E-mail: president@whitehouse.gov
Phone: (202) 456-1111
1600 Pennsylvania Avenue, NW
Washington, DC 20500
Includes numerous announcements—available on the web page—about the issue of racial profiling.

STATE AND LOCAL

California Highway Patrol (CHP)
URL: http://www.chp.ca.gov
E-mail: publicaffairs@chp.ca.gov
Phone: (916) 657-7261
2555 First Avenue
Sacramento, CA 95818

The CHP has been involved in incidents of alleged profiling of Latinos over concerns about illegal immigration and drug transportation and has settled a lawsuit by agreeing to make changes in stop-and-search procedures.

City of San Diego Police Department (SDPD)
URL: http://www.sannet.gov/police
E-mail: sdpdwebmaster@pd.sandiego.gov
Phone: (619) 531-2000
1401 Broadway
San Diego, CA 92101-5729
The SDPD has been a leader in collecting data on traffic stops, opposing racial profiling, and using community policing to improve relations with minority communities. However, these efforts have not had complete success, as accusations of racial profiling continue.

Florida Highway Patrol (FHP)
URL: http://www.fhp.state.fl.us
E-mail: fhp@hsmv.state.fl.us
Phone: (850) 487-2714
Neil Kirkman Building
2900 Apalachee Parkway
Tallahassee, FL 32399
Although accused of using racial profiling in efforts to apprehend those involved in drug transport, the Florida Highway Patrol now has a stated policy that race, ethnicity, gender, and economic status of the vehicle occupants will not be considered in making a stop or a search.

Illinois State Police (ISP)
URL: http://www.isp.state.il.us
E-mail: hector@isp.state.il.us
Phone: (217) 782-6637
125 Monroe Street
P.O. Box 19461
Springfield, IL 62794-19461
The Illinois State Police have been accused of using profiling of Hispanics in an effort to stop the transportation of drugs through the state, but lawsuits against the state agency have not been successful.

Justice Research and Statistics Association (JRSA)
URL: http://www.jrsa.org
E-mail: cjinfo@jrsa.org
Phone: (202) 842-9330
777 North Capitol Street, NE
Suite 801
Washington, DC 20002
This association of state statistical analysis center directors has conducted and published policy-relevant research on traffic stop data and racial profiling.

Maryland State Police (MDSP)
URL: http://www.mdsp.maryland.gov
Phone: (410) 486-3101
1201 Reisterstown Road
Pikesville, MD 21208
The first police agency to settle a suit over racial profiling, the Maryland State Police agreed to end racial profiling in 1995, but critics say the practice persists and have filed another suit.

National Conference of State Legislatures (NCSL)
URL: http://www.ncsl.org
E-mail: info@ncsl.org
Phone: (202) 642-5400
444 North Capitol Street, NW
Suite 515
Washington, DC 20001
The NCSL promotes sharing of information and resources among state legislatures, including those related to racial profiling and criminal justice issues.

New Jersey Department of Law and Public Safety (LPS)
URL: http://www.nj.gov/lps/oag
Phone: (609) 292-4791
Richard J. Hughes Justice Complex
P.O. Box 080
Trenton, NJ 08625
This New Jersey government agency, led by the state attorney general and in charge of the state police, has over the years been in the center of controversies concerning the use of racial profiling.

New Jersey State Police (NJSP)
URL: http://www.njsp.org
Phone: (609) 882-2000
P.O. Box 7068
West Trenton, NJ 08628
In the midst of racial profiling controversies since the 1990s, this police agency has been heavily criticized by minorities and civil rights groups. The controversy has led to instability in the leadership and a tarnished reputation of the agency.

New York City Police Department (NYPD)
URL: http://www.nyc.gov/html/nypd
Phone: (646) 610-5000
One Police Plaza
New York, NY 10038
After years of accusations by minorities that New York City police have used racial profiling, Commissioner Raymond W. Kelly and Mayor Michael Bloomberg have made it the policy of the department to prohibit this practice.

Seattle Police Department
URL: http://www.cityofseattle.net/police
E-mail: SPDinformation@seattle.gov
Phone: (606) 625-5011
610 Fifth Avenue
Seattle, WA 98104
The department has come under criticism for discrimination against minorities, and some police officers worry that the criticism will reduce their ability to prevent crime in minority communities.

ADVOCACY ORGANIZATIONS

Adversity.Net
URL: http://www.adversity.net
E-mail: editor@adversity.net
P.O. Box 7099
Silver Spring, MD 20907-7099
This organization opposes "reverse discrimination," racial preferences, and quotas—forms of prejudice and

discrimination in its view. It also includes a page critical of anti–racial profiling attacks on police.

American-Arab Anti-Discrimination Committee
URL: http://www.adc.org
E-mail: adc@adc.org
Phone: (202) 224-2990
4201 Connecticut Avenue, NW
Washington, DC 20008

In defending the civil rights of Arab Americans, the organization has strongly opposed racial profiling and recent actions of the Department of Justice to detain suspected terrorists. It urges that the government adopt even more stringent antiprofiling policies than it now has.

American Civil Liberties Union (ACLU)
URL: http://www.aclu.org
Phone: (212) 549-2500
125 Broad Street
18th Floor
New York, NY 10004

An organization devoted to the protection of rights and freedoms of citizens and opposed to racial profiling. It has participated in numerous suits against police agencies and states for use of racial profiling and maintains a web page on the issue.

Americans for Effective Law Enforcement (AELE)
URL: http://www.aele.org
E-mail: info@aele.org
Phone: (874) 685-0700
841 West Touhy Avenue
Park Ridge, IL 60068-3351

An organization that produces and disseminates legal information through seminars, electronic media, and direct contact, it includes case summaries on its web page relating to racial profiling and other legal issues.

American Muslim Council
URL: http://www.amconline.org
E-mail: amc@amconline.org
Phone: (202) 543-0095
721-R Second Street, NE
Washington, DC 20002

With a mission to increase effective participation of American Muslims in U.S. politics and public policy, the council opposes government detention of immigrants and supports the civil rights of Muslims.

Amnesty International
URL: http://www.amnesty.org
E-mail: admin-us@aiusa.org
Phone: (212) 807-8400
322 Eighth Avenue
New York, NY 10001

With goals of protecting human rights worldwide and opposing government-sponsored torture, political imprisonment, the death penalty, and racial and ethnic discrimination, Amnesty International has criticized American police agencies for use of racial profiling.

Arab American Institute
URL: http://www.aaiusa.org
E-mail: aai@aaiusa.org
Phone: (202) 429-9210
1600 K Street, NW
Suite 601
Washington, DC 20006

The institute provides policy, research, and public affairs services to support its goals of increasing the civic and political power of Americans of Arab descent. Under its president, James Zogby, it has strongly opposed profiling at airports.

Asian Law Caucus (ALC)
URL: http://www.asianlawcaucus.org
E-mail: alc@asianlawcaucus.org
Phone: (415) 896-1701
939 Market Street
Suite 201
San Francisco, CA 94103
As part of its goal to promote and represent the legal and civil rights of members of the Asian and Pacific Islander communities in America, particularly those with low income, the ALC has joined with other Asian organizations to oppose racial profiling.

Cato Institute
URL: http://www.cato.org
E-mail: service@cato.org
Phone: (202) 842-0200
1000 Massachusetts Avenue, NW
Washington, DC 20001-5403
A research and policy organization devoted to individual liberty, limited government, free markets, and peace, the Cato Institute has sponsored panels and papers on racial profiling. It has warned that the attacks of September 11 could threaten loss of individual liberty.

Center for Immigration Studies (CIS)
URL: http://www.cis.org
E-mail: center@cis.org
Phone: (202) 466-8185
1522 K Street, NW
Suite 820
Washington, DC 20005-1202
This research organization, generally supportive of lower rates of immigration, provides useful background information on a number of immigration topics related to racial profiling.

Center for Policy Alternatives (CFPA)
URL: http://www.stateaction.org
E-mail: info@cfpa.org
Phone: (202) 387-8529
1875 Connecticut Avenue, NW
Suite 710
Washington, DC 20009
This policy center serves state legislators, policy organizations, and grassroots leaders by providing policy information and developing communication networks. It has, for example, set up a web page on state action in the area of racial profiling.

Civil Rights Project (CRP)
URL: http://www.civilrightsproject.harvard.edu
E-mail: crp@harvard.edu
125 Mount Auburn Street
Third Floor
Cambridge, MA 02138
Part of the Harvard University Law School, the Civil Rights Project is devoted to civil rights research and policy studies. It has provided a guide for international students on racial profiling and hate crime.

Claremont Institute
URL: http://www.claremont.org
E-mail: info@claremont.org
Phone: (909) 621-6825
937 West Foothill Boulevard
Suite E
Claremont, CA 91711
Supports the principles of limited and accountable government, private property, stable family life, and a strong defense, and has opposed anti–racial profiling efforts, particularly as they relate to air safety.

Coalition for Peace Action (CFPA)
URL: http://www.princeton.edu/~cbli/profiles/cpa.html
E-mail: cfpa@peacecoalition.org
Phone: (609) 924-3052
40 Witherspoon Street
Princeton, NJ 08542-3208
An organization mostly concerned with issues of nuclear weapons, peace, and weapons trafficking, the CFPA is also interested in investigating instances of racial profiling in New Jersey.

Cypress Media Group
URL: http://www.cypressmedia.net
E-mail: cypressmedia@mindspring.com
Phone: (770) 640-9918
Box 53198
Atlanta, GA 30355-1198
This private firm offers a seminar on ethnic, racial, and cultural sensitivity issues that helps officers in dealing with the public and avoid racial profiling.

Drug Reform Coordination Network
URL: http://www.stopthedrugwar.org
E-mail: drcnet@drcnet.org
Phone: (202) 293-8340
23 Connecticut Avenue, NW
Third Floor
Washington, DC 20009
This organization views racial profiling as a consequence of an ineffective and mistaken drug war.

Fairness and Accuracy in Reporting (FAIR)
URL: http://www.fair.org
E-mail: fair@fair.org
Phone: (212) 633-6700
112 West 27th Street
New York, NY 10001
Concerned about media censorship, biased reporting, and control of the news by corporations, this organization views the media treatment of racial profiling as accurate but has criticized the media for promoting images of African Americans as drug users and criminals.

Fraternal Order of Police (FOP)
URL: http://www.grandlodgefop.org
E-mail: natlsecAtnip@grandlodgefop.org
Phone: (615) 399-0900
1410 Donelson Pike
Suite A-17
Nashville, TN 37217
The world's largest organization of law enforcement officers, it is committed to improving the working conditions of its members and has

opposed recent anti–racial profiling legislation.

Hispanic American Police Command Officers Association (HAPCOA)
URL: http://www.hapcoa.org
E-mail: villareal@hapcoa.org
Phone: (703) 534-2895
6055A Arlington Boulevard
Falls Church, VA 22044
This organization sponsors conferences for training, networking, and establishing relationships among Hispanic law enforcement officers. It favors anti–racial profiling legislation.

Human Rights Watch
URL: http://www.hrw.org
E-mail: hrwdc@hrw.org
Phone: (202) 612-4321
1630 Connecticut Avenue, NW
Suite 500
Washington, DC 20009
The largest human rights organization in the United States, it investigates and exposes human rights violations and works to end practices that encourage these violations. As such, it opposes racial profiling.

International Association of Chiefs of Police (IACP)
URL: http://www.theiacp.org
E-mail: spiveyk@theiacp.org
Phone: (703) 836-6767
515 North Washington Street
Alexandria, VA 22314
This organization supports law enforcement chiefs with research, training, policy representation, and a monthly magazine. It opposes police action based solely on race, ethnicity, or national origin and makes recommendations for how data on traffic stops should be collected.

Joint Center for Political and Economic Studies
URL: http://www.jointcenter.org
E-mail: dfarquharson@jointcenter.org
Phone: (202) 789-3500
1090 Vermont Avenue, NW
Suite 1100
Washington, DC 20005-4928
This center aids black government officials by conducting research, holding conferences, and publishing materials. It has sponsored surveys and research on the dangers of profiling.

Leadership Conference on Civil Rights (LCCR)
URL: http://www.civilrights.org/about/lccr
Phone: (202) 466-3311
1629 K Street, NW
10th Floor
Washington, DC 20006
Consisting of 180 organizations and an educational fund for effective civil rights and social justice policies, this coalition supports a web site with recent civil rights news and materials on racial profiling.

League of United Latin American Citizens (LULAC)
URL: http://www.lulac.org
E-mail: lquiroga@lulac.org

Phone: (292) 833-6130
2000 L Street, NW
Suite 610
Washington DC 20036
This organization works to advance the economic conditions, political influence, and civil rights of the Hispanic population in the United States. Its national assembly passed a resolution opposing racial profiling and favoring collection of data on the practice.

Manhattan Institute
URL: http://www.manhattan-institute.org
E-mail: mi@manhattan-institute.org
Phone: (212) 599-7000
112 West 31st Street
New York, NY 10001
In advancing greater economic choice and individual responsibility, this New York City think tank has supported efforts to improve the safety of cities and defended the police against accusations of racial profiling.

Mexican American Legal Defense and Educational Fund (MALDEF)
URL: http://www.maldef.org
Phone: (213) 629-2512
634 South Spring Street
Los Angeles, CA 90014
This fund supports litigation, advocacy, and educational outreach on behalf of Latinos living in the United States. It has been active in protecting the rights of immigrants and has opposed use of ethnic profiling by law enforcement officials.

National Asian Pacific American Legal Consortium (NAPALC)
URL: http://www.napalc.org
E-mail: veng@napalc.org
Phone: (202) 296-2300
1140 Connecticut Avenue, NW
Suite 1200
Washington, DC 20036
NAPALC has been active in protesting racial profiling in nuclear research laboratories and the prosecution of Wen Ho Lee for spying.

National Association for the Advancement of Colored People (NAACP)
URL: http://www.naacp.org
E-mail: webmaster@naacpnet.org
Phone: (877) 622-2798
4805 Mount Hope Drive
Baltimore, MD 21215
This well-known civil rights organization works to ensure compliance with civil rights laws, promote equitable treatment of all Americans, and empower African Americans. It has opposed racial profiling and been active in suits against the Maryland State Police for use of the practice.

National Association of Black Law Enforcement Executives (NOBLE)
URL: http://www.noblenatl.org
E-mail: noble@noblenatl.org
Phone: (703) 658-1529
4609 Pinecrest Office Park Drive
Suite F
Alexandria, VA 22312-1442

It aims to ensure equality in the administration of justice, improve the knowledge of its members, and promote effective policing policies. It has opposed racial profiling and supported federal legislation to collect data on racial differences in traffic stops.

National Association of Criminal Defense Lawyers (NACDL)
URL: http://www.nacdl.org
E-mail: assist@nacdl.org
Phone: (202) 872-8600
1150 18th Street, NW
Suite 950
Washington, DC 20036
NACDL provides an index of information on racial profiling that may be of possible interest to criminal defense lawyers.

National Association of Police Organizations (NAPO)
URL: http://www.napo.org
E-mail: info@napo.org
Phone: (202) 842-4420
750 First Street, NE
Suite 920
Washington, DC 20002-4241
A coalition of police unions and associations focusing on legislation, legal advocacy, political action, and education, NAPO opposes legislation requiring officers to gather information on racial profiling as unnecessary, likely to generate hostility toward officers, and worsen law enforcement.

National Black Police Association
URL: http://www.blackpolice.org
E-mail: nbpanatofc@worldnet.att.net
Phone: (202) 986-2070
3251 Mount Pleasant Street, NW
Second Floor
Washington, DC 20010-2103
This organization, which opposes racial profiling and favors legislation to collect traffic stop data, aims to improve the quality of life of the African-American community and promote fairness, justice, and effectiveness in law enforcement.

National Council of La Raza (NCLR)
URL: http://www.nclr.org
Phone: (202) 785-1670
1111 19th Street, NW
Washington, DC 20036
This national Hispanic advocacy group and policy analysis center represents Hispanic Americans and favors legislation to monitor and end racial profiling.

National District Attorneys Association (NDAA)
URL: http://www.ndaa.org
E-mail: webmaster@ndaa-apri.org
Phone: (703) 549-9222
99 Canal Center Plaza
Suite 510
Alexandria, VA 22314
This organization of U.S. prosecutors has condemned racial profiling and supports the equal treatment of all groups in the criminal justice system.

National Troopers Coalition (NTC)
URL: http://www.ntctroopers.com

E-mail: cperry@new.rr.com
Phone: (800) 232-1392
This coalition of state troopers and highway patrol officers aims to promote better policing standards and working conditions for officers. It has supported police in racial profiling hearings, arguing that they do not discriminate against minorities but use race, ethnicity, and national-origin characteristics only when they are associated with crime.

National Urban League
URL: http://www.nul.org
E-mail: info@nul.org
Phone: (212) 558-5300
120 Wall Street
New York, NY 10005
A charitable organization with the mission to enable African Americans to secure economic self-reliance, power, and civil rights, it has supported federal anti–racial profiling legislation.

Open Society Institute, Criminal Justice Initiative
URL: http://www.soros.org/crime
E-mail: jmort@sorosny.org
Phone: (212) 548-0100
400 West 59th Street
Third Floor
New York, NY 10019
Created and funded by philanthropist George Soros, the institute supports research and action to reduce the excessive reliance on punishment and imprisonment in the United States and to promote fair and equal treatment of people in the U.S. criminal justice system.

Organization of Chinese Americans (OCA)
URL: http://www.ocanatl.org
E-mail: oca@ocanatl.org
Phone: (202) 223-5500
1001 Connecticut Avenue, NW
#601
Washington, DC 20036-5527
This is an advocacy organization concerned with securing the rights of Chinese-American and Asian-American citizens and permanent residents through legislative and government policy initiatives. It has expressed concerns about racial profiling of Asian Americans.

People's Organization for Progress (POP)
URL: http://www.njpop.org
Phone: (973) 643-7711
P.O. Box 22505
Newark, NJ 07101
This New Jersey organization works to improve conditions in minority communities and to mobilize against racial profiling and police brutality.

Police Executive Research Forum (PERF)
URL: http://www.policeforum.org
E-mail: glove@policeforum.org or cwexler@policeforum.org
Phone: (202) 466-7820
1120 Connecticut Avenue, NW
Suite 930
Washington, DC 20036
This organization of police executives from the largest city, county, and state law enforcement agencies

uses research and public policy initiatives to improve the professionalism of police. It has opposed legislation to end racial profiling.

Police Foundation
URL: http://www.policefoundation.org
E-mail: pfinfo@policefoundation.org
Phone: (202) 833-1460
1210 Connecticut Avenue, NW
Washington, DC 20036-2636
This foundation advocates new ideas in policing toward the goal of strengthening the link between police and the public, and maintains information on legal issues relating to racial profiling.

Progressive Policy Institute (PPI)
URL: http://www.ppionline.org
Phone: (202) 546-0007
600 Pennsylvania Avenue, SE
Suite 400
Washington, DC 20003
This institute, associated with the Democratic Leadership Council, advocates modern progressive policies. In the area of criminal justice, it supports use of community policing techniques that can both deal with crime problems and protect the civil rights of citizens.

Public Entity Risk Institute (PERI)
URL: http://www.riskinstitute.org
E-mail: ghoetmer@riskinstitute.org
Phone: (703) 352-1846
11350 Random Hills Road
Suite 210
Fairfax, VA 22030
To help public officials and police executives deal with risk management, PERI has sponsored a symposium on racial profiling.

Racial Fairness Project
URL: http://www.racialfairness.org
E-mail: mwieser@racialfairness.org
Phone: (216) 323-9116
2401 Superior Viaduct
Cleveland, OH 44113-2342
This local organization is concerned with the unfair treatment of minorities by the criminal justice system, including the use of racial profiling.

Racial Profiling Data Collection Resource Center at Northeastern University
URL: http://www.racialprofilinganalysis.neu.edu
E-mail: racialprofilinganalysis@neu.edu
Phone: (617) 373-4678
Institute on Race and Justice
400 Churchill Hall
Northeastern University
Boston, MA 02115-5000
The Office of Justice Programs at the U.S. Department of Justice awarded funds to the Institute on Race and Justice at Northeastern University to construct a web-based resource center that serves as a clearinghouse for information and data on racial profiling.

Racial Profiling Legal Help (RPLH) Resource Center
URL: http://www.racialprofilinglegalhelp.com
E-mail: rplh@racialprofilinglegalhelp.com
Phone: (803) 831-7777
2930 Bent Twig Court
Clover, SC 29710
A privately funded project concerned about the loss of civil liberties after the September 11 attacks, it provides legal help to those subject to racial and ethnic profiling.

Rainbow/PUSH Coalition
URL: http://www.rainbowpush.org
E-mail: info@rainbowpush.org
Phone: (773) 373-3366
930 East 50th Street
Chicago, IL 60615-2702
A multiracial organization founded and led by Jesse Jackson, it works for social change and racial equality in the criminal justice system and elsewhere in society.

RAND Corporation
URL: http://www.rand.org
E-mail: correspondence@rand.org
P.O. Box 2138
1700 Main Street
Santa Monica, CA 90407-2138
An institution devoted to research and analysis for public policy decision making, RAND has studied police effectiveness and antiterrorism efforts—both issues related to racial profiling.

Reason Foundation
URL: http://www.reason.org
E-mail: feedback@reason.org
Phone: (310) 391-2245
3415 Sepulveda Boulevard
Los Angeles, CA 90034
Advocates positions and policies supportive of individual liberty, private property, and limited government, and publishes *Reason Magazine*. Based on a libertarian philosophy, it opposes racial profiling and has sponsored critical writings and discussion on the topic.

Sentencing Project
URL: http://www.sentencingproject.org
Phone: (202) 628-0871
514 10th Street, NW
Suite 1000
Washington, DC 20004
An organization devoted to the development of alternative sentencing programs and changes in criminal justice policy, it has been active in describing the high rates of imprisonment of African-American young men and has criticized police, prosecutors, judges, and lawmakers for the mistreatment of minorities.

TriTech Software Systems
URL: http://www2.trtech.com/internet
E-mail: sales@tritech.com
Phone: (858) 799-7000
9860 Mesa Rim Road
San Diego, CA 92121
The company has developed software that it believes can aid police in the use of audiovisual technol-

ogy to record contacts with the public and possible incidents of racial profiling.

Vera Institute of Justice
URL: http://www.vera.org
E-mail: info@vera.org
Phone: (212) 334-1300
233 Broadway
12th Floor
New York, NY 10279

The institute works closely with leaders in government and society to improve crime and justice services, and in so doing has conducted research on racial profiling.

PART III

APPENDICES

APPENDIX A

UNITED STATES V. BRIGNONI-PONCE, NO. 74-114 (1975)

CERTIORARI TO THE UNITED STATES COURT OF APPEALS FOR THE NINTH CIRCUIT

Note: Supreme Court of the United States, *Selected excerpts follow, with footnotes and most references deleted*

Argued February 18, 1975
Decided, June 30, 1975

MR. JUSTICE POWELL delivered the opinion of the Court.

This case raises questions as to the United States Border Patrol's authority to stop automobiles in areas near the Mexican border. It differs from our decision in *Almeida-Sanchez v. United States,* in that the Border Patrol does not claim authority to search cars, but only to question the occupants about their citizenship and immigration status.

I

As part of its regular traffic-checking operations in southern California, the Border Patrol operates a fixed checkpoint on Interstate Highway 5 south of San Clemente. On the evening of March 11, 1973, the checkpoint was closed because of inclement weather, but two officers were observing northbound traffic from a patrol car parked at the side of the highway. The road was dark, and they were using the patrol car's headlights to illuminate passing cars. They pursued respondent's car and stopped it, saying later that their only reason for doing so was that its three occupants appeared to be of Mexican descent. The officers questioned respondent and his two passengers about their citizenship and learned that the passengers were aliens who had entered the country illegally. All three were then arrested, and respondent was charged with two counts of knowingly transporting illegal immigrants, a violation of § 274 (a) (2) of the Immigration and Nationality Act, 66 Stat. 228, 8 U.S.C. § 1324 (a)(2). At trial respondent moved to suppress the testimony of and about the two passengers, claiming that this evidence was the fruit of an illegal seizure. The trial court denied the motion, the aliens testified at trial, and respondent was convicted on both counts.

Respondent's appeal was pending in the Court of Appeals for the Ninth Circuit when we announced our decision in *Almeida-Sanchez v. United States*, supra, holding that the Fourth Amendment prohibits the use of roving patrols to search vehicles, without a warrant or probable cause, at points removed from the border and its functional equivalents. The Court of Appeals, sitting en banc, held that the stop in this case more closely resembled a roving-patrol stop than a stop at a traffic checkpoint, and applied the principles of *Almeida-Sanchez*. The court held that the Fourth Amendment, as interpreted in *Almeida-Sanchez*, forbids stopping a vehicle, even for the limited purpose of questioning its occupants, unless the officers have a "founded suspicion" that the occupants are aliens illegally in the country. The court refused to find that Mexican ancestry alone supported such a "founded suspicion" and held that respondent's motion to suppress should have been granted. We granted certiorari and set the case for oral argument with No. 73-2050, *United States v. Ortiz*, and No. 73-6848, *Bowen v. United States*.

The Government does not challenge the Court of Appeals' factual conclusion that the stop of respondent's car was a roving-patrol stop rather than a checkpoint stop. Nor does it challenge the retroactive application of *Almeida-Sanchez*, or contend that the San Clemente checkpoint is the functional equivalent of the border. The only issue presented for decision is whether a roving patrol may stop a vehicle in an area near the border and question its occupants when the only ground for suspicion is that the occupants appear to be of Mexican ancestry. For the reasons that follow, we affirm the decision of the Court of Appeals.

II

The Government claims two sources of statutory authority for stopping cars without warrants in the border areas. Section 287 (a)(1) of the Immigration and Nationality Act, 8 U.S.C. § 1357 (a)(1), authorizes any officer or employee of the Immigration and Naturalization Service (INS) without a warrant, "to interrogate any alien or person believed to be an alien as to his right to be or to remain in the United States." There is no geographical limitation on this authority. The Government contends that, at least in the areas adjacent to the Mexican border, a person's apparent Mexican ancestry alone justifies belief that he or she is an alien and satisfies the requirement of this statute. Section 287 (a)(3) of the Act, 8 U.S.C. § 1357 (a)(3), authorizes agents, without a warrant,

> *"within a reasonable distance from any external boundary of the United States, to board and search for aliens any vessel within the territorial waters of the United States and any railway car, aircraft, conveyance, or vehicle..."*

Under current regulations, this authority may be exercised anywhere within 100 miles of the border. The Border Patrol interprets the statute as granting authority to stop moving vehicles and question the occupants about their citizenship, even when its officers have no reason to believe that the occupants are aliens or that other aliens may be concealed in the vehicle. But "no Act of Congress can authorize a violation of the Constitution," and we must decide whether the Fourth Amendment allows such random vehicle stops in the border areas.

III

The Fourth Amendment applies to all seizures of the person, including seizures that involve only a brief detention short of traditional arrest. "[W]henever a police officer accosts an individual and restrains his freedom to walk away, he has 'seized' that person," and the Fourth Amendment requires that the seizure be "reasonable." As with other categories of police action subject to Fourth Amendment constraints, the reasonableness of such seizures depends on a balance between the public interest and the individual's right to personal security free from arbitrary interference by law officers.

The Government makes a convincing demonstration that the public interest demands effective measures to prevent the illegal entry of aliens at the Mexican border. Estimates of the number of illegal immigrants in the United States vary widely. A conservative estimate in 1972 produced a figure of about one million, but the INS now suggests there may be as many as 10 or 12 million aliens illegally in the country. Whatever the number, these aliens create significant economic and social problems, competing with citizens and legal resident aliens for jobs, and generating extra demand for social services.

The aliens themselves are vulnerable to exploitation because they cannot complain of substandard working conditions without risking deportation.

The Government has estimated that 85% of the aliens illegally in the country are from Mexico. The Mexican border is almost 2,000 miles long, and even a vastly reinforced Border Patrol would find it impossible to prevent illegal border crossings. Many aliens cross the Mexican border on foot, miles away from patrolled areas, and then purchase transportation from the border area to inland cities, where they find jobs and elude the immigration authorities. Others gain entry on valid temporary border-crossing permits, but then violate the conditions of their entry. Most of these aliens leave the border area in private vehicles, often assisted by professional "alien smugglers." The Border Patrol's traffic-checking operations are designed to prevent this inland movement. They succeed in apprehending some illegal entrants and smugglers, and they deter the movement of others by threatening apprehension and increasing the cost of illegal transportation.

Against this valid public interest we must weigh the interference with individual liberty that results when an officer stops an automobile and questions its occupants. The intrusion is modest. The Government tells us that a stop by a roving patrol "usually consumes no more than a minute." There is no search of the vehicle or its occupants, and the visual inspection is limited to those parts of the vehicle that can be seen by anyone standing alongside. According to the Government, "[a]ll that is required of the vehicle's occupants is a response to a brief question or two and possibly the production of a document evidencing a right to be in the United States."

Because of the limited nature of the intrusion, stops of this sort may be justified on facts that do not amount to the probable cause required for an arrest. In *Terry v. Ohio*, the Court declined expressly to decide whether facts not amounting to probable cause could justify an "investigative 'seizure'" short of an arrest, but it approved a limited search—a pat-down for weapons—for the protection of an officer investigating suspicious behavior of persons he reasonably believed to be armed and dangerous. The Court approved such a search on facts that did not constitute probable cause to believe the suspects guilty of a crime, requiring only that "the police officer … be able to point to specific and articulable facts which, taken together with rational inferences from those facts, reasonably warrant" a belief that his safety or that of others is in danger.

We elaborated on Terry in *Adams v. Williams*, holding that a policeman was justified in approaching the respondent to investigate a tip that he was carrying narcotics and a gun.

> *"The Fourth Amendment does not require a policeman who lacks the precise level of information necessary for probable cause to arrest to simply shrug his*

shoulders and allow a crime to occur or a criminal to escape. On the contrary, Terry recognizes that it may be the essence of good police work to adopt an intermediate response. ... A brief stop of a suspicious individual, in order to determine his identity or to maintain the status quo momentarily while obtaining more information, may be most reasonable in light of the facts known to the officer at the time."

These cases together establish that in appropriate circumstances the Fourth Amendment allows a properly limited "search" or "seizure" on facts that do not constitute probable cause to arrest or to search for contraband or evidence of crime. In both *Terry* and *Adams v. Williams* the investigating officers had reasonable grounds to believe that the suspects were armed and that they might be dangerous. The limited searches and seizures in those cases were a valid method of protecting the public and preventing crime. In this case as well, because of the importance of the governmental interest at stake, the minimal intrusion of a brief stop, and the absence of practical alternatives for policing the border, we hold that when an officer's observations lead him reasonably to suspect that a particular vehicle may contain aliens who are illegally in the country, he may stop the car briefly and investigate the circumstances that provoke suspicion. As in *Terry*, the stop and inquiry must be "reasonably related in scope to the justification for their initiation." The officer may question the driver and passengers about their citizenship and immigration status, and he may ask them to explain suspicious circumstances, but any further detention or search must be based on consent or probable cause.

We are unwilling to let the Border Patrol dispense entirely with the requirement that officers must have a reasonable suspicion to justify roving-patrol stops. In the context of border area stops, the reasonableness requirement of the Fourth Amendment demands something more than the broad and unlimited discretion sought by the Government. Roads near the border carry not only aliens seeking to enter the country illegally, but a large volume of legitimate traffic as well. San Diego, with a metropolitan population of 1.4 million, is located on the border. Texas has two fairly large metropolitan areas directly on the border: El Paso, with a population of 360,000, and the Brownsville-McAllen area, with a combined population of 320,000. We are confident that substantially all of the traffic in these cities is lawful and that relatively few of their residents have any connection with the illegal entry and transportation of aliens. To approve roving-patrol stops of all vehicles in the border area, without any suspicion that a particular vehicle is carrying illegal immigrants, would subject the residents of these and other areas to potentially unlimited interference with their use of the highways, solely at the discretion of Border Patrol officers. The only formal limitation on that discretion appears to be the administrative regulation defining the term "reasonable distance" in § 287(a)(3) to mean within 100 air miles from the border. Thus, if we approved the Government's position in this case, Border Patrol officers could stop motorists at random for questioning, day or night, anywhere within 100 air miles of the 2,000-mile border, on a city street, a busy highway, or a desert road, without any reason to suspect that they have violated any law.

We are not convinced that the legitimate needs of law enforcement require this degree of interference with lawful traffic. As we discuss in Part IV, the nature of illegal alien traffic and the characteristics of smuggling operations tend to generate articulable grounds for identifying violators. Consequently, a requirement of reasonable suspicion for stops allows the Government adequate means of guarding the public interest and also protects residents of the border areas from indiscriminate official interference. Under the circumstances, and even though the intrusion incident to a stop is modest, we conclude that it is not "reasonable" under the Fourth Amendment to make such stops on a random basis.

The Government also contends that the public interest in enforcing conditions on legal alien entry justifies stopping persons who may be aliens for questioning about their citizenship and immigration status. Although we may assume for purposes of this case that the broad congressional power over immigration, see *Kleindienst v. Mandel*, authorizes Congress to admit aliens on condition that they will submit to reasonable questioning about their right to be and remain in the country, this power cannot diminish the Fourth Amendment rights of citizens who may be mistaken for aliens. For the same reasons that the Fourth Amendment forbids stopping vehicles at random to inquire if they are carrying aliens who are illegally in the country, it also forbids stopping or detaining persons for questioning about their citizenship on less than a reasonable suspicion that they may be aliens.

IV

The effect of our decision is to limit exercise of the authority granted by both § 287 (a)(1) and § 287 (a)(3). Except at the border and its functional equivalents, officers on roving patrol may stop vehicles only if they are aware of specific articulable facts, together with rational inferences from those facts, that reasonably warrant suspicion that the vehicles contain aliens who may be illegally in the country.

Any number of factors may be taken into account in deciding whether there is reasonable suspicion to stop a car in the border area. Officers may consider the characteristics of the area in which they encounter a vehicle. Its proximity to the border, the usual patterns of traffic on the particular road, and previous experience with alien traffic are all relevant. They also may consider information about recent illegal border crossings in the area. The driver's behavior may be relevant, as erratic driving or obvious attempts to evade officers can support a reasonable suspicion. Aspects of the vehicle itself may justify suspicion. For instance, officers say that certain station wagons, with large compartments for fold-down seats or spare tires, are frequently used for transporting concealed aliens. The vehicle may appear to be heavily loaded, it may have an extraordinary number of passengers, or the officers may observe persons trying to hide. The Government also points out that trained officers can recognize the characteristic appearance of persons who live in Mexico, relying on such factors as the mode of dress and haircut. In all situations the officer is entitled to assess the facts in light of his experience in detecting illegal entry and smuggling. In this case the officers relied on a single factor to justify stopping respondent's car: the apparent Mexican ancestry of the occupants. We cannot conclude that this furnished reasonable grounds to believe that the three occupants were aliens. At best the officers had only a fleeting glimpse of the persons in the moving car, illuminated by headlights. Even if they saw enough to think that the occupants were of Mexican descent, this factor alone would justify neither a reasonable belief that they were aliens, nor a reasonable belief that the car concealed other aliens who were illegally in the country. Large numbers of native-born and naturalized citizens have the physical characteristics identified with Mexican ancestry, and even in the border area a relatively small proportion of them are aliens. The likelihood that any given person of Mexican ancestry is an alien is high enough to make Mexican appearance a relevant factor, but standing alone it does not justify stopping all Mexican-Americans to ask if they are aliens.

The judgment of the Court of Appeals is Affirmed.

APPENDIX B

UNITED STATES V. STATE OF NEW JERSEY AND DIVISION OF STATE POLICE

CIVIL NO. 99-5970 (1999)

Note: United States District Court for District of New Jersey

Plaintiff, the United States, and Defendants, the State of New Jersey and the Division of State Police of the New Jersey Department of Law and Public Safety, respectfully move this Court for entry of the attached Consent Decree.

The United States has simultaneously filed its Complaint against the Defendants alleging violations of 42 U.S.C. § 14141 and 42 U.S.C. §3789d(c). The Complaint alleges a pattern or practice of conduct by troopers of the New Jersey State Police that deprives persons of rights, privileges, or immunities secured or protected by the Constitution and the laws of the United States. Defendants deny that the State Police has engaged in a pattern or practice of conduct that deprives persons of rights, privileges, or immunities secured or protected by the Constitution and laws of the United States.

The parties seek to enter into this Decree jointly for the purpose of avoiding the risks and burdens of litigation, and to support vigorous, lawful, and nondiscriminatory traffic enforcement that promotes traffic safety and assists law enforcement to interdict drugs and other contraband, arrest fugitives, and enforce firearms and other criminal statutes.

The United States and the State of New Jersey have agreed upon a proposed Consent Decree that would resolve all claims in the United States' Complaint. The proposed Decree would address the claims in the United States' Complaint by amending certain policies, practices, and procedures relating to the manner in which the State of New Jersey manages and operates the New Jersey State Police.

Appendix B

The proposed Decree addresses the following matters: policy requirements and limitations on the use of race in law enforcement activities and the procedures used for conducting motor vehicle searches; documentation of traffic stops including post-stop procedures and enforcement actions; supervisory measures to promote civil rights integrity; procedures for receiving, investigating, and resolving misconduct allegations; training; responsibilities of the Office of the New Jersey Attorney General concerning the New Jersey State Police; public reporting by the State Police about its law enforcement activities; and the establishment of an independent monitor to review and analyze implementation of the Decree by the State.

Specifically, the proposed Decree includes the following provisions:

1. *Policy Requirements (26–28):* State troopers may not rely to any degree on the race or national or ethnic origin of motorists in selecting vehicles for traffic stops and in deciding upon the scope and substance of post-stop actions, except where state troopers are on the look-out for a specific suspect who has been identified in part by his or her race or national or ethnic origin. The State Police shall continue to require that troopers make a request for consent to search only when they possess reasonable suspicion that a search will reveal evidence of a crime, and all consent searches must be based on the driver or passenger giving written consent prior to the initiation of the search.
2. *Traffic Stop Documentation (29–34):* State troopers engaged in patrol activities will document the race, ethnic origin, and gender of all motor vehicle drivers who are the subject of a traffic stop, and also will record information about the reason for each stop and any post-stop action that is taken (including the issuance of a ticket or warning, asking the vehicle occupants to exit the vehicle and frisking them, consensual and non-consensual vehicle searches, uses of force, and arrests).
3. *Supervisory Review of Individual Traffic Stops (35–39):* Supervisors regularly will review trooper reports concerning post-stop enforcement actions and procedures, and patrol car video tapes of traffic stops, to ensure that troopers are employing appropriate practices and procedures. Where concerns arise, supervisors may require that the trooper be counseled, receive additional training, or that some other non-disciplinary action be taken. Supervisors also can refer specific incidents for further investigation, where appropriate.
4. *Supervisory Review of Patterns of Conduct (40–56):* The State will develop and implement an early warning system, called the "Management

Awareness Program," that uses computerized information on traffic stops, misconduct investigations, and other matters to assist State Police supervisors to identify and modify potentially problematic behavior. At least quarterly, State Police supervisors will conduct reviews and analyses of computerized data and other information, including data on traffic stops and post-stop actions by race and ethnicity. These reviews and analyses, as appropriate, may result in supervisors implementing changes in traffic enforcement criteria, training, and practices, implementing non-disciplinary interventions for particular troopers (such as supervisory counseling or additional training), and/or requiring further assessment or investigation.

5. *Misconduct Allegations (57–92):* The State Police will make complaint forms and informational materials available at a variety of locations, will institute a 24-hour toll-free telephone hotline, and will publicize the State Police toll-free number at all State-operated rest stops located on limited access highways. The State also will institute procedures for ensuring that the State Police is notified of criminal cases and civil lawsuits alleging trooper misconduct. Allegations of discriminatory traffic stops, improper post-stop actions, and other significant misconduct allegations will be investigated by the Professional Standards Bureau inside the State Police or by the State Attorney General's Office. All investigations will be properly documented. Where a misconduct allegation is substantiated concerning prohibited discrimination or certain other serious misconduct, discipline shall be imposed. Where a misconduct allegation is not substantiated, the State Police will consider whether non-disciplinary supervisory steps are appropriate.
6. *Training (93–109):* The State Police will continue to implement measures to improve training for recruits and incumbent troopers. The training will address such matters as supervisory issues, communication skills, cultural diversity, and the nondiscrimination requirements of the Decree. The State Police also will take steps to continue to improve its trooper coach program for new troopers. The Independent Monitor selected by the parties will evaluate all training currently provided by the State Police regarding traffic stops, and will make recommendations for improvements.
7. *Auditing by the New Jersey Attorney General's Office (110–113):* The State Attorney General's Office will have special responsibility for ensuring implementation of the Decree. The Office will conduct various audits of State Police performance, which will include contacting samples of persons who were the subject of a State Police traffic stop to evaluate whether the stops were appropriately con-

ducted and documented. The Office also will audit State Police implementation of the Management Awareness Program, and procedures used for receiving, investigating, and resolving misconduct allegations.

8. *State Police Public Reports (114):* The State Police will issue semiannual public reports containing aggregate statistics on certain law enforcement activities, including traffic stop statistics.
9. *Independent Monitor (115–121):* An Independent Monitor, who will be an agent of the court, will be selected by the United States and the State of New Jersey to monitor and report on the State's implementation of the Decree. The responsibilities of the Monitor will include evaluating samples of trooper incident reports, supervisory reviews of incidents, and misconduct investigations, supervisors' use of the Management Awareness Program, and the use of non-disciplinary procedures to address at-risk conduct.
10. *Decree Term (131):* The basic term of the Decree will be five years, however, based on the State's record of compliance, the United States and the Independent Monitor may agree to a request by the State to shorten the term of the Decree if the State has been in substantial compliance for at least two years.

Joint entry of this Decree is in the public interest since it provides for expeditious remedial activity and avoids the diversion of federal and State resources to adversarial actions by the parties. Additionally, the proposed Decree does not conflict with the collective bargaining agreements between the State Police and its troopers, as noted in the Decree at 128.

For the reasons discussed above, entry of the Decree is lawful and appropriate. Therefore, the United States and the State jointly move for entry of the Consent Decree.

APPENDIX C

UNITED STATES OF AMERICA V. GERMAN ESPINOZA MONTERO-CAMARGO, NO. 97–50643 (1999); *UNITED STATES OF AMERICA V. LORENZO SANCHEZ-GUILLEN,* NO. 97-50645 (1999)

Note: Selected excerpts follow, with footnotes and most references deleted.

Argued and Submitted December 16, 1999—San Francisco, California
Filed April 11, 2000
Opinion by Judge Reinhardt.

The question before us is whether Border Patrol agents had reasonable suspicion to stop German Espinoza Montero-Camargo and Lorenzo Sanchez-Guillen. The defendants, who were driving separate automobiles in tandem, made U-turns on a highway at the only place where the view of the agents manning a permanent stationary checkpoint was obstructed. Following the turns, the two cars, both bearing Mexicali license plates, stopped briefly in an area that is often used as a drop-off and pick-up point for undocumented aliens and contraband. The U-turns occurred shortly after the cars passed a sign stating that the previously closed Border Patrol facility was now open. Based on these and other factors, the district court concluded that the stop, which occurred some fifty miles north of the Mexican border, was justified, as did the majority of the three judge panel that considered the question. We took the case en banc to reconsider the reasonable suspicion question. Although we affirm the result reached by both the district court and the panel majority, we reject some of the factors on which they relied.

FACTS

On the afternoon of October 15, 1996, a passing driver told border patrol agents at the Highway 86 permanent stationary checkpoint in El Centro, California, that two cars heading north, with Mexicali license plates, had just made U-turns on the highway shortly before the checkpoint. Upon receiving the tip, two Border Patrol Agents, Brian Johnson and Carl Fisher, got into separate marked patrol cars and headed south to investigate. Approximately one minute later (and about one mile from the checkpoint), the two agents saw a blue Chevrolet Blazer and a red Nissan sedan, both with Mexicali plates, pull off the shoulder and re-enter the highway heading south.

According to the agents, the area where they first observed the cars is used by lawbreakers to drop off and pick up undocumented aliens and illegal drugs, while evading inspection. Its use for such purposes is due in part to the fact that the view of that part of the highway area from the Border Patrol checkpoint is blocked. The location, according to Agent Johnson, is the only place where it is feasible to turn around both safely and with impunity. After that point, the road narrows and is in plain view of the checkpoint. The highway itself runs through the open desert and there is a fence on either side.

Both agents testified that almost all of the stops made by the Border Patrol at the turnaround site resulted in the discovery of "a violation of some sort ..." involving either illegal aliens or narcotics. In contrast, Agent Johnson said that similar stops made in connection with turnarounds near other checkpoints did not result in arrests nearly as frequently. He attributed the difference to the fact that travelers routinely miss their turnoffs to camping sites near those other checkpoints. Before the northbound Highway 86 checkpoint, however, there are no exits, driveways, or roads nearby that a driver might accidentally pass by. In fact, the only exit off of Highway 86 in that area is a private driveway to the Elmore Ranch, some two miles from the turnaround point.

The place where the agents saw that the vehicles had stopped following the U-turn was a deserted area on the side of the southbound highway located opposite the large sign on the northbound side advising drivers that the checkpoint was open. As Agent Johnson testified, the sign was the first indication to northbound drivers that the Border Patrol's facility was operational. The checkpoint in question had been closed for some time and had reopened only a day or two earlier.

At the suppression hearing, Agent Johnson testified that the majority of people going through the El Centro checkpoint are Hispanic. This demographic makeup is typical of the larger region of which the city El Centro is a part. In Imperial County, where El Centro is located, Hispanics make up roughly 73% of the population. See U.S. Census Bureau, "Population Estimates for Counties by Race and Hispanic Origin: July 1, 1999." Agent Johnson also testified that as he pulled behind the Blazer, he noted that both the driver and the passenger appeared to be Hispanic. Johnson stated that when the driver and passenger noticed him behind them, the passenger picked up a newspaper and began reading. This, according to Agent Johnson, further aroused his suspicions. Johnson then stopped the Blazer, identified himself as a Border Patrol agent, and asked about the citizenship of the two occupants. In response to Johnson's inquiries, the driver, Lorenzo Sanchez-Guillen, and his passenger, Sylvia Renteria-Wolff, showed Agent Johnson I-586 cards, which allow Mexican citizens to travel up to 25 miles inside the United States for no longer than 72 hours at a time. As the Blazer had been stopped approximately 50 miles from the border, Johnson then brought the two occupants to the checkpoint for processing.

In the meantime, Agent Fisher continued to follow the second car, a red Nissan sedan. According to Fisher, when he and Agent Johnson first drew near the two cars, the Nissan began to accelerate. As Fisher caught up with the vehicle, he could see that the second driver also appeared to be Hispanic. Fisher ultimately pulled the Nissan over after following it for approximately four miles. Appellant German Espinoza Montero-Camargo was the driver. After stopping the car, Agent Fisher, with the aid of Agent Johnson, who had returned to help him, searched the trunk and found two large bags of marijuana. A subsequent search of the Blazer back at the checkpoint turned up a loaded .32 caliber pistol in the glove compartment and an ammunition clip that fit the pistol in the passenger's purse.

Montero-Camargo, Sanchez-Guillen, and Renteria-Wolff were charged with conspiracy to possess marijuana with intent to distribute in violation of 21 U.S.C. §§ 846 and 841(a)(1), as well as possession of marijuana with intent to distribute in violation of 21 U.S.C. § 841(a)(1). Sanchez-Guillen was also charged with being an illegal alien in possession of ammunition in violation of 18 U.S.C. § 922(g)(5) and § 924(a)(2) and aiding and abetting the carrying of a firearm during the commission of a drug trafficking crime in violation of 18 U.S.C. § 924(c)(1) and (2). The three defendants filed a pretrial motion to suppress on the ground that the vehicle stop was not based on reasonable suspicion. When the district court denied the motion, Montero-Camargo entered a conditional guilty plea to conspiracy to possess and possession of marijuana with the intent to distribute; he reserved the right to challenge on appeal two of the district court's determinations, including the denial of the motion to suppress. Sanchez-Guillen went to trial, and a jury convicted him of conspiracy to possess and possession of marijuana with the intent to distribute, as well as being an illegal alien in possession of ammunition. He raises a number of issues on appeal.

In denying the motion to suppress, the district court conceded that the government's case "was somewhat weak," but concluded that, upon considering "all the factors that the officers had in their possession at the time that each of them made the stops, ... there was a sufficient founded suspicion to make an investigatory stop." Those factors, as the district court categorized them, included: 1) the tip about a U-turn made in the middle of the highway just before the checkpoint by two cars with Mexican license plates; 2) the alleged driving in tandem and the Mexicali license plates which supported the inference drawn by the officers that these were the two cars identified by the tipster; 3) the area in question, which, based on the officers' experience with previous stops, is "a notorious spot where smugglers turn around to avoid inspection" just before the first sign indicating that the checkpoint was in fact open; 4) the fact that the occupants of both cars appeared to be of Hispanic descent; and 5) the fact that the passenger in the Blazer picked up a newspaper as the Border Patrol car approached. The district judge concluded that when these factors were considered in light of the officers' experience, they supported a finding of reasonable suspicion.

On appeal, Montero-Camargo and Sanchez-Guillen argued that the district court erred in denying the motion to suppress. The panel majority agreed, however, with the district court's conclusion. It did so by listing, without further explication, a number of factors, including: apparent avoidance of a checkpoint, tandem driving, Mexicali license plates, the Hispanic appearance of the vehicles' occupants, the behavior of Renteria-Wolff, the agent's prior experience during stops after similar turnarounds, and the pattern of criminal activity at the remote spot where the two cars stopped. Although we reach the same result as both the district judge and the panel majority, we do so on the basis of a more selective set of factors.

ANALYSIS

1. The Reasonable Suspicion Calculus

[1] The Fourth Amendment "applies to all seizures of the person, including seizures that involve only a brief detention short of traditional arrest." Accordingly, the Fourth Amendment requires that such seizures be, at a minimum, "reasonable." In order to satisfy the Fourth Amendment's strictures, an investigatory stop by the police may be made only if the officer in question has "a reasonable suspicion supported by articulable facts that criminal activity may be afoot..."

[2] Like probable cause determinations, the reasonable suspicion analysis is "not 'readily, or even usefully, reduced to a neat set of legal rules'" and, also like probable cause, takes into account the totality of the circumstances. Although the level of suspicion required for a brief investigatory stop is less demanding than that for probable cause, the Fourth Amendment nevertheless requires an objective justification for such a stop. As a result, the officer in question "must be able to articulate more than an inchoate and unparticularized suspicion or 'hunch' of criminal activity." Rather, reasonable suspicion exists when an officer is aware of specific, articulable facts which, when considered with objective and reasonable inferences, form a basis for particularized suspicion.

[3] The requirement of particularized suspicion encompasses two elements. First, the assessment must be based upon the totality of the circumstances. Second, that assessment must arouse a reasonable suspicion that the particular person being stopped has committed or is about to commit a crime. See *Terry v. Ohio* ("[t]his demand for specificity in the information upon which police action is predicated is the central teaching of this Court's Fourth Amendment jurisprudence"). Accordingly, we have rejected profiles that are "likely to sweep many ordinary citizens into a generality of suspicious appearance..." *United States v. Rodriguez* (concluding that the factors cited in the case—namely, a Hispanic man carefully driving an old Ford with a worn suspension who looked in his rear view mirror while being followed by agents in a marked car—described "too many individuals to create a reasonable suspicion that this particular defendant was engaged in criminal activity"); see also *United States v. Rodriguez-Sanchez* (holding that reasonable suspicion cannot be based "on broad profiles which cast suspicion on entire categories of people without any individualized suspicion of the particular person to be stopped").

In *Brignoni-Ponce*, the Court listed factors which officers might permissibly take into account in deciding whether reasonable suspicion exists to stop a car. Those factors include: (1) the characteristics of the area in which they encounter a vehicle; (2) the vehicle's proximity to the border; (3) patterns of traffic on the particular road and information about previous illegal border crossings in the area; (4) whether a certain kind of car is frequently used to transport contraband or concealed aliens; (5) the driver's "erratic behavior or obvious attempts to evade officers;" and (6) a heavily loaded car or an unusual number of passengers. With time, however, "[s]ubsequent interpretations of these factors have created a highly inconsistent body of law," and we have given them varying weight in varying contexts.

[4] As the list of factors set out in *Brignoni-Ponce* suggests, sometimes conduct that may be entirely innocuous when viewed in isolation may properly be considered in arriving at a determination that reasonable sus-

picion exists. in *United States v. Sokolow*, the Supreme Court held that: "'[i]n making a determination of probable cause the relevant inquiry is not whether particular conduct is 'innocent' or 'guilty,' but the degree of suspicion that attaches to particular types of noncriminal acts.' That principle applies equally well to the reasonable suspicion inquiry." In short, conduct that is not necessarily indicative of criminal activity may, in certain circumstances, be relevant to the reasonable suspicion calculus. At the same time, however, innocuous conduct does not justify an investigatory stop unless there is other information or surrounding circumstances of which the police are aware, which, when considered along with the otherwise innocuous conduct, tend to indicate criminal activity has occurred or is about to take place.

[5] In all circumstances, "the officer is entitled to assess the facts in light of his experience in detecting illegal entry and smuggling." Nevertheless, "[w]hile an officer may evaluate the facts supporting reasonable suspicion in light of his experience, experience may not be used to give the officers unbridled discretion in making a stop." In other words, an officer's experience may furnish the background against which the relevant facts are to be assessed, as long as the inferences he draws are objectively reasonable; but "experience" does not in itself serve as an independent factor in the reasonable suspicion analysis.

2. The Factors Considered by the District Court

As noted above, the district court based its determination that reasonable suspicion existed on a series of factors: 1) the U-turn made before the checkpoint by the two cars; 2) the driving in tandem and the Mexicali license plates; 3) the area at which the U-turn occurred included a well-known drop-off point for smugglers; 4) the Hispanic appearance of the three defendants; and 5) Renteria-Wolff's picking up the newspaper after glancing back at the patrol cars. Although we agree with the district court that reasonable suspicion did exist to justify an investigatory stop, we conclude that some of the factors on which the district court relied are not relevant or appropriate to the reasonable suspicion analysis. We begin by considering the factors in that category, before turning to address those which the district court properly considered.

[6] In concluding that reasonable suspicion existed, both the district court and the panel majority relied in part upon the Hispanic appearance of the three defendants. We hold that they erred in doing so. We first note that Agent Johnston [sic] testified at the suppression hearing that the majority of people who pass through the El Centro checkpoints are Hispanic, and thus, presumably have a Hispanic appearance.

As we stressed earlier, reasonable suspicion requires particularized suspicion. Where, as here, the majority (or any substantial number) of people share a specific characteristic, that characteristic is of little or no probative value in such a particularized and context-specific analysis. See *Rodriguez-Sanchez* (holding that reasonable suspicion cannot be based "on broad profiles which cast suspicion on entire categories of people without any individualized suspicion of the particular person to be stopped"). As we put it in *Rodriguez*, "[w]e are not prepared to approve the wholesale seizure of miscellaneous persons ... in the absence of well-founded suspicion based on particular, individualized, and objectively observable factors which indicate that the person is engaged in criminal activity." See *Rodriguez* (holding that a stop cannot be upheld where the factors tendered as justification are "calculated to draw into the law enforcement net a generality of persons unmarked by any really articulable basis for reasonable suspicion...").

[7] The likelihood that in an area in which the majority—or even a substantial part—of the population is Hispanic, any given person of Hispanic ancestry is in fact an alien, let alone an illegal alien, is not high enough to make Hispanic appearance a relevant factor in the reasonable suspicion calculus. As we have previously held, factors that have such a low probative value that no reasonable officer would have relied on them to make an investigative stop must be disregarded as a matter of law. Moreover, as we explain below, Hispanic appearance is not, in general, an appropriate factor.

In reaching our conclusion, we are mindful of *Brignoni-Ponce*, in which, a quarter-century ago, the Supreme Court affirmed this court's decision reversing the denial of Brignoni-Ponce's motion to suppress and held that a stop could not be justified by ethnic appearance alone. In that case, the Court held that "[e]ven if [Border Patrol officers] saw enough to think that the occupants were of Mexican descent, this factor alone would justify neither a reasonable belief that they were aliens, nor a reasonable belief that the car concealed other aliens who were illegally in the country." In a brief dictum consisting of only half a sentence, the Court went on to state, however, that ethnic appearance could be a factor in a reasonable suspicion calculus.

In arriving at the dictum suggesting that ethnic appearance could be relevant, the Court relied heavily on now-outdated demographic information. In a footnote, the Court noted that:

> *"The 1970 census and the INS figures for alien registration in 1970 provide the following information about the Mexican-American population in the border States. There were 1,619,064 persons of Mexican origin in Texas, and 200,004 (or 12.4%) of them registered as aliens from Mexico. In New Mexico there were 119,049 persons of Mexican origin, and 10,171 (or 8.5%) registered as aliens. In Arizona there were 239,811 persons of Mex-*

ican origin, and 34,075 (or 14.2%) registered as aliens. In California there were 1,857,267 persons of Mexican origin, and 379,951 (or 20.4%) registered as aliens."

Brignoni-Ponce was handed down in 1975, some twenty-five years ago. Current demographic data demonstrate that the statistical premises on which its dictum relies are no longer applicable. The Hispanic population of this nation, and of the Southwest and Far West in particular, has grown enormously—at least five-fold in the four states referred to in the Supreme Court's decision. According to the U.S. Census Bureau, as of January 1, 2000, that population group stands at nearly 34 million. Furthermore, Hispanics are heavily concentrated in certain states in which minorities are becoming if not the majority, then at least the single largest group, either in the state as a whole or in a significant number of counties. According to the same data, California has the largest Hispanic population of any state—estimated at 10,112,986 in 1998, while Texas has approximately 6 million. As of this year, minorities—Hispanics, Asians, blacks and Native Americans—comprise half of California's residents; by 2021, Hispanics are expected to be the Golden State's largest group, making up about 40% of the state's population. Today, in Los Angeles County, which is by far the state's biggest population center, Hispanics already constitute the largest single group.

One area where Hispanics are heavily in the majority is El Centro, the site of the vehicle stop. As Agent Johnson acknowledged, the majority of the people who pass through the El Centro checkpoint are Hispanic. His testimony is in turn corroborated by more general demographic data from that area. The population of Imperial County, in which El Centro is located, is 73% Hispanic. In Imperial County, as of 1998, Hispanics accounted for 105,355 of the total population of 144,051. More broadly, according to census data, five Southern California counties are home to more than a fifth of the nation's Hispanic population. During the current decade, Hispanics will become the single largest population group in Southern California, and by 2040, will make up 59% of Southern California's population. Accordingly, Hispanic appearance is of little or no use in determining which particular individuals among the vast Hispanic populace should be stopped by law enforcement officials on the lookout for illegal aliens. Reasonable suspicion requires particularized suspicion, and in an area in which a large number of people share a specific characteristic, that characteristic casts too wide a net to play any part in a particularized reasonable suspicion determination.

Moreover, the demographic changes we describe have been accompanied by significant changes in the law restricting the use of race as a criterion in government decision-making. The use of race and ethnicity for such purposes has been severely limited. Relying on the principle that "[o]ur Constitution is color-blind, and neither knows nor tolerates classes among citizens," the Supreme Court has repeatedly held that reliance "on racial or ethnic criteria must necessarily receive a most searching examination to make sure that it does not conflict with constitutional guarantees." In invalidating the use of racial classifications used to remedy past discrimination in Croson, the Court applied strict scrutiny, stating that its rigorousness would ensure that:

> *"The means chosen 'fit' this compelling goal so closely that there is little or no possibility that the motive for the classification was illegitimate racial prejudice or stereotype. Classifications based on race carry a danger of stigmatic harm. Unless they are strictly reserved for remedial settings, they may in fact promote notions of racial inferiority and lead to a politics of racial hostility."*

The danger of stigmatic harm of the type that the Court feared overbroad affirmative action programs would pose is far more pronounced in the context of police stops in which race or ethnic appearance is a factor. So, too, are the consequences of "notions of racial inferiority" and the "politics of racial hostility" that the Court pointed to. Stops based on race or ethnic appearance send the underlying message to all our citizens that those who are not white are judged by the color of their skin alone. Such stops also send a clear message that those who are not white enjoy a lesser degree of constitutional protection—that they are in effect assumed to be potential criminals first and individuals second.

It would be an anomalous result to hold that race may be considered when it harms people, but not when it helps them.

We decide no broad constitutional questions here. Rather, we are confronted with the narrow question of how to square the Fourth Amendment's requirement of individualized reasonable suspicion with the fact that the majority of the people who pass through the checkpoint in question are Hispanic. In order to answer that question, we conclude that, at this point in our nation's history, and given the continuing changes in our ethnic and racial composition, Hispanic appearance is, in general, of such little probative value that it may not be considered as a relevant factor where particularized or individualized suspicion is required. Moreover, we conclude, for the reasons we have indicated, that it is also not an appropriate factor.

[8] We now turn to another factor on which the United States relies, namely Renteria-Wolff's behavior. Both the district court judge as well as the panel majority concluded that Renteria-Wolff's behavior—more specif-

ically, her picking up a newspaper after glancing at the patrol car in the rear-view mirror—was a relevant factor in the reasonable suspicion analysis. We disagree. In general, although eye contact, or the lack thereof, may be considered as a factor establishing reasonable suspicion, we have noted that whether the contact is suspicious or not "is highly subjective and must be evaluated in light of the circumstances of each case." The skepticism with which this factor is treated is in large part due to the fact that reliance upon "suspicious" looks can so easily devolve into a case of damned if you do, equally damned if you don't. Accordingly, we have noted that that factor is "of questionable value … generally."

[9] In this case, Agent Johnson testified that, as he approached the Blazer from behind, he observed that Renteria-Wolff appeared to glance quickly in the rear view mirror before picking up a newspaper and reading it. It is unclear from the record whether Johnson could in fact have seen such a glance as he drove up behind the Blazer. In any event, it is a common, if not universal, practice for drivers and passengers alike to take note of a law enforcement vehicle coming up behind them. In fact, the most law-abiding of citizens frequently adjust their driving accordingly.

[10] Further, we give no weight to the fact that Sylvia Renteria-Wolff picked up a newspaper after glancing at the patrol car. Agent Johnson did not suggest that by this action she sought to conceal her face so that he would not recognize her. Had Renteria-Wolff continued to keep her eyes on the patrol car behind them after her initial glance, Agent Johnson might well have found it equally suspicious—because she paid too much, rather than too little attention to him. It is, in fact, difficult to imagine what Renteria-Wolff could have done at that point that might not have appeared suspicious to a Border Patrol agent. It is for this very reason that we reached the conclusion we did in then-Judge Kennedy's opinion in *Munoz*.

We recognize that in its recent decision in *Wardlow*, the Supreme Court noted that evasive behavior may be a "pertinent factor in determining reasonable suspicion." However, nothing in *Wardlow*—or the three Supreme Court cases it cites to illustrate that proposition—runs contrary to our conclusion that Renteria-Wolff's conduct provides no basis for reasonable suspicion. The three earlier cases all involved obvious, unambiguous attempts to evade contact with law enforcement officials—conduct very different from what was observed by the Border Patrol agent as he followed the car in which Renteria-Wolff was riding. In the first case, namely *Brignoni-Ponce*, the Supreme Court categorized evasive behavior as "obvious attempts to evade officers" or to hide. In the second case, *Sokolow*, the Court held that evidence that the suspect took an evasive or erratic path through an airport in an apparent attempt to avoid police might also be relevant to the reasonable suspicion determination. In the third, *Florida v. Rodriguez*, the Supreme

Court held that articulable suspicion existed where three men spoke furtively among themselves after seeing officers approaching them, where one was twice overheard during that conversation urging the others to "get out of here," and where one of the three, Rodriguez, in fact turned around and attempted to flee. As noted above, all three cases described actual—and obvious—attempts to evade or to hide from law enforcement officers. Moreover, *Wardlow* itself, of course, involved head-long flight, which the Court termed "the consummate act of evasion..." We do not mean to suggest that these cases establish the outer parameters for what is evasive behavior. Rather, we conclude only that glancing in a rear view mirror and then picking up a newspaper to read is not. Such actions are simply not the sort of evasive conduct that the Supreme Court has held is properly part of the reasonable suspicion calculus, nor did the officers suggest that it was the type of behavior they had observed in the past when wrongdoing was afoot. Accordingly, we conclude that, like Hispanic appearance, Renteria-Wolff's behavior was not a relevant or appropriate factor to consider in determining reasonable suspicion.

[11] The question then is what factors are both relevant and appropriate to the reasonable suspicion analysis in this case. Those factors are, in a certain sense, interwoven, and they draw their significance, in part, from one another. The first of these factors to consider is the U-turn or turnaround. In *United States v. Ogilvie* this Court held that "turning off the highway and turning around [are] not in themselves suspicious..." Accordingly, "the proximity of the turn to the checkpoint, regardless of the legality of the checkpoint, [is] not a sufficient foundation on which to rest reasonable suspicion."

[12] In the panel decision, the majority and the dissenting judge disagreed as to whether Ogilvie prohibited reliance on the U-turn in this case. We side with the majority and conclude that it does not. Ogilvie simply holds that a turnaround alone is not enough in and of itself to create reasonable suspicion. Indeed, in subsequent decisions, this Court has made it clear that a turnaround combined with other factors may be considered as part of a reasonable suspicion analysis. See *United States v. Garcia-Barron* ("[a]pparent efforts to avoid checkpoints combined with other factors have generally been found to constitute 'reasonable suspicion'"). Even more so, a U-turn.

[13] In concluding that the U-turn in this case constitutes a significant factor, we note a number of circumstances that combine to make it so, some of which also constitute independent factors in the reasonable suspicion analysis. First, a U-turn on a highway is very different from reversing direction by using a designated highway exit. The use of a highway exit is both frequent and legal; in contrast, a U-turn on a highway is unusual and often

illegal. While it is not clear whether the U-turn here was legal, the other surrounding circumstances render the reversal-in-direction one that may properly be given significant weight in our reasonable suspicion analysis. One of those circumstances is the fact that the two cars made their U-turn and immediately stopped at the side of the highway in an isolated, desert area frequently used to drop off or pick up undocumented aliens or contraband. Another is that the U-turn occurred just after a sign indicating that an upcoming checkpoint had been re-opened. Finally, it is highly unlikely that the reason for the U-turn was that the cars had accidentally passed their exit point. There is only one turn-off anywhere in the area before the checkpoint, and that turn-off leads to a private road rather than one that members of the general public might use.

[14] We also rely on the characteristics of the area in which the cars stopped after the reversal-in-direction as an independent factor. We note initially that an individual's presence in a high crime area is not enough to support reasonable, particularized suspicion that the individual in question has committed or is about to commit a crime. See *Brown v. Texas* (holding that an investigatory stop was not justified when police officers detained two men walking away from each other in an alley in an area with a high rate of drug trafficking because "the appellant's activity was no different from the activity of other pedestrians in that neighborhood"). Still, "officers are not required to ignore the relevant characteristics of a location in determining whether the circumstances are sufficiently suspicious to warrant further investigation."

[15] The citing of an area as "high-crime" requires careful examination by the court, because such a description, unless properly limited and factually based, can easily serve as a proxy for race or ethnicity. District courts must carefully examine the testimony of police officers in cases such as this, and make a fair and forthright evaluation of the evidence they offer, regardless of the consequences. We must be particularly careful to ensure that a "high crime" area factor is not used with respect to entire neighborhoods or communities in which members of minority groups regularly go about their daily business, but is limited to specific, circumscribed locations where particular crimes occur with unusual regularity. In this case, the "high crime" area is in an isolated and unpopulated spot in the middle of the desert. Thus, the likelihood of an innocent explanation for the defendants' presence and actions is far less than if the stop took place in a residential or business area.

Finally, we consider the tandem driving as well as the Mexicali license plates. The panel majority treated the two as independent factors giving rise to reasonable suspicion. In contrast, the district court took a different approach, relying on the "tandem driving" and Mexicali license plates solely for the purposes of linking the cars described by the tipster to the ones observed by the Border Patrol officers. We conclude that, under the circumstances present here, both occurrences may be given some direct weight in the reasonable suspicion analysis. They do not, however, constitute substantial factors, either singly or collectively.

[16] With respect to tandem driving, we have held that two or more cars traveling together, although not sufficient in itself to establish reasonable suspicion, may nonetheless "be indicative of illegal smuggling activity." However, the circumstances of the tandem driving will in the end determine whether that factor is relevant. While two cars driving together is intrinsically innocuous, here the fact that the two cars not only turned around in tandem in the middle of a highway, but then pulled off the shoulder together and stopped where criminal activity often took place, makes the tandem driving relevant. The fact that the cars had Mexicali license plates may also provide some additional weight, given all the other circumstances. While having Mexican plates is ordinarily of no significance, where the criminal act suspected involves border-crossing, the presence of foreign license plates may be afforded some weight in determining whether a stop is reasonable.

CONCLUSION

In this case, the two cars driven in tandem by Montero-Camargo and Sanchez-Guillen made U-turns on a highway, at a place where the view of the border officials was obstructed, and stopped briefly at a locale historically used for illegal activities, before proceeding back in the direction from which they had come. The U-turn occurred at a place at a location where it was unlikely that the cars would have reversed directions because they had missed an exit. Moreover, the vehicles in question bore Mexicali license plates and the U-turn occurred just after a sign indicating that a Border Patrol checkpoint that had been closed for some time was now open. We conclude that these factors, although not overwhelming, are sufficient to constitute reasonable suspicion for the stop. In reaching that result, however, we firmly reject any reliance upon the Hispanic appearance or ethnicity of the defendants. We also do not consider Renteria-Wolff's behavior in glancing at the Border Patrol car in the rear view mirror and then picking up and reading a newspaper.

In affirming the district court's ruling, we note that the agents' initial decision to investigate the tip and to pursue the two vehicles was made without any knowledge on their part of the defendants' ethnicity or Hispanic appearance. Agents Johnson and Fisher observed that appearance only when the officers subsequently caught up with the defendants' cars. Moreover, the agents had enough information to justify the stop before they became aware of the defendants' likely ethnicity. Under these circumstances, there is no need to remand the matter to the district court for reconsideration of its decision. Instead, we AFFIRM the district court's denial of the motion to suppress.

APPENDIX D

107TH CONGRESS 1ST SESSION, H. R. 2074, JUNE 6, 2001

Mr. CONYERS (for himself, Mr. SHAYS, Mr. SCOTT, Ms. JACKSON-LEE of Texas, Mr. SERRANO, Mr. WU, Mr. PAYNE, Mr. MENENDEZ, Mr. HONDA, Mr. STARK, Mrs. MORELLA, Mr. GREENWOOD, Mr. FRELINGHUYSEN, Mr. JOHNSON of Illinois, Mr. FERGUSON, and Mr. WALSH) introduced the following bill; which was referred to the Committee on the Judiciary

A BILL

To prohibit racial profiling.

Be it enacted by the Senate and House of Representatives of the United States of America in Congress assembled,

SECTION 1. SHORT TITLE; TABLE OF CONTENTS.

(a) SHORT TITLE.—This Act may be cited as the "End Racial Profiling Act of 2001".

(b) TABLE OF CONTENTS.—The table of contents of this Act is as follows:

SEC. 2. FINDINGS AND PURPOSES.

(a) FINDINGS.—Congress makes the following findings:

(1) The vast majority of law enforcement agents nationwide discharge their duties professionally, without bias, and protect the safety of their communities.

(2) The use by police officers of race, ethnicity, or national origin in deciding which persons should be subject to traffic stops, stops and frisks, questioning, searches, and seizures is a problematic law enforcement tactic. Statistical evidence from across the country demonstrates that such racial profiling is a real and measurable phenomenon.

(3) As of November 15, 2000, the Department of Justice had 14 publicly noticed, ongoing, pattern or practice investigations involving allegations of racial profiling and had filed five pattern and practice lawsuits involving allegations of racial profiling, with four of those cases resolved through consent decrees.

(4) A large majority of individuals subjected to stops and other enforcement activities based on race, ethnicity, or national origin are found to be law-abiding and therefore racial profiling is not an effective means to uncover criminal activity.

(5) A 2001 Department of Justice report on citizen-police contacts in 1999 found that, although African-Americans and Hispanics were more likely to be stopped and searched, they were less likely to be in possession of contraband. On average, searches and seizures of African-American drivers yielded evidence only eight percent of the time, searches and seizures of Hispanic drivers yielded evidence only 10 percent of the time, and searches and seizures of white drivers yielded evidence 17 percent of the time.

(6) A 2000 General Accounting Office report on the activities of the United States Customs Service during fiscal year 1998 found that black

women who were United States citizens were 9 times more likely than white women who were United States citizens to be X-rayed after being frisked or patted down and, on the basis of X-ray results, black women who were United States citizens were less than half as likely as white women who were United States citizens to be found carrying contraband. In general, the report found that the patterns used to select passengers for more intrusive searches resulted in women and minorities being selected at rates that were not consistent with the rates of finding contraband.

(7) Current local law enforcement practices, such as ticket and arrest quotas, and similar management practices, may have the unintended effect of encouraging law enforcement agents to engage in racial profiling.

(8) Racial profiling harms individuals subjected to it because they experience fear, anxiety, humiliation, anger, resentment, and cynicism when they are unjustifiably treated as criminal suspects. By discouraging individuals from traveling freely, racial profiling impairs both interstate and intrastate commerce.

(9) Racial profiling damages law enforcement and the criminal justice system as a whole by undermining public confidence and trust in the police, the courts, and the criminal law.

(10) Racial profiling violates the Equal Protection Clause of the Constitution. Using race, ethnicity, or national origin as a proxy for criminal suspicion violates the constitutional requirement that police and other government officials accord to all citizens the equal protection of the law. Arlington Heights v. Metropolitan Housing Development Corporation, 429 U.S. 252 (1977).

(11) Racial profiling is not adequately addressed through suppression motions in criminal cases for two reasons. First, the Supreme Court held, in Whren v. United States, 517 U.S. 806 (1996), that the racially discriminatory motive of a police officer in making an otherwise valid traffic stop does not warrant the suppression of evidence. Second, since most stops do not result in the discovery of contraband, there is no criminal prosecution and no evidence to suppress.

(12) Current efforts by State and local governments to eradicate racial profiling and redress the harms it causes, while laudable, have been limited in scope and insufficient to address this national problem.

(b) PURPOSES.—The independent purposes of this Act are—

(1) to enforce the constitutional right to equal protection of the laws, pursuant to the Fifth Amendment and section 5 of the 14th Amendment to the Constitution of the United States;

(2) to enforce the constitutional right to protection against unreasonable searches and seizures, pursuant to the Fourth Amendment to the Constitution of the United States;

(3) to enforce the constitutional right to interstate travel, pursuant to section 2 of article IV of the Constitution of the United States; and

(4) to regulate interstate commerce, pursuant to clause 3 of section 8 of article I of the Constitution of the United States.

TITLE I—PROHIBITION OF RACIAL PROFILING

SEC. 101. PROHIBITION.

No law enforcement agent or law enforcement agency shall engage in racial profiling.

SEC. 102. ENFORCEMENT.

(a) REMEDY.—The United States, or an individual injured by racial profiling, may enforce this title in a civil action for declaratory or injunctive relief, filed either in a State court of general jurisdiction or in a District Court of the United States.

(b) PARTIES.—In any action brought pursuant to this title, relief may be obtained against: any governmental unit that employed any law enforcement agent who engaged in racial profiling; any agent of such unit who engaged in racial profiling; and any person with supervisory authority over such agent.

(c) NATURE OF PROOF.—Proof that the routine investigatory activities of law enforcement agents in a jurisdiction have had a disparate impact on racial or ethnic minorities shall constitute prima facie evidence of a violation of this title.

(d) ATTORNEYS' FEES.—In any action or proceeding to enforce this title against any governmental unit, the court may allow a prevailing plaintiff, other than the United States, reasonable attorneys' fees as part of the costs, and may include expert fees as part of the attorney's fee.

TITLE II—PROGRAMS TO ELIMINATE RACIAL PROFILING BY FEDERAL LAW ENFORCEMENT AGENCIES

SEC. 201. POLICIES TO ELIMINATE RACIAL PROFILING.

(a) IN GENERAL.—Federal law enforcement agencies shall —

(1) maintain adequate policies and procedures designed to eliminate racial profiling; and

(2) cease existing practices that encourage racial profiling.

(b) POLICIES.—The policies and procedures described in subsection (a)(1) shall include the following:

(1) A prohibition on racial profiling.

(2) The collection of data on routine investigatory activities sufficient to determine if law enforcement agents are engaged in racial profiling and submission of that data to the Attorney General.

(3) Independent procedures for receiving, investigating, and responding meaningfully to complaints alleging racial profiling by law enforcement agents of the agency.

(4) Procedures to discipline law enforcement agents who engage in racial profiling.

(5) Such other policies or procedures that the Attorney General deems necessary to eliminate racial profiling.

TITLE III—PROGRAMS TO ELIMINATE RACIAL PROFILING BY STATE AND LOCAL LAW ENFORCEMENT AGENCIES

SEC. 301. POLICIES REQUIRED FOR GRANTS.

(a) IN GENERAL.—An application by a State or governmental unit for funding under a covered program shall include a certification that such unit and any agency to which it is redistributing program funds —

(1) maintains adequate policies and procedures designed to eliminate racial profiling; and

(2) has ceased existing practices that encourage racial profiling.

(b) POLICIES.—The policies and procedures described in subsection (a) shall include the following:

(1) A prohibition on racial profiling.

(2) The collection of data on routine investigatory activities sufficient to determine if law enforcement agents are engaged in racial profiling and submission of that data to the Attorney General.

(3) Independent procedures for receiving, investigating, and responding meaningfully to complaints alleging racial profiling by law enforcement agents.

(4) Procedures to discipline law enforcement agents who engage in racial profiling.

(5) Such other policies or procedures that the Attorney General deems necessary to eliminate racial profiling.

(c) NONCOMPLIANCE.—If the Attorney General determines that a grantee is not in compliance with conditions established pursuant to this title, the Attorney General shall withhold the grant, in whole or in part, until the grantee establishes compliance. The Attorney General shall provide notice regarding State grants and opportunities for private parties to present evidence to the Attorney General that a grantee is not in compliance with conditions established pursuant to this title.

SEC. 302. BEST PRACTICES DEVELOPMENT GRANTS.

(a) GRANT AUTHORIZATION.—The Attorney General may make grants to States, law enforcement agencies and other governmental units, Indian tribal governments, or other public and private entities to develop and implement best practice devices and systems to ensure the racially neutral administration of justice.

(b) USES.—The funds provided pursuant to subsection (a) may be used to support the following activities:

(1) Development and implementation of training to prevent racial profiling and to encourage more respectful interaction with the public.

(2) Acquisition and use of technology to facilitate the collection of data regarding routine investigatory activities in order to determine if law enforcement agents are engaged in racial profiling.

(3) Acquisition and use of technology to verify the accuracy of data collection, including in-car video cameras and portable computer systems.

(4) Development and acquisition of early warning systems and other feedback systems that help identify officers or units of officers engaged in or at risk of racial profiling or other misconduct, including the technology to support such systems.

(5) Establishment or improvement of systems and procedures for receiving, investigating, and responding meaningfully to complaints alleging racial or ethnic bias by law enforcement agents.

(6) Establishment or improvement of management systems to ensure that supervisors are held accountable for the conduct of their subordinates.

(c) EQUITABLE DISTRIBUTION.—The Attorney General shall ensure that grants under this section are awarded in a manner that reserves an equitable share of funding for small and rural law enforcement agencies.

(d) AUTHORIZATION OF APPROPRIATIONS.—The Attorney General shall make available such sums as are necessary to carry out this section from amounts appropriated for programs administered by the Attorney General.

TITLE IV—DEPARTMENT OF JUSTICE REPORTS ON RACIAL PROFILING IN THE UNITED STATES

SEC. 401. ATTORNEY GENERAL TO ISSUE REPORTS ON RACIAL PROFILING IN THE UNITED STATES.

(a) REPORTS. —

(1) IN GENERAL.—Not later than two years after the enactment of this Act, and each year thereafter, the Attorney General shall submit to Congress a report on racial profiling by Federal, State, and local law enforcement agencies in the United States.

(2) SCOPE.—The reports issued pursuant to paragraph (1) shall include —

(A) a summary of data collected pursuant to sections 201(b)(2) and 301(b)(2) and any other reliable source of information regarding racial profiling in the United States;

(B) the status of the adoption and implementation of policies and procedures by Federal law enforcement agencies pursuant to section 201;

(C) the status of the adoption and implementation of policies and procedures by State and local law enforcement agencies pursuant to sections 301 and 302; and

(D) a description of any other policies and procedures that the Attorney General believes would facilitate the elimination of racial profiling.

(b) DATA COLLECTION.—Not later than six months after the enactment of this Act, the Attorney General shall by regulation establish standards for the collection of data pursuant to sections 201(b)(2) and 301(b)(2), including standards for setting benchmarks against which collected data shall be measured. Such standards shall result in the collection of data, including data with respect to stops, searches, seizures, and arrests, that is sufficiently detailed to determine whether law enforcement agencies are engaged in racial profiling and to monitor the effectiveness of policies and procedures designed to eliminate racial profiling.

(c) PUBLIC ACCESS.—Data collected pursuant to section 201(b)(2) and 301(b)(2) shall be available to the public.

SEC. 402. LIMITATION ON USE OF DATA.

Information released pursuant to section 401 shall not reveal the identity of any individual who is detained or any law enforcement officer involved in a detention.

TITLE V—DEFINITIONS AND MISCELLANEOUS PROVISIONS

SEC. 501. DEFINITIONS.

In this Act:

(1) COVERED PROGRAM.—The term "covered program" means any program or activity funded in whole or in part with funds made available under any of the following:

(A) The Edward Byrne Memorial State and Local Law Enforcement Assistance Programs (part E of title I of the Omnibus Crime Control and Safe Streets Act of 1968 (42 U.S.C. 3750 et seq.)).

(B) The "Cops on the Beat" program under part Q of title I of the Omnibus Crime Control and Safe Streets Act of 1968 (42 U.S.C. 3796dd et seq.), but not including any program, project, or other activity specified in section 1701(d)(8) of that Act (42 U.S.C. 3796dd(d)(8)).

(C) The Local Law Enforcement Block Grant program of the Department of Justice as described in appropriations Acts.

(2) GOVERNMENTAL UNIT.—The term "governmental unit" means any department, agency, special purpose district, or other instrumentality of Federal, State, local, or Indian tribal government.

(3) LAW ENFORCEMENT AGENCY.—The term "law enforcement agency" means a Federal, State, local, or Indian tribal public agency engaged

in the prevention, detection, or investigation of violations of criminal, immigration, or customs laws.

(4) LAW ENFORCEMENT AGENT.—The term "law enforcement agent" means any Federal, State, local, or Indian tribal official responsible for enforcing criminal, immigration, or customs laws, including police officers and other agents of Federal, State, and local law enforcement agencies.

(5) RACIAL PROFILING.—The term "racial profiling" means the practice of a law enforcement agent relying, to any degree, on race, ethnicity, or national origin in selecting which individuals to subject to routine investigatory activities, or in deciding upon the scope and substance of law enforcement activity following the initial routine investigatory activity, except that racial profiling does not include reliance on such criteria in combination with other identifying factors when the law enforcement agent is seeking to apprehend a specific suspect whose race, ethnicity, or national origin is part of the description of the suspect.

(6) ROUTINE INVESTIGATORY ACTIVITIES.—The term "routine investigatory activities" includes the following activities by law enforcement agents: traffic stops; pedestrian stops; frisks and other types of body searches; consensual or nonconsensual searches of the persons or possessions (including vehicles) of motorists or pedestrians; inspections and interviews of entrants into the United States that are more extensive than those customarily carried out; and immigration-related workplace investigations.

SEC. 502. SEVERABILITY.

If any provision of this Act, an amendment made by this Act, or the application of such provision or amendment to any person or circumstance is held to be unconstitutional, the remainder of this Act, the amendments made by this Act, and the application of the provisions of such to any person or circumstance shall not be affected thereby.

SEC. 503. SAVINGS CLAUSE.

Nothing in this Act shall be construed to limit legal or administrative remedies under section 1979 of the Revised Statutes of the United States (42 U.S.C. 1983), section 210401 of the Violent Crime Control and Law Enforcement Act of 1994 (42 U.S.C. 14141), the Omnibus Crime Control and Safe Streets Act of 1968 (42 U.S.C. 3701 et seq.), and title VI of the Civil Rights Act of 1964 (42 U.S.C. 2000d et seq.).

SEC. 504. EFFECTIVE DATES.

(a) IN GENERAL.—Except as provided in subsection (b), the provisions of this Act shall take effect on the date of the enactment of this Act.

(b) CONDITIONS ON FUNDING.—Section 301 shall take effect 1 year after the date of enactment of this Act.

APPENDIX E

GUIDANCE REGARDING THE USE OF RACE BY FEDERAL LAW ENFORCEMENT AGENCIES, JUNE 2003

Note: From the U.S. Department of Justice Civil Rights Division

INTRODUCTION AND EXECUTIVE SUMMARY

In his February 27, 2001, Address to a Joint Session of Congress, President George W. Bush declared that racial profiling is "wrong and we will end it in America." He directed the Attorney General to review the use by Federal law enforcement authorities of race as a factor in conducting stops, searches and other law enforcement investigative procedures. The Attorney General, in turn, instructed the Civil Rights Division to develop guidance for Federal officials to ensure an end to racial profiling in law enforcement.

"Racial profiling" at its core concerns the invidious use of race or ethnicity as a criterion in conducting stops, searches and other law enforcement investigative procedures. It is premised on the erroneous assumption that any particular individual of one race or ethnicity is more likely to engage in misconduct than any particular individual of another race or ethnicity.

Racial profiling in law enforcement is not merely wrong, but also ineffective. Race-based assumptions in law enforcement perpetuate negative racial stereotypes that are harmful to our rich and diverse democracy, and materially impair our efforts to maintain a fair and just society.[1]

The use of race as the basis for law enforcement decision-making clearly has a terrible cost, both to the individuals who suffer invidious discrimination and to the Nation, whose goal of "liberty and justice for all" recedes with every act of such discrimination. For this reason, this guidance in many cases imposes more restrictions on the consideration of race and ethnicity in Federal law enforcement than the Constitution requires.[2] This guidance prohibits racial profiling in law enforcement practices without hindering the important work of our Nation's public safety officials, particularly the intensified anti-terrorism efforts precipitated by the events of September 11, 2001.

I. Traditional Law Enforcement Activities. Two standards in combination should guide use by Federal law enforcement authorities of race or ethnicity in law enforcement activities:

- In making routine or spontaneous law enforcement decisions, such as ordinary traffic stops, Federal law enforcement officers may not use race or ethnicity to any degree, except that officers may rely on race and ethnicity in a specific suspect description. This prohibition applies even where the use of race or ethnicity might otherwise be lawful.
- In conducting activities in connection with a specific investigation, Federal law enforcement officers may consider race and ethnicity only to the extent that there is trustworthy information, relevant to the locality or time frame, that links persons of a particular race or ethnicity to an identified criminal incident, scheme, or organization. This standard applies even where the use of race or ethnicity might otherwise be lawful.

II. National Security and Border Integrity. The above standards do not affect current Federal policy with respect to law enforcement activities and other efforts to defend and safeguard against threats to national security or the integrity of the Nation's borders,[3] to which the following applies:

- In investigating or preventing threats to national security or other catastrophic events (including the performance of duties related to air transportation security), or in enforcing laws protecting the integrity of the Nation's borders, Federal law enforcement officers may not consider race or ethnicity except to the extent permitted by the Constitution and laws of the United States.

Any questions arising under these standards should be directed to the Department of Justice.

THE CONSTITUTIONAL FRAMEWORK

"[T]he Constitution prohibits selective enforcement of the law based on considerations such as race." *Whren v. United States,* 517 U.S. 806, 813

(1996). Thus, for example, the decision of federal prosecutors "whether to prosecute may not be based on 'an unjustifiable standard such as race, religion, or other arbitrary classification.'"[4] *United States v. Armstrong*, 517 U.S. 456, 464 (1996) (quoting *Oyler v. Boles*, 368 U.S. 448, 456 (1962)). The same is true of Federal law enforcement officers. Federal courts repeatedly have held that any general policy of "utiliz[ing] impermissible racial classifications in determining whom to stop, detain, and search" would violate the Equal Protection Clause. *Chavez v. Illinois State Police*, 251 F.3d 612, 635 (7th Cir. 2001). As the Sixth Circuit has explained, "[i]f law enforcement adopts a policy, employs a practice, or in a given situation takes steps to initiate an investigation of a citizen based solely upon that citizen's race, without more, then a violation of the Equal Protection Clause has occurred." *United States v. Avery*, 137 F.3d 343, 355 (6th Cir. 1997). "A person cannot become the target of a police investigation solely on the basis of skin color. Such selective law enforcement is forbidden." *Id.* at 354.

As the Supreme Court has held, this constitutional prohibition against selective enforcement of the law based on race "draw[s] on 'ordinary equal protection standards.'"*Armstrong*, 517 U.S. at 465 (quoting *Wayte v. United States*, 470 U.S. 598, 608 (1985)). Thus, impermissible selective enforcement based on race occurs when the challenged policy has "'a discriminatory effect and . . . was motivated by a discriminatory purpose.'"*Id.* (quoting *Wayte*, 470 U.S. at 608).[5] Put simply, "to the extent that race is used as a proxy" for criminality, "a racial stereotype requiring strict scrutiny is in operation." *Cf. Bush v. Vera*, 517 U.S. at 968 (plurality).

I. GUIDANCE FOR FEDERAL OFFICIALS ENGAGED IN LAW ENFORCEMENT ACTIVITIES

A. Routine or Spontaneous Activities in Domestic Law Enforcement

In making routine or spontaneous law enforcement decisions, such as ordinary traffic stops, Federal law enforcement officers may not use race or ethnicity to any degree, except that officers may rely on race and ethnicity in a specific suspect description. This prohibition applies even where the use of race or ethnicity might otherwise be lawful.

Federal law enforcement agencies and officers sometimes engage in law enforcement activities, such as traffic and foot patrols, that generally do not involve either the ongoing investigation of specific criminal activities or the prevention of catastrophic events or harm to the national security. Rather, their activities are typified by spontaneous action in response to the activities of individuals whom they happen to encounter in the course of their patrols and about whom they have no information other than their observations. These general enforcement responsibilities should be carried out without *any* consideration of race or ethnicity.

- ***Example***: While parked by the side of the George Washington Parkway, a Park Police Officer notices that nearly all vehicles on the road are exceeding the posted speed limit. Although each such vehicle is committing an infraction that would legally justify a stop, the officer may not use race or ethnicity as a factor in deciding which motorists to pull over. Likewise, the officer may not use race or ethnicity in deciding which detained motorists to ask to consent to a search of their vehicles.

Some have argued that overall discrepancies in certain crime rates among racial groups could justify using race as a factor in general traffic enforcement activities and would produce a greater number of arrests for non-traffic offenses (*e.g.*, narcotics trafficking). We emphatically reject this view. The President has made clear his concern that racial profiling is morally wrong and inconsistent with our core values and principles of fairness and justice. Even if there were overall statistical evidence of differential rates of commission of certain offenses among particular races, the affirmative use of such generalized notions by federal law enforcement officers in routine, spontaneous law enforcement activities is tantamount to stereotyping. It casts a pall of suspicion over every member of certain racial and ethnic groups without regard to the specific circumstances of a particular investigation or crime, and it offends the dignity of the individual improperly targeted. Whatever the motivation, it is patently unacceptable and thus prohibited under this guidance for Federal law enforcement officers to act on the belief that race or ethnicity signals a higher risk of criminality. This is the core of "racial profiling" and it must not occur.

The situation is different when an officer has specific information, based on trustworthy sources, to "be on the lookout" for specific individuals identified at least in part by race or ethnicity. In such circumstances, the officer is not acting based on a generalized assumption about persons of different races; rather, the officer is helping locate specific individuals previously identified as involved in crime.

- ***Example***: While parked by the side of the George Washington Parkway, a Park Police Officer receives an "All Points Bulletin" to be on the lookout for a fleeing bank robbery suspect, a man of a particular race and particular hair color in his 30s driving a blue automobile. The Officer may use this description, including the race of the particular suspect, in deciding which speeding motorists to pull over.

B. Law Enforcement Activities Related to Specific Investigations

In conducting activities in connection with a specific investigation, Federal law enforcement officers may consider race and ethnicity only to the extent that there is trustworthy information, relevant to the locality or time frame, that links persons of a particular race or ethnicity to an identified criminal incident, scheme, or organization. This standard applies even where the use of race or ethnicity might otherwise be lawful.

As noted above, there are circumstances in which law enforcement activities relating to particular identified criminal incidents, schemes or enterprises may involve consideration of personal identifying characteristics of potential suspects, including age, sex, ethnicity or race. Common sense dictates that when a victim describes the assailant as being of a particular race, authorities may properly limit their search for suspects to persons of that race. Similarly, in conducting an ongoing investigation into a specific criminal organization whose membership has been identified as being overwhelmingly of one ethnicity, law enforcement should not be expected to disregard such facts in pursuing investigative leads into the organization's activities.

Reliance upon generalized stereotypes is absolutely forbidden. Rather, use of race or ethnicity is permitted only when the officer is pursuing a specific lead concerning the identifying characteristics of persons involved in an *identified* criminal activity. The rationale underlying this concept carefully limits its reach. In order to qualify as a legitimate investigative lead, the following must be true:

- The information must be relevant to the locality or time frame of the criminal activity;
- The information must be trustworthy;
- The information concerning identifying characteristics must be tied to a particular criminal incident, a particular criminal scheme, or a particular criminal organization.

The following policy statements more fully explain these principles.

1. *Authorities May Never Rely on Generalized Stereotypes, But May Rely Only on Specific Race- or Ethnicity-Based Information*

This standard categorically bars the use of generalized assumptions based on race.

- ***Example:*** In the course of investigating an auto theft in a federal park, law enforcement authorities could not properly choose to target individuals of a particular race as suspects, based on a generalized assumption that those individuals are more likely to commit crimes.

This bar extends to the use of race-neutral pretexts as an excuse to target minorities. Federal law enforcement may not use such pretexts. This prohibition extends to the use of other, facially race-neutral factors as a proxy for overtly targeting persons of a certain race or ethnicity. This concern arises most frequently when aggressive law enforcement efforts are focused on "high crime areas." The issue is ultimately one of motivation and evidence; certain seemingly race-based efforts, if properly supported by reliable, empirical data, are in fact race-neutral.

- ***Example:*** In connection with a new initiative to increase drug arrests, local authorities begin aggressively enforcing speeding, traffic, and other public area laws in a neighborhood predominantly occupied by people of a single race. The choice of neighborhood was not based on the number of 911 calls, number of arrests, or other pertinent reporting data specific to that area, but only on the general assumption that more drug-related crime occurs in that neighborhood because of its racial composition. This effort would be improper because it is based on generalized stereotypes.
- ***Example:*** Authorities seeking to increase drug arrests use tracking software to plot out where, if anywhere, drug arrests are concentrated in a particular city, and discover that the clear majority of drug arrests occur in particular precincts that happen to be neighborhoods predominantly occupied by people of a single race. So long as they are not motivated by racial animus, authorities can properly decide to enforce all laws aggressively in that area, including less serious quality of life ordinances, as a means of increasing drug-related arrests. *See, e.g., United States v. Montero-Camargo*, 208 F.3d 1122, 1138 (9th Cir. 2000) ("We must be particularly careful to ensure that a 'high crime' area factor is not used with respect to entire neighborhoods or communities in which members of minority groups regularly go about their daily business, but is limited to specific, circumscribed locations where particular crimes occur with unusual regularity.").

By contrast, where authorities are investigating a crime and have received *specific information* that the suspect is of a certain race (*e.g.*, direct observations by the victim or other witnesses), authorities may reasonably use that information, even if it is the only descriptive information available. In such an instance, it is the victim or other witness making the racial classification, and federal authorities may use reliable incident-specific identifying information to apprehend criminal suspects. Agencies and departments, however, must use caution in the rare instance in which a suspect's race is the only available information. Although the use of that information may not be unconstitutional, broad targeting of discrete racial or ethnic groups always raises serious fairness concerns.

- *Example:* The victim of an assault at a local university describes her assailant as a young male of a particular race with a cut on his right hand. The investigation focuses on whether any students at the university fit the victim's description. Here investigators are properly relying on a description given by the victim, part of which included the assailant's race. Although the ensuing investigation affects students of a particular race, that investigation is not undertaken with a discriminatory purpose. Thus use of race as a factor in the investigation, in this instance, is permissible.

2. ***The Information Must be Relevant to the Locality or Time Frame***
Any information concerning the race of persons who may be involved in specific criminal activities must be locally or temporally relevant.

- *Example:* DEA issues an intelligence report that indicates that a drug ring whose members are known to be predominantly of a particular race or ethnicity is trafficking drugs in Charleston, SC. An agent operating in Los Angeles reads this intelligence report. In the absence of information establishing that this intelligence is also applicable in Southern California, the agent may not use ethnicity as a factor in making local law enforcement decisions about individuals who are of the particular race or ethnicity that is predominant in the Charleston drug ring.

3. ***The Information Must be Trustworthy***
Where the information concerning potential criminal activity is unreliable or is too generalized and unspecific, use of racial descriptions is prohibited.

- *Example:* ATF special agents receive an uncorroborated anonymous tip that a male of a particular race will purchase an illegal firearm at a Greyhound bus terminal in a racially diverse North Philadelphia neighborhood. Although agents surveilling the location are free to monitor the movements of whomever they choose, the agents are prohibited from using the tip information, without more, to target any males of that race in the bus terminal. *Cf. Morgan v. Woessner*, 997 F.2d 1244, 1254 (9th Cir. 1993) (finding no reasonable basis for suspicion where tip "made all black men suspect"). The information is neither sufficiently reliable nor sufficiently specific.

4. ***Race- or Ethnicity-Based Information Must Always be Specific to Particular Suspects or Incidents, or Ongoing Criminal Activities, Schemes, or Enterprises***
These standards contemplate the appropriate use of both "suspect-specific" and "incident-specific" information. As noted above, where a

crime has occurred and authorities have eyewitness accounts including the race, ethnicity, or other distinguishing characteristics of the perpetrator, that information may be used. Federal authorities may also use reliable, locally relevant information linking persons of a certain race or ethnicity to a particular incident, unlawful scheme, or ongoing criminal enterprise—even absent a description of any particular individual suspect. In certain cases, the circumstances surrounding an incident or ongoing criminal activity will point strongly to a perpetrator of a certain race, even though authorities lack an eyewitness account[.]

- ***Example:*** The FBI is investigating the murder of a known gang member and has information that the shooter is a member of a rival gang. The FBI knows that the members of the rival gang are exclusively members of a certain ethnicity. This information, however, is not suspect-specific because there is no description of the particular assailant. But because authorities have reliable, locally relevant information linking a rival group with a distinctive ethnic character to the murder, Federal law enforcement officers could properly consider ethnicity in conjunction with other appropriate factors in the course of conducting their investigation. Agents could properly decide to focus on persons dressed in a manner consistent with gang activity, but ignore persons dressed in that manner who do not appear to be members of that particular ethnicity.

It is critical, however, that there be reliable information that ties persons of a particular description to a specific criminal incident, ongoing criminal activity, or particular criminal organization. Otherwise, any use of race runs the risk of descending into reliance upon prohibited generalized stereotypes.

- ***Example:*** While investigating a car theft ring that dismantles cars and ships the parts for sale in other states, the FBI is informed by local authorities that it is common knowledge locally that most car thefts in that area are committed by individuals of a particular race. In this example, although the source (local police) is trustworthy, and the information potentially verifiable with reference to arrest statistics, there is no particular incident- or scheme- specific information linking individuals of that race to the particular interstate ring the FBI is investigating. Thus, without more, agents could not use ethnicity as a factor in making law enforcement decisions in this investigation.

Note that these standards allow the use of reliable identifying information about planned future crimes. Where federal authorities receive a credible tip from a reliable informant regarding a planned crime that has not yet occurred, authorities may use this information under the same restrictions applying to information obtained regarding a past incident. A prohibition on the use of reliable prospective information would severely hamper law enforcement efforts by essentially compelling authorities to wait for crimes to occur, instead of taking pro-active measures to prevent crimes from happening.

- ***Example:*** While investigating a specific drug trafficking operation, DEA special agents learn that a particular methamphetamine distribution ring is manufacturing the drug in California, and plans to have couriers pick up shipments at the Sacramento, California airport and drive the drugs back to Oklahoma for distribution. The agents also receive trustworthy information that the distribution ring has specifically chosen to hire older couples of a particular race to act as the couriers. DEA agents may properly target older couples of that particular race driving vehicles with indicia such as Oklahoma plates near the Sacramento airport.

II. Guidance for Federal Officials Engaged in Law Enforcement Activities Involving Threats to National Security or the Integrity of the Nation's Borders

In investigating or preventing threats to national security or other catastrophic events (including the performance of duties related to air transportation security), or in enforcing laws protecting the integrity of the Nation's borders, Federal law enforcement officers may not consider race or ethnicity except to the extent permitted by the Constitution and laws of the United States.

Since the terrorist attacks on September 11, 2001, the President has emphasized that federal law enforcement personnel must use every legitimate tool to prevent future attacks, protect our Nation's borders, and deter those who would cause devastating harm to our Nation and its people through the use of biological or chemical weapons, other weapons of mass destruction, suicide hijackings, or any other means. "It is 'obvious and unarguable' that no governmental interest is more compelling than the security of the Nation." *Haig v. Agee*, 453 U.S. 280, 307 (1981) (quoting *Aptheker v. Secretary of State*, 378 U.S. 500, 509 (1964)).

The Constitution prohibits consideration of race or ethnicity in law enforcement decisions in all but the most exceptional instances. Given the incalculably high stakes involved in such investigations, however, Federal law enforcement officers who are protecting national security or preventing catastrophic events (as well as airport security screeners) may consider race, ethnicity, and other relevant factors to the extent permitted by our laws and the Constitution. Similarly, because enforcement of the laws protecting the Nation's borders may necessarily involve a consideration of a person's alienage in certain circumstances, the use of race or ethnicity in such circumstances is properly governed by existing statutory and constitutional standards. *See, e.g., United States v. Brignoni-Ponce*, 422 U.S. 873, 886-87 (1975).[6] This policy will honor the rule of law and promote vigorous protection of our national security.

As the Supreme Court has stated, all racial classifications by a governmental actor are subject to the "strictest judicial scrutiny."*Adarand Constructors, Inc. v. Peña*, 515 U.S. 200, 224-25 (1995). The application of strict scrutiny is of necessity a fact-intensive process. *Id.* at 236. Thus, the legality of particular, race-sensitive actions taken by Federal law enforcement officials in the context of national security and border integrity will depend to a large extent on the circumstances at hand. In absolutely no event, however, may Federal officials assert a national security or border integrity rationale as a mere pretext for invidious discrimination. Indeed, the very purpose of the strict scrutiny test is to "smoke out" illegitimate use of race, *Adarand*, 515 U.S. at 226 (quoting *Richmond v. J.A. Croson Co.*, 488 U.S. 469, 493 (1989)), and law enforcement strategies not actually premised on *bona fide* national security or border integrity interests therefore will not stand.

In sum, constitutional provisions limiting government action on the basis of race are wide-ranging and provide substantial protections at every step of the investigative and judicial process. Accordingly, and as illustrated below, when addressing matters of national security, border integrity, or the possible catastrophic loss of life, existing legal and constitutional standards are an appropriate guide for Federal law enforcement officers.

- ***Example:*** The FBI receives reliable information that persons affiliated with a foreign ethnic insurgent group intend to use suicide bombers to assassinate that country's president and his entire entourage during an official visit to the United States. Federal law enforcement may appropriately focus investigative attention on identifying members of that ethnic insurgent group who may be present and active in the United States and who, based on other available information, might conceivably be involved in planning some such attack during the state visit.
- ***Example:*** U.S. intelligence sources report that terrorists from a particular ethnic group are planning to use commercial jetliners as weapons by

hijacking them at an airport in California during the next week. Before allowing men of that ethnic group to board commercial airplanes in California airports during the next week, Transportation Security Administration personnel, and other federal and state authorities, may subject them to heightened scrutiny.

Because terrorist organizations might aim to engage in unexpected acts of catastrophic violence in any available part of the country (indeed, in multiple places simultaneously, if possible), there can be no expectation that the information must be specific to a particular locale or even to a particular identified scheme.

Of course, as in the example below, reliance solely upon generalized stereotypes is forbidden.

- ***Example:*** At the security entrance to a Federal courthouse, a man who appears to be of a particular ethnicity properly submits his briefcase for x-ray screening and passes through the metal detector. The inspection of the briefcase reveals nothing amiss, the man does not activate the metal detector, and there is nothing suspicious about his activities or appearance. In the absence of any threat warning, the federal security screener may not order the man to undergo a further inspection solely because he appears to be of a particular ethnicity.

---

[1] *See United States v. Montero-Camargo*, 208 F.3d 1122, 1135 (9th Cir. 2000) ("Stops based on race or ethnic appearance send the underlying message to all our citizens that those who are not white are judged by the color of their skin alone.").

[2] This guidance is intended only to improve the internal management of the executive branch. It is not intended to, and does not, create any right, benefit, trust, or responsibility, whether substantive or procedural, enforceable at law or equity by a party against the United States, its departments, agencies, instrumentalities, entities, officers, employees, or agents, or any person, nor does it create any right of review in an administrative, judicial or any other proceeding.

[3] This guidance document does not apply to U.S. military, intelligence, protective or diplomatic activities conducted consistent with the Constitution and applicable Federal law.

[4] These same principles do not necessarily apply to classifications based on alienage. For example, Congress, in the exercise of its broad powers over immigration, has enacted a number of provisions that apply only to aliens, and enforcement of such provisions properly entails consideration of a person's alien status.

[5] Invidious discrimination is not necessarily present whenever there is a "disproportion" between the racial composition of the pool of persons prosecuted and the general public at large; rather, the focus must be the pool of "*similarly situ-*

ated individuals of a different race [who] were not prosecuted."*Armstrong*, 517 U.S. at 465 (emphasis added). "[R]acial disproportions in the level of prosecutions for a particular crime may be unobjectionable if they merely reflect racial disproportions in the commission of that crime."*Bush v. Vera*, 517 U.S. 952, 968 (1996) (plurality).

6 Moreover, as in the traditional law enforcement context described in the second standard, *supra*, officials involved in homeland security may take into account specific, credible information about the descriptive characteristics of persons who are affiliated with identified organizations that are actively engaged in threatening the national security.

INDEX

Locators in **boldface** indicate main topics. Locators followed by *g* indicate glossary entries. Locators followed by *b* indicate biographical entries. Locators followed by *c* indicate chronology entries.

Index

Index

Index

Index

Index

Index

Index